The Inspired Traveller

OUR WORLD IN 100 CULTURAL PLACES

The Inspired Traveller

OUR WORLD IN 100 CULTURAL PLACES

SARAH BAXTER AND SUSIE HODGE
ILLUSTRATED BY AMY GRIMES

Contents

INTRODUCTION	6

PART ONE: EUROPE — 10

ST IVES, ENGLAND – *ARTISTIC* — 12
ROME, ITALY – *CINEMATIC* — 16
MARSEILLE, FRANCE – *FOODIE* — 18
DUBLIN, IRELAND – *LITERARY* — 22
LIVERPOOL, ENGLAND – *MUSICAL* — 24
CASCAIS & ESTORIL, PORTUGAL – *ARTISTIC* — 28
VENICE, ITALY – *FOODIE* — 30
ELBE SANDSTONE MOUNTAINS, GERMANY – *ARTISTIC* — 34
OOSTDUINKERKE, BELGIUM – *FOODIE* — 38
CATALONIA, SPAIN – *ARTISTIC* — 42
GÖRLITZ, GERMANY – *CINEMATIC* — 44
LYON, FRANCE – *FOODIE* — 48
LA MANCHA, SPAIN – *LITERARY* — 50
REYKJAVÍK, ICELAND – *MUSICAL* — 54
DELFT, NETHERLANDS – *ARTISTIC* — 58
BOLOGNA, ITALY – *FOODIE* — 60
BATH, ENGLAND – *LITERARY* — 64
GUERNICA, SPAIN – *ARTISTIC* — 68
NORDLAND, NORWAY – *LITERARY* — 72
COPENHAGEN, DENMARK – *FOODIE* — 74
DAVOS, SWITZERLAND – *LITERARY* — 78
LAKE ATTERSEE, AUSTRIA – *ARTISTIC* — 82
BELCHITE & THE SIERRA DE GUADARRAMA, SPAIN – *CINEMATIC* — 84
PARIS, FRANCE – *LITERARY* — 88
NUREMBERG, GERMANY – *FOODIE* — 92
LONDON, ENGLAND – *CINEMATIC* — 94
BRUSSELS, BELGIUM – *ARTISTIC* — 98
GALWAY, IRELAND – *MUSICAL* — 100
FÅRÖ, SWEDEN – *CINEMATIC* — 104
VENICE, ITALY – *ARTISTIC* — 106
YORKSHIRE MOORS, ENGLAND – *LITERARY* — 110

LISBON, PORTUGAL – *FOODIE* — 114
BERN, SWITZERLAND – *ARTISTIC* — 118
SALZBURG, AUSTRIA – *CINEMATIC* — 120
BERLIN, GERMANY – *LITERARY* — 124
WELLS, ENGLAND – *CINEMATIC* — 128
VIENNA, AUSTRIA – *MUSICAL* — 130
TUSHETI, GEORGIA – *FOODIE* — 134
OSLO, NORWAY – *ARTISTIC* — 136
ST PETERSBURG, RUSSIA – *LITERARY* — 140
LAKE MÄLAREN, SWEDEN – *ARTISTIC* — 142
KRAKÓW, POLAND – *FOODIE* — 146
ANDALUCÍA, SPAIN – *MUSICAL* — 148
LONDON, ENGLAND – *LITERARY* — 152
ARLES, FRANCE – *ARTISTIC* — 154
MONTMARTE, FRANCE – *CINEMATIC* — 158
LONDON, ENGLAND – *ARTISTIC* — 160
NAPLES, ITALY – *LITERARY* — 164
VALENCIA, SPAIN – *FOODIE* — 166
DUMFRIES & GALLOWAY, SCOTLAND – *CINEMATIC* — 170
GIVERNY, FRANCE – *ARTISTIC* — 172
BRUGES, BELGIUM – *CINEMATIC* — 176
FLORENCE, ITALY – *ARTISTIC* — 178
SAN SEBASTIAN, SPAIN – *FOODIE* — 182
EAST BERGHOLT, ENGLAND – *ARTISTIC* — 184

PART TWO: NORTH AMERICA — 186

MONTEREY, USA – *LITERARY* — 188
JAMAICA – *CINEMATIC* — 190
BROOKLYN, USA – *CINEMATIC* — 194
NEW MEXICO, USA – *ARTISTIC* — 196
MONTRÉAL, CANADA – *FOODIE* — 200
MISSISSIPPI RIVER, USA – *LITERARY* — 202
NEW YORK, USA – *ARTISTIC* — 206
CUBA – *MUSICAL* — 208
PHILADELPHIA, USA – *CINEMATIC* — 212

NEW ORLEANS, USA – *FOODIE*	214
NEW YORK, USA – *LITERARY*	218
ALBERTA, CANADA – *CINEMATIC*	222
MONROEVILLE, USA – *LITERARY*	226
DEAD HORSE POINT STATE PARK, USA – *CINEMATIC*	228
COYOACÁN, MEXICO – *ARTISTIC*	232
MEMPHIS, USA – *MUSICAL*	234

PART THREE: SOUTH AMERICA	238
CARTAGENA, COLOMBIA – *LITERARY*	240
LIMA, PERU – *FOODIE*	244
SALVADOR, BRAZIL – *MUSICAL*	246
LA PAMPA, ARGENTINA – *FOODIE*	250
CHILE – *LITERARY*	254
CUSCO & MACHU PICCHU, PERU – *CINEMATIC*	256

PART FOUR: ASIA	260
KABUL, AFGHANISTAN – *LITERARY*	262
JEONJU, SOUTH KOREA – *FOODIE*	266
TOKYO, JAPAN – *CINEMATIC*	268
KERALA, INDIA – *LITERARY*	272
SICHUAN, CHINA – *FOODIE*	276
MOUNT FUJI, JAPAN – *ARTISTIC*	280
SEOUL, SOUTH KOREA – *MUSICAL*	282
HONG KONG, CHINA – *CINEMATIC*	286
UDUPI, INDIA – *FOODIE*	288
SAIGON (HO CHI MINH CITY), VIETNAM – *LITERARY*	292
OSAKA, JAPAN – *FOODIE*	294
MUMBAI, INDIA – *CINEMATIC*	298

PART FIVE: AUSTRALASIA	300
MELBOURNE, AUSTRALIA – *FOODIE*	302
KAREKARE BEACH, NEW ZEALAND – *CINEMATIC*	304
TAHITI, FRENCH POLYNESIA – *ARTISTIC*	308
HANGING ROCK, AUSTRALIA – *LITERARY*	310
OUTBACK, AUSTRALIA – *CINEMATIC*	314

PART SIX: AFRICA	316
TANGIER, MOROCCO – *ARTISTIC*	318
SOWETO, SOUTH AFRICA – *LITERARY*	322
MATMATA & TOZEUR, TUNISIA – *CINEMATIC*	324
DAKAR, SENEGAL – *MUSICAL*	328
MARRAKESH, MOROCCO – *FOODIE*	332

PART SEVEN: MIDDLE EAST	334
CAIRO, EGYPT – *LITERARY*	336
TEL AVIV, ISRAEL – *FOODIE*	340
WADI RUM, JORDAN – *CINEMATIC*	342

INDEX	346
AUTHOR AND ILLUSTRATOR BIOGRAPHIES	351

Introduction

What's the best way into the world? The deep way. What's the best way to dive head-first into a destination? Not the pass-through-and-buy-the-T-shirt, gloss-the-surface type of travel, but the richer kind, the stuff of back streets, lock-ins, hidden corners.

What is it? It's culture: 'the arts and other manifestations of human intellectual achievement regarded collectively'. That is, the force that shapes our identities, influences our behaviours, defines our communities. Culture encompasses stories told, songs sung, rituals celebrated, legends passed down through generations, the distinctive flavour of a great-grandmother's secret recipe. These are the things that make each place unique but unite us as a global family; reminders that, while we all come from different places, we share the same quests for meaning and beauty, the same yearning to belong.

This book looks at the world through a cultural lens. From the dishes on its tabletops to the spines on its shelves, the stories flickering on its cinema screens, the rhythms floating through its windows and the paintings hung on its walls. Food, literature, films, music, art – all keys to unlocking the globe. Universal languages in a polyglot world.

Why do this? Because, well, it just makes sense. For example: take the Eiffel Tower. A famous spire of wrought iron, a fine spot for a selfie. But you'll learn more – and love more – about what makes France tick by ripping apart a fresh, crusty baguette, sticking some Serge Gainsbourg on the record player and getting stuck into Victor Hugo's *Les Misérables*. Tourist sites are all well and good, but a meal, a melody or a work of art can move us in other, much more powerful ways.

These things are all excellent 'modes of transport' for the armchair traveller, too. If we can't physically make it across the globe to visit faraway places, we can be taken there by the genius of authors, directors, composers and chefs. The best place to experience a country's culture is in situ of course, but the second best is anywhere else, with a fantastic movie playing or a great book open on our laps.

Let's start with literature. Books have always been portals to other worlds, inviting us into the minds and lives of characters who walk different streets, speak different tongues, dream different dreams. Skilled authors construct palaces with words, worlds with sentences, planets with paragraphs. Places are rendered rich, vivid and three-dimensional with just pen and ink. Moreover, travel fiction has no boundaries. The literary locations included in this book – from the wind-whipped moors of Emily Brontë's *Wuthering Heights* (p110) to the steamy Keralan backwaters of Arundhati Roy's *The God of Small Things* (p272) – are imbued with realism but are allowed to take flight. The best books traverse physical landscapes and immerse us in rich historical and social contexts, while also telling a damn-good tale.

Similarly, cinema. The magic of the movies is that they can whisk us, frame by frame, to places we've never been. And sometimes, even to places we'll never go – no one's about to visit the planet of Tatooine, though *Star Wars* fans can play make-believe in the Tunisian desert (p324). But more than that, in many films, the location doesn't simply set the scene, it drives the action, influences the feel, shapes the entire mood. The place can even become the main character of the piece. This is the case in a film such as *The Revenant* (p222), where even superstar Leonardo DiCaprio must play second fiddle to the brutal beauty of the North American Wild West. The landscape is like an A-list actor, one with such an arresting presence it seems you can feel, hear and smell its icy breath through the screen.

And while the movies featured within these pages roam from sinister folk horror to arthouse thrillers to martial arts flicks and more, what they share is a very definite sense of place. Be it the wild sands of Jordan in *Lawrence of Arabia* (p342), the desolate coastline of New Zealand in *The Piano* (p304) or the neon-crazy streets of Tokyo in *Lost in Translation* (p268), in each case it's almost impossible to imagine any of these movies being set anywhere else.

This very certain sense of place also pours out of the artistic entries. In this book we travel to a very varied set of landscapes that have inspired the greatest works of art; locales where a genius has captured a specific moment with masterful brushstrokes, distilling its essence within a frame. Entering the real worlds of these pictures is to enter the minds of the artists themselves, and to understand the history, circumstances and context in which they worked.

For instance, the small Spanish town of Guernica (p68) looks nothing like Pablo Picasso's surrealist take on it. But his disturbing image – black and white, full of violence and chaos – captures the horrors of the day

INTRODUCTION 7

in April 1937, when German and Italian planes attacked, killing around 1,650 people. Meanwhile, to walk in the gardens of Giverny, France (p172), is not only to inhale the scent of its exquisite rose bushes and admire its iconic waterlilies, but to see this floral wonderland through the gaze and, later, failing vision of Claude Monet; to behold the details he transformed into swirling impressions. Both place and paintings are magnificent. But Giverny – and the other artistic places included here – aren't merely feasts for the eyes, they are places where great creatives have been inspired, sought refuge and maybe altered the entire course of art history.

Music, like art, speaks to us all. Just as a symphony unites disparate notes into a harmonious whole, music unites humanity; it is a powerful storyteller. It doesn't even matter whether you can understand the lyrics being uttered – the beat, the tone, the soul can be enough to bridge gaps, join hearts, connect minds.

This book listens in on a host of diverse locations. From the passionate strains of a flamenco guitar echoing around a sun-drenched Spanish plaza (p148) to the ethereal sounds of Iceland, which seem to mimic the very nature of the land itself (p54), to the grand concert halls of Vienna (p130), where the masterpieces of Mozart and Beethoven continue to fill the air. Each one has its own unique soundtrack; a musical heritage that shapes its identity and offers insights into its past. There are also cities so utterly entwined with the music they've produced that it's almost impossible to imagine them without it: Liverpool (p24) without The Beatles feels like Disney World without Mickey Mouse.

And then there's food. The great universal. For we all must eat. Is there any better way to understand another human than to pull up a chair at their table? To break bread, scoop stew, drink tea, chew fat with them? To share a meal with another person is to share a little of life itself.

Also, nothing tells the story of a destination in such a delicious way. Slice into the speciality of a nation, take a big bite, slurp every morsel, and you can uncover an entire history. A simple-seeming dish can contain the stories of empires, exiles and expansions, conflict and commerce, oppression and innovation. For instance, the ethnic smorgasbord spread out in Melbourne (p302) – Italian, Greek, Indian, Vietnamese, Ethiopian and a hundred more – tells the tale of the city's backstory of immigration. Meanwhile, the age-old vegan dishes of Udupi in southern India (p288) speak of spirituality, worship and the footsteps of centuries of pilgrims. In following these various culinary trails, we embark on journeys that enrich our understanding; food, with its ability to evoke memories and emotions like nothing else can, becomes a guide to seeing places afresh.

In total, there are 100 exciting, dynamic, mesmerising, appetising locations gathered here, supported by rich, evocative illustrations that aim to give a taster of what makes each place so great. Ultimately, this book is a virtual banquet. A Technicolor epic condensed into a handful of pages; we've tried to cram it with real cultural treasures that will hopefully inspire you to look at things from a slightly different perspective. It's a way for you to travel from the comfort of your sofa, put yourself quite literally into the picture – and perhaps feel inspired to plot real adventures.

Remember, music, art, movies, books, food – these are not merely supplementary to travel; these are some of the essential mediums for truly understanding the world. At their best, they offer deep and nuanced perspectives, foster empathy, preserve unique heritage, encourage transformation and shrink divides. Embarking on journeys through these cultural lenses – tasting that local delicacy, listening to that haunting tune – can mean opening ourselves up to a richer, more meaningful experience of the world.

Part One:
Europe

St Ives

Where? Cornwall, England
Which? Pelagos (1946) by Barbara Hepworth
What? Renowned hub for artists inspired by light, sea, wind and hills

Even on a cloudy day, the light is clear. It slants down to the earth, highlighting and intensifying all it touches. Ferns, mosses, liverworts, lichens and fungi spread across the rich soil and rockier areas, bristling in the gentle breeze or sometimes stronger winds, catching the same dazzling light that shines on the sea, the fishing harbour, the narrow streets of the old part of town, and the soft sandy beaches, and even silhouettes the distant, undulating hills.

This is St Ives, a place where ancient history exudes from every rock and grassy mound. Approximately 10,000 years ago, Cornwall began to be occupied, and even today, it retains a uniqueness and a spiritual distance from England. Despite its fluctuating fortunes, since its first settlers moved in, Cornwall has drawn people to live and work, and St Ives, to the north of Penzance, on the coast of the Celtic Sea, has held an enduring attraction for many. Named after a fifth-century Irish princess and missionary called St Ia, St Ives initially flourished through mining and fishing, with its peak in the nineteenth century, when there was huge demand for tin, copper and locally caught pilchards. In 1877, the extension of the Great Western Railway from Paddington to Penzance made the remote town more accessible, and St Ives became a popular destination for tourists and artists – the latter settling all over the town.

Captivated by the shimmering light and landscape, these original thinkers immersed themselves in St Ives – and thrived, establishing a community of artists and writers. Among the first to travel there were Walter Sickert and Whistler, while the Finnish painter Helene Schjerfbeck and the Swedish artist Anders Zorn spent the winter in 1887–88. Other early settlers established the St Ives Arts Club in 1890 and by the mid-1890s, St Ives was known as a destination for landscape and marine artists. Later it was made more famous by innovative potters Shōji Hamada and Bernard Leach, who opened the world-renowned Leach Pottery in 1920.

One particular artist to become synonymous with the area was Barbara Hepworth (1903–75) who arrived there with her then-husband, the painter Ben Nicholson, in 1939. From the time she moved in, Hepworth's art expressed her surroundings with a passion. In a time when female artists were rare, she evolved innovative ideas, using a wide range of materials, and investigating textures and negative spaces as much as positive shapes in her sculpture, as well as focusing on the relationships of her sculptures to the landscapes around them. Although much of her work was abstract, most referred to aspects of nature. 'All my sculpture comes out of landscape' she wrote, and 'I'm sick of sculptures in galleries . . . no sculpture really lives until it goes back to the landscape, the trees, air and clouds.' She also wrote: 'Finding Trewyn Studio was a sort of magic. Here was a studio, a yard and garden where I could work in open air and space.' One of her best-known pieces, *Pelagos* (meaning sea in Greek), 1946, is a curving, rounded, spiral wooden sculpture, inspired by a view of the bay, where two stretches of land surround the sea on either side. The hollowed-out sculpture also recalls a shell or the roll of a hill, while the strings suggest music and musical instruments, which Hepworth used to convey 'the tension I felt between myself and the sea, the wind or the hills.'

Other artists added to the legendary status of the St Ives School, and nowadays the town continues to draw artists and art lovers to its many art galleries, including Tate St Ives and the Barbara Hepworth Sculpture Garden, as well as its surrounding scenery. As soon as you experience the sparkling, jewel-bright light, rugged landscape and breathtaking beaches, including the splendid Pendour Cove – with its curved, rocky coastline that inspired Hepworth's 1947 *Pendour* wooden sculpture – and the working port and harbour of Porthminster, you'll be drawn in. With miles of well-marked trails through the countryside and pelagic panorama, St Ives is wonderful for walking or boating from the bay. Old town and new, from narrow cobbled streets to more modern buildings, all appeals to the senses.

ARTISTIC   13

Rome

Where? Italy
Which? La Dolce Vita (Federico Fellini, 1960)
Why? Glorious glimpse of the Italian capital at its most gay and gorgeous

Look at the Eternal City. All champagne and cappuccinos, outrageous parties with beautiful people, Vespas and sports cars, glamorous gowns, designer sunglasses that are worn even in the dead of night. Libertarian, hedonistic, orgiastic, OTT. A sweet life indeed . . .

With its distinct vision of Rome – sexy and sensational – *La Dolce Vita* may be the most stylish movie ever made. A portmanteau of episodes that occur in the Italian capital over seven days and nights, it revolves around Marcello Rubini (Marcello Mastroianni), a well-coiffed, sharp-suited gossip columnist who reports on the scandalous capers of the city's celebrities, social climbers, intercontinental aristocrats and nouveaux-riches. Marcello flirts with a movie star, reports on a 'miracle', has an affair with an heiress, deals with his girlfriend's overdose; he dreams of greater things but is stuck in this 'sweet' life of excess, extravagance and emptiness.

Released in 1960, *La Dolce Vita* showed a new Italy: post-Fascism and post-war, surfacing from poverty, booming economically, developing a different morality. Indeed, with its sex, adultery, homosexuality and blasphemy, *La Dolce Vita* was condemned by the Church – not least for the opening image of a statue of Christ being helicoptered over the ruined aqueducts of Parco degli Acquedotti, viewed by some as a sacrilegious depiction of Christ's second coming.

While the movie's biggest star is Rome, Fellini filmed most of *La Dolce Vita* on the sound stages of the city's Cinecittà Studios rather than out on its streets. In a way, the studios themselves – originally founded by Mussolini – explain the film's existence. Cinecittà attracted many big American productions in the 1950s, earning it the nickname 'Hollywood on the Tiber'. This drew showbiz types to Rome – just the sorts of people Marcello is fraternising with on the chi-chi Via Veneto.

Back then the Via Veneto was THE place to be seen, an exclusive boulevard of plush palazzi, five-star hotels and high-end boutiques. This is where the paparazzi – a term coined after hound-like photographer Paparazzo (Walter Santesso) in this very film – would stalk stars such as Brando, Hepburn, Sinatra and Fellini himself at hip hangouts like Harry's Bar. Though enduringly elegant, these days Veneto has lost its cool, but it's still worth strolling: start at Piazza Barberini, with its fine Bernini fountains, and finish at Harry's, where a certain Dolce Vita vibe is kept alive in the chic, piano-tinkled bar, still patronised by a jet-set clientele.

Just as Fellini recreated Via Veneto at Cinecittà, he did likewise for another classic location: St Peter's. There are aerial shots filmed above the real basilica – that aforementioned statue of Christ flies in over the Vatican City – but the interiors of the church, where blonde bombshell Sylvia (Anita Ekberg) climbs up to the cupola, were a set. You can still make the real ascent, though: 231 stairs lead to the first level; another 320 narrow, spiralling steps head inside Michelangelo's monumental dome, where you can step out onto the roof – like Marcello and Sylvia – to see the Eternal City below.

Somewhere down there, east over the Tiber, is the site of *La Dolce Vita*'s most iconic scene. After storming out of a party amid the magnificent ruins of the Baths of Caracalla – Rome's second-biggest bathhouse, dating from 212 CE – Marcello and Sylvia wander the city until they reach the Trevi Fountain, a Baroque flounce of white travertine that depicts the sea-god Oceanus in a shell-shaped chariot pulled by mermen and hippocamps. The cobbled streets are dark and empty, and Sylvia, in her strapless black gown, wades into the water, every bit as mythical and divine as the sculpted figures behind.

It is, unsurprisingly, illegal to leap into the fountain yourself. And it is rarely so quiet as the film finds it, now heaving with tourists at all hours. But it remains the place to indulge in another bit of movie lore. The tradition of tossing in a coin comes from the 1954 film *Three Coins in the Fountain*: they say it means you'll return to Rome. Maybe not to Fellini's decadent, swinging, surreal version of the city, but it's worth a throw all the same.

CINEMATIC 17

Foodie

Marseille

Where? Provence-Alpes-Côte d'Azur, France
Why? Find the fine fish stew that symbolises the soul of the city

A whole sea of dishes swirls here. Flavours from across the globe, washed into this storied, vivid, ancient port. But one remains THE dish. The gritty city's culinary signature. A make-do of scrag-ends. The bottom of the tank. The ugliest, boniest and least prepossessing of the fisherman's haul, boiled up into something beautiful indeed . . .

Founded by the Greeks in 600 BCE, Marseille is the oldest and second-biggest city in France. It's staunchly Mediterranean in feel – salt-spritzed and perpetually bathed in intense, shimmering light. It's also rebellious, good-natured, spirited and seaward-looking; a long history of trade and exchange with southern Europe, North Africa, the Middle East and beyond means Marseille feels less of France, more of the world.

This multicultural legacy has suffused the city's cuisine. Grapes and olive trees, brought by the colonising Greeks, and coffee, introduced later by Venetian merchants, first entered France via Marseille. Today, one of the best-loved local eats is pizza, brought by Neapolitan immigrants in the early twentieth century and – as befits a port city – typically topped with anchovies. But you'll also find couscous rolled by Algerian Berbers, fish-filled pastries from Senegal, Tunisian chickpeas, Lebanese flatbreads, merguez sausage, Moroccan pastilla...This sprawling city of 111 districts has something for every taste.

However, the most Marseille of meals is bouillabaisse. The name of this fine fish stew comes from the Provençal Occitan word *bolhabaissa*, a compound of *bolhir* (to boil) and *abaissar* (to simmer). Some say it developed from *kakavia*, a traditional soup brought to the port by Greek settlers. Others claim it was invented by Venus, Roman goddess of love, to put her husband, Vulcan, to sleep so she could sneak off with her lover, Mars. But despite this divine conjecture, it more likely began as a dish of the working class. Fishermen would make their own suppers from the cheaper, less saleable dregs of their catch – flavoursome

FOODIE 19

but spiny and unattractive species such as scorpion fish, conger eel, red mullet, venomous weever fish, gurnard and John Dory (aka Saint Pierre); sea urchins, mussels, langoustines and crabs might feature too. The fishermen's wives would light a fire on the beach and boil up the lot in a cast-iron pot of seawater, chucking in onions, fennel, Provençal bouquet garni, garlic, olive oil and saffron. From the seventeenth century, tomatoes, newly arrived from the Americas, were added in. Over time, this rustic fuel became a fancy feast.

While there are as many bouillabaisse as there are chefs that make it, there are rules. In 1980 a group of restaurateurs drew up the Marseille Bouillabaisse Charter to help protect the dish's authenticity: for example, it must contain fresh, not frozen, ingredients, and should include at least four of the traditional types of 'ugly' fish. It should also be served in a certain way, in two courses. First comes a bowl of the steaming broth, accompanied by toasted bread, raw garlic cloves and a saffron-mayonnaise rouille – rub the toasts with the garlic, dollop on the rouille and place them in the soup. The second course is the fish itself, drizzled in the remaining broth. The cooked fish should be presented to your table whole before being filleted within sight – that way you know exactly what's been put in the mix.

Marseille has changed greatly in the past decade. One of the biggest regeneration schemes in Europe has smartened the Vieux-Port, built new tramways and cultural spaces and improved its prior reputation as a den of crime. It's now much nicer to walk the historic waterfront, where merchant ships once brought their exotic cargoes and where boat masts still sway and clink.

Finding proper bouillabaisse can be tricky and expensive – seek out dining spots signed up to the Charter and brace yourself for the bill. But it's worth it; the dish still manages to distill the immutable colour and character of the city.

Literary

Dublin

Where? Ireland
Which? *Ulysses* by James Joyce (1922)
What? The world in miniature, for the humdrum events of one epic Irish day

The pub is warm and beery. Grog glasses – drained, foam stained – scatter sticky veneer. Red-wine lips, hoppy breath, a slurry of slurring; laughter like gunfire, craic-ing off the wood panels, mirror walls and ranks of whiskey bottles. Bar talk is of theology and adultery, literature and death, soap and sausages. Everything and nothing, discussed or daydreamed over a quick cheese sandwich. A nothing old day. But the stuff of life – infinitesimal yet essential – all the same . . .

James Joyce's *Ulysses* – variously considered the most momentous, accomplished, infuriating and unreadable book in the English language – is the ordinary made extraordinary. It's a modernist reworking of Homer's *Odyssey*, but while the Ancient Greek poem tells of Odysseus' incident-packed return from the Trojan War, Joyce makes an epic out of a single, unremarkable day.

Ulysses follows Leopold Bloom, a Jewish ad canvasser for *The Freeman's Journal*, as he wanders around Dublin on 16 June 1904. He attends a funeral, goes to the pub, ducks into a museum (to avoid the man sleeping with his wife), pleasures himself by Sandymount Strand, enters the red-light district. The novel is a chaotic stream of consciousness, performing stylistic acrobatics to try to render the human experience. But it is grounded in the streets of Dublin. Joyce, writing from self-exile in Paris, slavishly researched the physicality of the city. Though he seldom returned, he remained tethered: 'When I die,' he once said, 'Dublin will be written in my heart'.

At the turn of the century, the city was changing. The well-to-do had moved to the suburbs as the overcrowded centre decayed. Dublin had some of Europe's worst slums; almost one in every four children died before their first birthday. A Celtic Revival was promoting Irish culture and language while in politics the Irish Parliamentary Party was

22   EUROPE

pressing for Home Rule (rather than independence). But more radical movements were fermenting, and the Great War (1914–1918), Easter Rising (1916) and IRA violence were imminent. Though published in 1922, the 'action' of *Ulysses* predates this tumult. Joyce concerns himself, not with the struggles of nations but rather the little battles an Everyman faces, every day. Dublin becomes a microcosm of the world.

Joyce's geographic diligence makes it possible to trace Bloom's footsteps. Start at No. 7 Eccles Street, Bloom's home, where he fries kidneys and contemplates his wife's infidelity. The building was knocked down in the 1960s but a plaque marks the spot and the original doorway is preserved within a fine townhouse on North Great George's Street, now the James Joyce Centre.

O'Connell Street lies around the corner, a fashionable address in Georgian times, though faded by the 1900s and damaged during the Easter Rising. No more the horse-drawn cabs and clanking trams; a stroll down its leafy central mall these days is accompanied by car din and a mishmash of architectural styles. Bloom wouldn't have passed Joyce, who now leans nonchalantly in bronze at the corner with North Earl Street, but he did note the monument to Irish leader Daniel O'Connell – 'the hugecloaked Liberator's form' – which stares across the River Liffey.

Bloom buys Banbury cakes to feed the wheeling gulls as he walks over the wide span of O'Connell Bridge, the divide between dingier north Dublin and the more affluent south. This crossing takes you and Bloom into the heart of Dublin, home to the Bank of Ireland (originally the Irish Parliament building), prestigious Trinity College (where Catholic Joyce didn't go), the National Library (where he frequently did). It leads to narrow, shop-lined Grafton Street, still gay with awnings, where locals and outsiders alike still come for the craic – Dublin's social essence.

Bloom is hungry when he hits Duke Street. His first choice, The Burton – establishment of 'pungent meatjuice, slop of greens' – is no more. But Davy Byrnes pub, a traditional boozer, first opened in 1889, still serves Gorgonzola sandwiches and glasses of Burgundy (Bloom's lunch of choice), providing a tangible taste of Joyce's sometimes indigestible masterpiece.

LITERARY   23

Musical

Liverpool

Where? North-west England
Why? A fabulous pilgrimage for the Fab Four, and more

Music flows through Liverpool as surely as the Mersey – the city is simply unthinkable without either. These two constitute the lifeblood of Liverpool, mighty river and musical rhythms, both intrinsic to its gritty and gregarious nature. Sound and water percolate through the city, influencing its voices and vocations, its sense of both itself and its standing on the world stage. Of course, a certain Fab Four steal much of the cultural limelight, but the history of music here runs much deeper than that . . .

Liverpool's name – originally *Liuerpul* – links back to the river, derived from the Old English *liver* (muddy) and *pol* (pool or creek). It gained its Royal Charter in 1207, making a proper town of this settlement by the Irish Sea. Thus, began centuries of maritime commerce: government-funded privateers set sail to plunder enemy vessels; whalers headed north for the Arctic; ships embarked for West Africa on the first leg of the Trans-Atlantic trade triangle – goods from northern England were swapped for enslaved people; exotic cargo, such as sugar and tobacco, was brought back from the Caribbean. By the early nineteenth century, 40 per cent of the entire world's trade passed through Liverpool's docks.

It seems like a story of economics, but it's also one of culture. A port this busy and far-reaching – with settlers hailing from everywhere from Europe to China – became a playbook of global sounds. For a start, Liverpool's proximity to Ireland bequeathed a rich tradition of Irish folk music – and plenty of Irish pubs. And being a maritime hub awash with sailors, sea shanties thrived. Take 'Maggie May' (once covered by The Beatles), a fo'c'sle ditty about a seaman returned home to Liverpool who is robbed by a prostitute; the lyrics roam around from Lime Street (now the site of the main railway station) to Canning Place, once home to the Liverpool Sailors' Home. At the other end of the social scale, the city's prosperity helped fund the Liverpool Philharmonic Society, founded for the elite in 1840, and now one of the world's oldest orchestras.

MUSICAL   25

Liverpool was also a first port of call for new influences – which found an eagerly receptive population. The mid-twentieth century saw the city in a post-industrial slump, with factories shutting down and unemployment high. But it also saw the arrival of jazz and skiffle, country, blues and rock and roll – sounds of hope and release; young musicians lapped them up, putting their own spin on these foreign rhythms. The result was Merseybeat, the era-defining, guitar-led pop phenomenon of working-class Liverpudlians shaking up the world music scene. Merseybeat's most famous proponents were two lads, John and Paul, who first played together in 1957 at St Peter's Church Hall in the suburb of Woolton. Within a few years they'd formed The Beatles, and the rest is history. The group solidified Liverpool's reputation as a musical powerhouse – it's now a designated UNESCO City of Music – and is probably the most influential band there's ever been.

The Beatles dominate Liverpool's music culture still. Hop on a Magical Mystery Bus tour from the impressive Victorian-built Royal Albert Dock and you'll be whisked around locations from the band's formative years. These include the childhood homes of Paul McCartney and John Lennon – two ordinary post-war houses (now museums), where iconic tracks such as 'She Loves You' were written. Also, George Harrison's birthplace, the Toxteth terrace where Ringo Starr lived, the band's former schools and colleges; Penny Lane's 'shelter in the middle of a roundabout'; the red-painted gates of Strawberry Field. A good place to finish is the Cavern Club, the legendary warehouse cellar, with its barrel-vaulted arches, where The Beatles first performed on 9 February 1961. The original building was knocked down in the 1970s, but reconstructed in the 1980s in the same place, to the same design, with most of the original bricks.

Liverpool is more than The Beatles though. Merseybeat spawned other stars like Gerry and the Pacemakers and The Swinging Blue Jeans. Suddenly, being from Liverpool was the in thing, and while Merseybeat itself was short-lived, the city's talent factory didn't stop producing. In the following decades, the city has given the world the likes of Echo and the Bunnymen, OMD, Frankie Goes To Hollywood, The La's, The Farm and Atomic Kitten. Music, of all genres, is still very much alive here and can be heard floating out of cafés, arenas, backyards and dive bars. Iconic clubs, such as the Jacaranda – which hosted The Beatles – are still venues for new artists. Or pop into the Jacaranda's record store: it has a rare 1948 Voice-O-Graph on which you can record yourself straight onto vinyl and make your own piece of Liverpool music history.

Cascais and Estoril

Artistic

Where? Lisbon coast, Portugal
Which? The Dance (1988) by Paula Rego
What? Rugged coastline with ancient fishing town and royal bay

As the afternoon moves towards evening, and the sun begins to lower over the distant mountains, the bay of Cascais and Estoril feels calm and relaxed. Golden light slides over the rockroses, heathers, gorse and lavender, and warms the stone of the mansions, built during the nineteenth and early twentieth centuries to house the many wealthy visitors who flocked there. Several of these are now museums, including the Casa das Histórias de Paula Rego (Paula Rego House of Stories), a building with an unusual design that houses several of the works of the expressive Portuguese artist. Also nearby is the Portuguese Music Museum, at Casa Verdades de Faria. Closer to the sea, is the Citadel Palace, the former House of the Cascais governor and once the king of Portugal's summer residence, currently under the authority of the Presidency of the Portuguese Republic.

Directly to the west of Lisbon, the Estoril coastline has remained one of the most popular and cosmopolitan parts of Portugal since the late nineteenth century, when the king of Portugal spent his summers there and other European royals joined him and his family. The scenic route hugs the coast and the River Tagus, passing several forts that were erected to defend Lisbon. Originally a little fishing town, Cascais now bustles with colourful shops and lively restaurants and bars. A large marina dominates the southern edge of town, frequented by yacht- and catamaran-owners travelling to the Mediterranean, fishermen who take advantage of the deep waters off the coast, surfers and windsurfers, and golfers who come to play on its world-championship courses.

At the northern end of town, Boca do Inferno (Hell's Mouth) comprises a dark and conspicuous rock formation, resembling the steep and craggy cliff that can be seen in the background of Paula Rego's haunting 1988 painting The Dance. On the top of this cliff in Rego's painting is the silhouette of an imposing fortress, set against a deep-blue sky filled with ominous dark clouds and a full moon. This fort was used as a prison and torture site during the Estado Novo (1933–74), a period of authoritarian rule in Portugal. With this and its dark, long shadows, the rhythmic, intriguing painting contrasts with the bright holiday atmosphere of the coastal paradise. Born in Lisbon in 1935, Rego moved to Estoril with her family when she was three years old. Yet at the time she painted *The Dance*, she was living in London, having moved there permanently in 1976. The work was the largest painting she had created at that time and represents several of her memories of growing up. She produced 11 preparatory ink drawings for the shadow-filled painting, each exploring various combinations of dancing figures, from seven young women jumping in the air to a mixed group walking along a beach, all featuring elements of her beloved homeland.

With its balmy climate and rugged shorelines, Cascais is an ideal place for family holidays or for walking or cycling along the promenade between Azarujinha and Nossa Senhora da Conceição beaches. Between June and September, the oldest arts-and-crafts fair in the country, FIARTIL, is held every year, offering an opportunity to discover traditional crafts and to taste the wide variety of regional produce – not least the internationally renowned regional speciality, *Tarte de Natas*. As well as Cascais and Estoril, this coastline is lined with other charming Portuguese resort towns, including Paço de Arcos, Oeiras and Carcavelos. Fishing boats are moored on the sands of the Praia Velha in the picturesque town of Paço de Arcos, while the golden beaches that nestle along this coast include the Praia de Caxias, guarded by two forts, the Forte da Giribita and the Forte de São Bruno de Caxias. These medieval military forts were built at the same time as the Fort of São Pedro do Estoril, or the Fort of Poça, that appears in Rego's *The Dance*. Strolling in the moonlight, past the craggy cliffs and windswept beaches of Cascais, illuminated by the silvery moonlight, you can experience the mystical atmosphere captured in Rego's enigmatic artwork.

Foodie

Venice

Where? Veneto, Italy
Why? Graze like a local around this most serene city

Cicchetti isn't eating, it's living. Cheap, informal finger food as social sustenance; the oil that helps Venice run. It's young friends catching up. It's old men chewing crostini while they chew the fat. It's off-duty gondoliers comparing notes over meatballs. It's colleagues and brothers and neighbours and acquaintances exchanging the news with a swig of wine or shot of grappa. It's early snack, light lunch, golden-hour aperitivo. It's a quick way to slow down. As the old Venetian saying goes, *'magna e bevi che la vita xé un lampo'* – 'eat and drink because life is a lightning flash' . . .

Nothing about Venice is like anywhere else. Founded, according to tradition, at noon on 25 March in 421 CE, when the site was nothing more than a scattering of marshy islets in an estuarine lagoon, *La Serenissima* – the 'most serene' – floats on its own current. A city both sublime and sinking; a one-time maritime superpower where water has replaced roads; an artistic hub par excellence, where even the tiniest chapel or palazzo probably contains a Renaissance masterpiece. So why shouldn't its eating habits be out of the ordinary too?

Cicchetti is a very Venice thing. Some say the word (pronounced 'chi-KET-tee') derives from the Latin *ciccus,* (meaning little or small amount). Whatever the root, cicchetti are bite-size morsels, designed to be eaten standing up, no cutlery required. Offerings might include cured meat and cheese stabbed onto toothpicks, fried *polpette* (balls of meat or fish), *fritto misto* on skewers, neat little *tramezzini* (triangular sandwiches) or crusty crostini topped with anything from tuna mayo to gorgonzola, radicchio, tomato or fresh shrimp. Real specialities include *baccalà mantecato*, a whipped mousse of salt cod, olive oil and garlic served on a grilled polenta slice, as well as *sarde in saor*, sardines marinated in vinegar, which harks back to when sailors had to preserve food for long voyages at sea.

30   EUROPE

The origins of cicchetti lie in wine. The Rialto Market was established in 1087 and, by the thirteenth century, had become one of the most cosmopolitan trading hubs in medieval Europe. Vintners sold their wares to the throng of merchants, bankers, travellers and pilgrims here; businessmen would seal their deals with a quick glass. The wine traders also roamed elsewhere in Venice, selling direct from their barrels in the shade of the Piazza di San Marco's campanile; it's said they'd shift with the sun as it moved around the bell tower throughout the day in order to keep their wine cool. Thus, the small glasses they sold became known as *un'ombra* – a shadow.

Venetians don't like to imbibe on an empty stomach, so cicchetti were invented – little snacks to keep patrons drinking for longer. Eventually, the vintners sought more permanent premises, shifting into *bàcari*. These were small, rustic, inexpensive taverns without chairs and tables, maybe just a few old barrels on which to lean, where nibbles were served. Some say they got their name from Bacchus, Roman god of wine, or that it stems from the local phrase *'far bàcara'*: to eat, drink and be jolly together.

The character of these no-frills hangouts has changed over the centuries, but cicchetti culture is flourishing. Away from the main squares, you'll still find *bàcari* that are more Venetian than tourist. Where you still have to push your way in through the gesticulating locals; where you have to yell *'un'ombra, per favore!'* at the bartender, browse the snacks behind the counter and simply point at what you want.

Indeed, a slow-grazing *giro de ombre* – a pub crawl, Venetian style – is the best way to see this meandering, magnificent city. Rather than dashing between big sites, wander willy-nilly. Get lost in the *calli* (streets) and *campi* (squares), admire the grandiose and the crumbling buildings, listen to the oar-splash of the gondoliers, watch the people ebb and flow like the lagoon's own waters. And pause now and then for a morsel of something delicious, washed down by honest, earthy wine. This is how Venice should be consumed.

Elbe Sandstone Mountains

Where? Germany

Which? Wanderer Above the Sea of Fog (1818) by Caspar David Friedrich

What? Mountainous region of magnificence and mystery

The River Elbe flows through a steep, narrow valley of sandstone, carved by erosion through mountains on the border of the state of Saxony in south-eastern Germany and the North Bohemian region of the Czech Republic. Formed of forested areas, plains and ravines, the breathtaking scenery of the region attracts hikers, cyclists and rock climbers – as well as writers and artists. The varied terrain is also home to a broad range of flora and fauna. Predominantly comprised of sandstone, the mountains were formed millions of years ago, when rivers carried deposits of minerals including sand, clay and other eroded debris and deposited them on the seabed. Over millennia, these deposits hardened together in layers, building up to create the dramatic mountainous region so loved by artists such as Caspar David Friedrich (1774–1840).

Best known for his allegorical, atmospheric and often ambiguous landscapes with enigmatic figures, Friedrich frequently depicted the Elbe Sandstone Mountains. Rather than objectively capturing the drama and contrasts of the scenery, however, his underlying themes were commonly spirituality and the contemplation of nature, and he often featured anonymous figures and ruins silhouetted against moonlit or misty skies. Through his expressive, introspective approach, he conveyed the infinite power and timelessness of nature, reminding viewers of their frailty and insignificance within the universe. Nowhere was this more apparent than in his 1818 painting *Wanderer Above the Sea of Fog.*

Friedrich was working as the Romantic movement was evolving in art and literature, and he infused his landscapes with deep religious and mystical significance, conveying the power and magnificence of the divine through the natural world. Inspired by the Elbe Sandstone Mountains, Friedrich's inventive portrayal of landscape was his major innovation. He did not just capture the grandeur and extraordinariness of the vista, but suggested through it that close contemplation of nature enables us all to achieve an appreciation of spirituality. In this way, he helped to transform landscape painting from an overlooked background setting to an autonomous, emotive subject.

The integration of spiritual significance within the landscape attracted wide acclaim. In *Wanderer Above the Sea of Fog*, a man wearing a frock coat and holding a cane stands on a crag, surveying the rocks and mist before him. He is a Rückenfigur, or a person seen from behind. Through the Rückenfigur's contemplation of the scene, the viewer is forced to share the experience. The unknown world before him is vast and immeasurable. The outline of the mountains is barely visible through the fog. Worryingly, it seems that with one false step, the figure could plunge to his death. Or if he lingers longer, will he be enveloped by the fog?

Although this painting is atmospheric and lifelike, Friedrich never painted directly from nature. He made detailed sketches of the land, but back in his studio, he used elements of these from different settings, building up an entirely imagined view. For instance, the Zirkelstein, a rock that appears in the background mist of the painting, is real but in a changed location. This small table mountain offers spectacular views across the countryside, especially at sunrise and sunset. Located near the River Elbe, only 2 kilometres (1 mile) from Schöna train station in Saxony, hikers can reach the summit and admire the scenery that inspired Friedrich's mysterious works.

During his early career, Friedrich achieved great success; a fellow artist described him as a man who had discovered 'the tragedy of landscape' but later, his art became perceived as fanciful, melancholy and old-fashioned, and he died in obscurity. In the 1920s and 1930s, however, the Expressionists and Surrealists admired his work and he once again came to the fore, only for his equivocal art – and especially his *Wanderer Above the Sea of Fog* – to be adopted by the Nazi regime to symbolise German nationalism during the Second World War. It was not until the 1970s that his dramatic renditions of places such as the Elbe Sandstone Mountains were reassessed and admired once more.

Foodie

Oostduinkerke

Where? West Flanders, Belgium
Why? Watch the world's last horse fishermen working the North Sea waves

The heavy, gentle horse clomps across the endless-seeming sand and into the blue-grey brew. Submerged to its barrel, it wades steadfastly against the surf. The rider on its back sways in unison, feels the power of both swell and steed, their bright sou'wester pushed back by the salty breeze. On through the water they press, steadily, mindfully, working the sand below. Gulls look on, unfazed by this yellow-clad man and this beast of the land trudging out at sea. This has been happening here for centuries. The ultimate slow food . . .

Travel back 500 years and this scene would have been common right along the North Sea coast. Paardenvissers (horse fishermen) once worked the flat, sloping shores all the way from France to Germany. Most were farmers, who would use their sturdy draft breeds to trawl for shrimp to make some extra money, selling the spoils directly from their carts. It was a family affair, the expertise passed down from fathers to sons. But from the mid-twentieth century, the coast was developed, farms were pushed further inland and commercial boats took over the shrimping trade. Now, the Belgian village of Oostduinkerke is the paardenvissers' last stand.

Oostduinkerke lies 30 kilometres (19 miles) east of Dunkirk. In fact, its wide, white-sand beach stretches all the way to its French namesake, while a rippling system of high, horseshoe-shaped dunes rises behind, sprinkled with marram grass, sea buckthorn and crested larks. It's a quiet, no-rush kind of place, where families come for summer holidays and a few passionate locals keep shrimp-fishing traditions alive.

What they're after is *cangon cangon*, little *crevettes grises* (grey shrimp). Harvested from the North Sea, they're found in dishes across Belgium: perhaps fried in an oozy sauce as *croquettes aux crevettes*, mixed up with mayonnaise for *tomates aux crevettes* or simply boiled and served on buttered bread with strong Belgian beer. Most shrimp are

38   EUROPE

trawler-dredged these days but a handful of paardenvissers persevere. Their age-old practice is far kinder on the seabed; the crustaceans they harvest somehow purer, and supremely fresh. A labour of love infused in every bite.

Their methods haven't altered much over the centuries. Wearing high rubber boots and oilskins, the fishermen head out on their horses, often Belgian Brabants, renowned for their great strength. The mutual trust between man and steed is key. The horse drags a chain, followed by a large funnel-shaped net. The chain creates vibrations, prompting the shrimp to jump right into the trap. At low tide, the paardenvissers plough back and forth for a few hours, periodically coming ashore to empty their nets into the wicker baskets that are slung across the horse's back. The catch must be sorted: crabs, jellyfish and unwanted fishes are thrown back in, the shrimps are sieved, as only fully grown crustaceans will do. Finally, the shrimp must be washed, boiled and peeled. It's not enough to be able to fish, paardenvissers must also be experts in tides and currents, weaving nets, equestrianism and cooking.

In 2013, shrimp fishing on horseback in Oostduinkerke was added to UNESCO's Intangible Cultural Heritage of Humanity list. This has helped safeguard it for the future, and also spurred the biggest sea change. Since this designation, the Orde van de Paardenvisser (Royal Order of Horse Fishers) and other organisations have, for the first time, allowed women into the profession.

Oostduinkerke's shrimping season runs from March to November. During these months you might see the paardenvissers out plying the waves; you will certainly see the statues commemorating them, which rise from the silky sand. In summer the shrimp fishers give public demonstrations and, in June, a two-day Shrimp Festival is held, Oostduinkerke's liveliest celebration. You can also visit Navigo, the national fisheries museum, housed in a nineteenth-century fisherman's cottage. Here, there's a rustic café run by a horse fisherman and his wife, where you can order a house peerdevisscher beer and a plate of shrimp croquettes and taste yourself back a few hundred years.

Artistic

Catalonia

Where? Spain
Which? *The Persistence of Memory* (1931) by Salvador Dalí
What? Relaxing, chilled, historic and cultural region

Rich with culture and history, Catalonia is part of the Costa Brava, in the north-eastern corner of Spain, comprising the four provinces of Barcelona, Girona, Lleida and Tarragona. Inviting and colourful, several languages are spoken here, including Catalan, Spanish and the Aranese dialect of Occitan. The capital city of Catalonia is Barcelona, with many magical attractions, including the towering, still incomplete basilica La Sagrada Família, Park Güell and Casa Batlló, all created by the visionary architect Antoni Gaudí, and to the north, in the province of Girona, close to Southern France and the Mediterranean Sea, is Figueres, the birthplace of Salvador Dalí (1904–89).

Near Figueres, nestling in a sheltered bay on the southern side of the Cap de Creus peninsula, is Cadaqués, the easternmost port in Spain. Dalí, who later described it as the most beautiful town in the world, used to stay here as a child during family holidays. With its elegant waterfront, narrow, meandering streets, abundance of bougainvillea and dazzling whitewashed houses with blue front doors and windows, Cadaqués sparkles in the sunlight and gleams above the sapphire sea. It became a popular retreat for writers and artists during the twentieth century, and visitors included René Magritte, Henri Matisse, Joan Miró, Marcel Duchamp, Luís Buñuel and Pablo Picasso – and, of course, Dalí himself. Aspects of Cadaqués and the surrounding coastline feature in some of Dalí's most famous works, including his paintings *The Spectre of Sex Appeal* (1932) and *The Persistence of Memory* (1931).

The first settlers of Cadaqués were Iberian and ancient Egyptians, Greeks and Romans used the natural harbour as a stopping-off point during voyages around the Mediterranean. Evidence of the fortified medieval town remain in the Torre de sa Fusta des Baluard, an imposing tower overlooking the bay, the Portal de Mar de la Muralla, the arched gateway entrance to the old town, and the Casa del Baró de la Roda, a

42   EUROPE

medieval house built into the old town wall. The background landscape in *The Persistence of Memory* depicts elements of both Figueres and Cadaqués, as well as Portlligat, where Dalí painted this. The craggy Cap de Creus can be seen, while the clear Catalonian light enhances all the colours. Dalí joined the Surrealist movement in 1929, and from the start, he imbued his art with a sense of the fantastic, deliberately painting with meticulous precision to create a sense of confusing reality, which he called 'hand-painted dream photographs'. In *The Persistence of Memory* he explored his own psychological issues and phobias, such as his unconscious fear of death and his belief that our unconscious minds are present in all we do in our daily lives. Before joining the Surrealists, Dalí had studied Sigmund Freud's theories on psychoanalysis, which may explain why this work also contains a strangely distorted self-portrait. Overall, the painting suggests the transitory or fluid nature of time.

In the same year in which he joined the Surrealist movement, Dalí met his love, inspiration, muse and future wife Gala (real name Elena Ivanovna Diakonova). In 1930, Dalí purchased a *barraca* (small fisherman's hut) in Portlligat, where he and Gala lived for over 40 years, gradually extending and adding to it. Dalí lived there until Gala's death in 1982, and it is now a museum, maintained exactly as it was when the couple lived there, housing many of their personal belongings and photographs of famous friends taken there, including Coco Chanel, Ingrid Bergman and Walt Disney (with whom Dalí collaborated in 1946 on the animated short film *Destino*, and which was finally completed and released in 2003). If you visit, you will be shown round in groups of up to eight people, who are taken into the house every ten minutes. In this way, the tranquil atmosphere, beautiful bay views from every window and the individual exhibits can be fully appreciated.

A few miles inland from glittering Cadaqués and Portlligat, is Figueres, where Dalí grew up. The name Figueres translates to Fig Tree, as copious numbers of these trees used to grow across the town that comprises a central Old Town, where most of the cultural attractions are located, and a central avenue of La Rambla that connects the old quarter with the newer parts of town that were developed in the nineteenth and twentieth centuries. Across Figueres are various public squares. Each square has its own architecture and character – in some, markets are held regularly, others are quieter. Dalí devotees will want to head to the Teatre-Museu Dalí; a quirky, extravagant, permanent exhibition of his work, which attracts tourists from all over the world. Opened in 1974, the museum was designed by Dalí himself, and it contains work from the entire expanse of his career, from his early beginnings to his utterly ostentatious late works of the early twentieth century.

ARTISTIC   43

Cinematic

Görlitz

Where? Germany

Which? *The Grand Budapest Hotel* (Wes Anderson, 2014)

What? Perfectly preserved old border town where much movie magic is made

Outside the ornate windows, snow swirls, soft and dreamlike as a watercolour picture. Inside, the champagne flows. Bell-hops in bright purple dash between exquisitely coutured dowagers, tycoons and nobles, balancing hatboxes, shifting trunks and scooping up diamanté-collared poodles. The heady scent of L'Air de Panache wafts around the potted palms and colonnades, while money and nostalgia drip off everything from the fur stoles and furnishings to the larger-than-life people. It's a grande dame hotel in its pomp, a vivid bygone world to which it's bewitching to return, even if only for an hour or two . . .

The Grand Budapest Hotel recalls the inter-war exploits of legendary concierge Monsieur Gustave H. (Ralph Fiennes) and his trusted lobby boy Zero Moustafa (Tony Revolori) at the titular landmark retreat in the Alpine Sudetenwaltz of the Republic of Zubrowka. The plot involves death, theft, murder, exquisite baking, incarceration, jail-breaking and gunfighting, all played out against the backdrop of a continent that is changing fast, and will never be the same again. Although the movie doesn't specifically name-check real events, the rise of Nazism – in the guise of the grey-uniformed 'ZZ' soldiers – looms large.

Zubrowka is fictional, but fully realised. Writer-director Wes Anderson fashions a fully-fleshed world for his bittersweet comedy caper: not only does Zubrowka have towns and hotels but also its own currency (the klübeck) and newspaper (the *Trans-Alpine Yodel*). It is a delicious confection, fashioned – in trademark Anderson style – from detailed research and a child-like imagination. But Zubrowka is also part-bedded in reality, with much of the filming taking place in the fairytale-like town of Görlitz.

Located in East Saxony, on the banks of the Lusatian Neisse, Görlitz is Germany's easternmost town. Indeed, half of it lies over the border:

CINEMATIC   45

Görlitz and Zgorzelec, just across the river in Poland, used to be one united city but were divided after the Second World War. This real crossroads location makes Görlitz ideal for make-believe Zubrowka, a place of unidentified Central/Eastern European-ness on the brink of war, in a state of flux, in its last gasp of aristocratic decadence.

Görlitz survived the Second World War virtually untouched and, as such, its Old Town of tightly packed streets and squares is still lined with some 4,000 monuments and buildings encompassing 500 years of architectural history, from Gothic, Renaissance and Baroque to Wilhelminian and Jugendstil. The whole place is a traveller's joy and a movie-maker's dream – so it's no surprise that many other films have been shot here, including Tarantino's *Inglourious Basterds* and *The Reader*, also starring Ralph Fiennes.

The look of the Grand Budapest itself is based on early twentieth-century photochrome prints of Europe's historic Alpine and spa hotels, with their mountain funiculars, bathhouses, Neo-Baroque flounce and ice-cream parlour shades. A scale model – more rose-iced wedding cake than life-like building – was made. But the interiors were provided by Kaufhaus Görlitz, not a hotel but an Art Nouveau department store, opened in Görlitz in 1913. Although disused since 2010, it has retained its palatial feel, comprising a three-tier atrium, grand staircases, arched galleries, functioning elevators and ornate chandeliers, topped with a great enamelled-glass dome. It provided a spectacular skeleton onto which the crew could construct two iterations of the hotel: one, all 1930s glamour, in vibrant reds, purples and pinks; the other, 1960s brown-orange communist chic. The movie even revived the Kaufhaus' fortunes: since filming, new buyers have pledged to reopen it as a store once more. In the meantime, it's open for tours on certain days of the week – a must, if you can time it right.

Take a leisurely wander around Görlitz and the essence of Zubrowka can be found elsewhere. The keen-eyed will recognise the striking sandstone façade of the Schönhof, the town's oldest Renaissance building (now home to the Silesian Museum), the magnificent portal of the Ratsapotheke (townhall pharmacy) and the view to the fortified Reichenbach Tower along Brüderstrasse, or Brother Street, which links the Upper and Lower Market Squares – Zero picks up copies of the *Trans-Alpine Yodel* here but in reality it's a good place to shop for trinkets or stop for coffee and cake.

At one point Zero's sweetheart, Agatha (Saoirse Ronan), cycles down cobbled Fischmarkt, past the pastel-hued shopfront of Mendl's patisserie. Mendl's doesn't exist, and its elaborately tiled interiors were filmed in Dresden's Pfunds Molkerei, but the street is a delight to stroll along, and the movie's signature cream-filled Courtesan au Chocolat choux pastries were created by a local baker, at Görlitz's Café CaRe.

Also, in the background of this shot is the Dreifaltigkeitskirche (Trinity Church) tower, the town's oldest Gothic structure, established in 1234 by Franciscan monks – its high vaulted ceilings and elaborate altarpiece stand in for the movie's mountaintop convent, seemingly only reachable by cable car. The exterior of that convent is played by the elegant cloth merchants' arcades outside the Brauner Hirsch (Brown Stag) townhouse. Once an esteemed inn and brewery, this vast Baroque house has hosted many illustrious guests over the years, from Russian Tsar Nicholas I to German Emperor Wilhelm I. And it hosted Grand Budapest too: several sets were constructed within its cavernous interior, from Zero's spartan bedroom to Agatha's attic; spa scenes were also staged in the old baths. These days the Brauner Hirsch is empty but there are plans to open it up as a film museum, an apt way to celebrate 'Görliwood's' rich cinematic legacy.

Foodie

Lyon

Where? Auvergne-Rhône-Alpes, France
Why? Unique establishments offering the finest French dining in humble and hearty places

Walk in and it hits you: air thick with heat, meat and bonhomie. The space itself is small and simple. Just a shiny counter and a few red-check-draped tables, tightly packed in. Thick-bottomed carafes are lined up; wine glasses wait to be filled, raised and clinked. Saucepans and sausages dangle from the ceiling while faded photos and old posters decorate the walls. On a chalkboard menu, the flouncy ronde script peddles eel stew, pike dumplings and *tête de veau* (calf's head). Michelin stars may spangle this city, but it's these timeless bistros that really shine . . .

That Lyon is deemed the gastronomic capital of a country as gastronomic as France makes it a strong contender for gastronomic king of the world. A bold but fair claim: this sophisticated city has long been renowned for its excellent eating. Today, it boasts innumerable patisseries, charcuteries, boulangeries and fromageries, and a reputed 4,000 restaurants, giving it one of the highest per capita concentrations in the country.

Lyon's location helps. In the centre-east of France, on the edge of the Alps, at the meeting of the Rhône and Saône rivers, it's the country's larder. All the best produce is in easy reach: fruit, vegetables and olive oil from the south, freshwater fish from the Dombes marshlands, lauded chicken from Bresse, pork from the Monts du Lyonnais massif, cheese from nearby Alpine meadows, wines from Beaujolais and the Rhône. Indeed, it's been a major wine hub since the Romans arrived, christening it Lugdunum in 43 BCE. In the Middle Ages many trade fairs were held here. Then, from the fifteenth century, Lyon developed as a silk-producing centre – one of the reasons for the city's extensive network of *traboules*, the covered, cobbled, secretive passages once used by weavers to protect the precious fabrics from inclement weather. Much business was done here, many people came through, and they all needed feeding.

48   EUROPE

The tradition of *bouchons* – Lyon's trademark family-run bistros – began in Croix-Rousse, the *canut* (silk workers) district. The name 'bouchon' supposedly derives from the bundles of tree branches that innkeepers would hang on their doors to signal their offerings to peckish passers-by. These rustic establishments were allowed to serve wine with food, and specialised in hearty, honest fare. This was developed from the mid-eighteenth century by les *Mères Lyonnaises* (mothers of Lyons), humble but pioneering home cooks who started opening their own restaurants, having worked in the households of the upper classes. The most famous was Mère Brazier (born in 1895), who became the first woman in France to be awarded three Michelin stars. She went on to teach the local-born goliath of French gastronomy, Paul Bocuse.

Accustomed to making use of the offal and offcuts unwanted by the bourgeoise, the mothers didn't waste a thing. Still today, classic bouchon dishes include ripely odoured *andouillette* sausage, made with pig intestines, *tablier de sapeur* (fried and breaded tripe), *clapotons* (sheep's feet cooked in a vinaigrette) and *quenelles de brochet* (carp paste dumplings). Less challenging specialities are *salade Lyonnaise* (with croutons, bacon and poached egg), *cervelle de canut* ('silk worker's brain', though actually a type of herby cheese spread), *tarte praline* and *bugnes* (twisted doughnuts).

There is still an abundance of bouchons in Lyon, especially in the districts of Part-Dieu (also home to the enormous Halles de Lyon-Paul Bocuse food hall) and colourful Croix-Rousse. However, not all of them are members of Les Bouchons Lyonnais, the association founded in 2012 to ensure the traditions of these historic establishments are upheld. Les Bouchons Lyonnais is not a registered trademark, more a manifesto for how bouchons should be. That is, warm and convivial; a menu of simple, homemade dishes; Beaujolais served in pot *Lyonnais* pitchers; pushed-close wooden tables and rustic decor; and a zinc countertop, behind which a larger-than-life owner holds court. Look out for the association's Gnafron logo. This ruddy-cheeked bon vivant puppet, created in the nineteenth century, marks out affiliated bouchons and symbolises their motto: good food and wine, in good spirits.

FOODIE   49

Literary

La Mancha

Where? Spain
Which? *Don Quixote* by Miguel de Cervantes (1615)
Why? Windswept Spanish plains of windmills, wheatfields and literary giants

The sun slips earthwards, its last rays caressing the endless plateau of nodding wheat, saffron blooms and ancient olive groves. The light glows, too, on a phalanx of hulking white giants, lording the hillside and waving their long arms as if urging a fight. Yet these mighty monsters, so pugnacious from a distance, prove harmless up close. Not ogres but windmills, transformed by the day's late haze and the flights of a fanciful mind . . .

The late Middle Ages heralded Spain's *Siglo de Oro* – Golden Age. From around 1492, following the end of the Reconquest, to the middle of the seventeenth century, the arts, architecture and exploration flourished here. Columbus set off for the New World, Velázquez and El Greco dazzled with their paintbrushes, the royal monastery at El Escorial was built. And writer Miguel de Cervantes penned *Don Quixote* – not only the best-ever Spanish novel, but arguably the best novel of all time.

Cervantes' hefty tale follows Alonso Quixano, a middle-aged *hidalgo* (nobleman) and reader of medieval romances who titles himself Don Quixote, pulls on a suit of armour and sets out – with his squat squire Sancho Panza – like a Renaissance, horse-riding Batman to right wrongs and resurrect chivalry. But his escapades seldom go to plan; the 'Knight of the Sorrowful Countenance' frequently gets painfully trampled or beaten. In his magnum opus, Cervantes spoofs the genre Alonso so loves, and introduces the world of literature – hitherto fixated on myths and monsters – to universal truths and a fat dose of reality.

Don Quixote's domain is La Mancha, the wild, fertile plateau south of Madrid, and Spain's least densely populated region. Like the novel, the landscape here is epic: big deep-blue skies stretching over a near-infinite roll of red earth, flaxen crops and vine stripes, the occasional whitewashed windmill, the odd ruined castle, a scatter of country inns.

It's a place where grand adventures might be had, or where the scale and the heat and the teasing horizon – always seeming just out of reach – might simply drive you mad.

Cervantes names few specific places; also, his settings can be slippery, transformed in Quixote's florid imagination, which turns inns into castles and farm girls into princesses. But it's still possible to trace a quixotic route across La Mancha – not least thanks to professors at a Madrid university, who spent years deciphering clues and postulating donkey speeds in order to pinpoint Don Quixote's home, 'somewhere in La Mancha, in a place whose name I do not care to remember'. The scholars settled on the town of Villanueva de los Infantes, stranded on the tableland 225 kilometres (140 miles) south of Madrid. Regardless of whether the Cervantes connection is valid, it's a charming little town, with many sixteenth- and seventeenth-century churches and palaces, and statues of Quixote, Panza and their steeds wandering across the handsome Plaza Mayor.

The foothills village of Puerto Lápice is explicitly mentioned in the novel. Here, Quixote persuades an innkeeper to knight him; today, a reconstructed inn gives flavour if not authenticity. Also named in the book is El Toboso, home of Dulcinea, the 'superhuman beauty' with whom Quixote is infatuated. The traditional sixteenth-century farmhouse once belonging to the woman who inspired Dulcinea is now a museum, complete with old iron and copper kitchenware, horse tack and a wine cellar and olive press. It's a place more befitting the peasant girl Dulcinea really is rather than the highborn lady that delusional Quixote believes her to be.

However, perhaps the most Quixote moment is to be found by driving across La Mancha's mind-messing emptiness towards Campo de Criptana. The town looms like a ghost, its whitewashed old Moorish centre seeping over a slope below a handful of hilltop 'giants' – site of Quixote's 'fearful and never imagined adventure of the windmills'. In Cervantes' time, around 30 or 40 windmills were clustered here; now 13 remain, waving their sails at the featureless plain, still stirring visions of Spain's great, flawed hero.

LITERARY 51

Musical

Reykjavik

Where? Iceland
Why? Haunting, high-performing sounds, formed alongside the island itself

This youthful land – a strange, nascent place, still in the process of being forged – has its own distinct soundtrack. A discordant symphony of creaking fissures, calving ice, crashing waves, belching mud pools, thunderous waterfalls, exploding geysers; even the eerie whistles and hisses of the aurora borealis. Iceland is like a boxer cracking his knuckles before a fight with a steam engine; it's the audible growing pains of an acned teen, sprouting into their skin, popping their pimples. But it's not only geological groans filling the air; this island far from anywhere, subject to far-north furies, has developed a most singular sound. The reverberations of which are felt and heard around the world, punching well above their weight . . .

Iceland is a hardscrabble sort of place. Those that chose to live here a millennium or so ago had to cope with savage weather, volatile mountains and the earth literally splitting beneath their feet. Perhaps because of this – due to a survivalist need for close-knit community or a desire to try to make some sense of their challenging world – music has always been central to Icelandic life.

The origins of Icelandic music lie in *rímur*, the folkloric narratives brought here by the Vikings. Intrepid Norsemen first sailed to this rugged Atlantic outpost in the ninth century, bringing with them their songs and sagas – tales of love and loss, life at sea, endurance, conflict, mythical hidden folk and mighty heroes. The sorts of tales that would be shared around the peat fire; low, alliterative, hypnotic rhymes chanted as families sat winnowing and weaving, while outside the wind howled around the gargantuan glaciers and the active volcanoes.

Because few instruments made it here, the human voice was long the island's chief musical tool. And, due to Iceland's extreme isolation, the singing style remained little altered by external fashions and influences,

MUSICAL   55

leaving the sound scarcely changed from the fourteenth to the twentieth century. Indeed, a simplified timeline of major moments in Icelandic musical development would probably skip from around 1208 – when the oldest hymn still sung today was put on to parchment – to the late 1980s, when the debut album by alt-rock band The Sugarcubes (*Life's Too Good*, 1988) became a global hit.

After this, though, that timeline explodes, not least thanks to one Sugarcube, a certain Björk Guðmundsdóttir, whose raw, spectral, unearthly vocals became Iceland's biggest export since cod. In the following decades, Iceland – population a mere 360,000 – has massively overachieved in the music world, producing mesmeric etherealists Sigur Rós, folk-rockers Of Monsters and Men, multi-instrumentalist Ólafur Arnalds, bluesy Kaleo and a host of other artists of whom countries a hundred times the size would be proud.

Reykjavík, Iceland's culturally cool, geothermally smouldering capital, is the heartland of the country's music scene. It's home to Bad Taste (*Smekkleysa*), the indie label that propelled The Sugarcubes, and which is still flying the flag for local musicians and artists; it has a shop on the capital's Hjartatorg (Heart Square). Reykjavík is also where you'll find the striking glass-clad Harpa Music Hall (home to the Iceland Symphony Orchestra), a multitude of bars and cafés that host live bands, eclectic creatives collaborating year-round and, come early November, the massive and immersive Iceland Airwaves music festival.

But it's really the land beyond the city that's done most to nurture this upswell of musical magnificence. It's the great roar of Gullfoss, the enormous exhalations of Geysir, the Atlantic swell smacking Reynisfjara's jet-black sand, the spurt and spew of Eyjafjallajökull. Artists coming of age in this cut-off, untampered-with natural landscape, ears still ringing with folk traditions, inevitably found distinctive styles. Iceland the island has a dynamism, a naked power, a wild unpredictability – and so does the music it shapes. It is a sound built on a bedrock of *rímur* that bounces off glaciers and snow-capped peaks; sounds composed by the experimental and the curious, to be shouted into the wind or whispered into the utter silence of a place barely inhabited. Because, in a nation that's developed in virtual isolation, only independent since 1944, and still being moulded by Mother Nature, every Icelander is determining for themselves what Icelandic music actually is.

Delft

Where? Netherlands
Which? View of Delft (c.1660–61) by Johannes Vermeer
What? Charming city of soft, fluid light

The word 'Delft' itself is derived from delven, (meaning to dig), as a great deal of digging led to the intricate network of canals that hold this charming city together, rather like a painting by famous Dutch artist Piet Mondrian. Part of the original city planning, the canals of Delft were built to serve as both defence systems and lifelines for the inhabitants. Even today, the canals – or *grachten* – are the veins of the city, keeping its heart beating.

Suffused with artistic imagery through its connections with the glowing, meticulous paintings of Johannes Vermeer (1632–75) and the delicate blue patterned pottery that has been made there since the sixteenth century, Delft is a visual feast. Small enough to walk around, much of it is closed to cars, so the peaceful canals, bridges, churches, mansions and courtyards can be enjoyed alongside the livelier museums, markets, pubs and bars. In close-up, the elegant splendour of the place conveys the pride of a nation that had fought for – and gained – its own autonomy. Officially a city since 1246, Delft is nestled between The Hague and Rotterdam. When, in 1572, William of Orange (often called the 'Father of the Fatherland') moved to Delft, it served as headquarters for the Dutch resistance against Spain during the Eighty Years' War (1568–1648). Ultimately, this resulted in Dutch independence, which in turn led to the cultural zenith of the Dutch Golden Age in the seventeenth century, when the Netherlands rose politically and economically. Everywhere you walk in the city, you can feel the allure of that gilded period, and recall the paintings of the Dutch Golden Age, particularly the light-filled works of Vermeer.

While strolling around Delft, be sure to admire the beautifully preserved, mostly seventeenth-century buildings that look just as they did when Vermeer was painting there, alongside other great artists of the Dutch Golden Age such as Pieter de Hooch, Carel Fabritius and Jan

Steen. The Oude Kerk (Old Church, consecrated in 1306), nicknamed Oude Jan (Old John) or Scheve Jan (Skewed John), has a 75-metre-high (246-feet-high) brick tower that leans about 2 metres from the vertical. Climb to the top and marvel at the glorious panorama beneath you, watching boats glide along the canals. Among other notable Delft residents, such as the painter Hendrick Cornelisz van Vliet and scientist Antonie van Leeuwenhoek, Vermeer is buried in the Oude Kerk, while he was baptised in the Nieuwe Kerk (New Church, built in 1496).

Born in Delft in 1632, Vermeer spent his entire life in the city. Now one of the best-known Dutch artists, he experimented endlessly to create the illusion of three-dimensional space and render the effects of natural light in paint. While not a single drawing by him has survived, his compositions are complex and accurate in scale and perspective. To begin a work, he drew, then applied 'dead colouring' or underpainting; a monochrome version of the final painting. Colour was applied next in layers and glazes to achieve a variety of effects, and his insight into how the eye registers optical effects can be seen in his careful rendering of textures and tones. His two paintings *The Little Street* (c.1657–58) and *View of Delft* (c.1660–61) portray the city that he knew and loved so well, while his *Girl with a Pearl Earring* (c.1665) and *The Milkmaid* (c.1660) are studies of (anonymous) Delft residents. The Vermeer Centrum Delft brings together life-size reproductions of all 37 of Vermeer's paintings that have survived (it is thought that he painted around 50 in total), with information about each work and about his life. From a high vantage point, looking down on the calm waterfront, *View of Delft* shows both how little and, contrastingly, how much the city has changed. Vermeer included the area of river that had been widened to serve as the harbour, the distant tower of the Oude Kerk and the dazzlingly sunlit Nieuwe Kerk. His painstaking approach of precise details, diffused highlights and lustrous light effects appear to have sunk deep into the psyche of the city – *View of Delft* is probably the most recognised cityscape in western art – and visitors to this charmed city can still admire this same view in the soft, fluid light of Delft today.

ARTISTIC   59

Foodie

Bologna

Where? Emilia-Romagna, Italy
Why? Feast on the Fat One

Spaghetti bolognese? Don't even dare whisper it. Not among these porticoed streets. The globally ubiquitous dish – that student stalwart, that first-date plate, that child-pleasing slurry – may have taken the name of this fine old city, but it certainly doesn't have its blessing. 'Spag bol' is a cuss word here; culinary blasphemy; an unholy mangling of meat and wheat. This is a place of history, intellect and industry with a prodigious belly. A place where terracotta towers meet elasticated trousers. Food here is rich and calorific, cooked with time and love, infused with tradition, and messed with at your peril . . .

Bologna, capital of the north Italian province of Emilia-Romagna, was first established by the Etruscans in the sixth century BCE. And since then, it has garnered many nicknames. To some it's *La Dotta* (the 'Learned One'), for its ancient university, founded in 1088 and still going strong. To others it's *La Rossa* (the 'Red One'), borne of its long history of left-leaning politics: the *Paradisum Voluptatis* act, passed here in 1256, made it the first city in the world to abolish slavery while, more recently, Bologna was the centre of anti-fascist sentiment during the Second World War. But to absolutely everyone it is *La Grassa* (the 'Fat One') – the city that loves its food. Dieters, look elsewhere: the Bolognese menu is unapologetically meaty, creamy, buttery, oily, indulgent and delicious.

A prosperous trade and agriculture hub since Roman times, Bologna sits amid a land of plenty. The surrounding countryside is awash with olive groves, vineyards and productive farmland. The city itself, a compact maze of medieval lanes, red rooftops and endless porticoes (arched arcades), is positively obese, full to bursting with food plucked, produced and perfected in the region.

Take a walk around and you'll get it. There are stalls hawking gargantuan vegetables and shops full of yolk-yellow pasta, hand-rolled into every shape and size. There are cheesemongers proffering superbly stinky Parmigiano Reggiano from nearby Parma, grocers' shelves sticky

FOODIE   61

with aceto balsamico from nearby Modena and musky delis hung with huge hams and local mortadella cheese. There are homely *osterie* (wine bars that serve a simple menu) crammed with check-clothed tabletops and kitchens full of women in dark aprons pinching globs of pork into tiny tortellini – just as they have for generations.

But one dish has come to define Bologna's stomach more than any other: spaghetti bolognese. Or, more correctly, *tagliatelle al ragú Bolognese* – the original recipe to which all others must bow. The roots of the dish aren't entirely clear. Ragù stems from the French *ragout*, itself from *ragoûter* ('to revive the taste'), describing the method of cooking meat and vegetables over a low heat for a long time. *'Piano piano'*, as an Italian *nonna* might say: 'little by little'.

This slow-cooking concept found its way from medieval France to Italy, at first without tomatoes – they don't appear in ragù recipes until the mid-nineteenth century – and as more of a stew than a sauce. Cookbook author Pellegrino Artusi is credited as the first to serve ragù on pasta, in 1891. Though he also advocated chucking in chicken livers, sliced truffles and a half-cup of cream – additions that may be frowned upon by purists today.

In fact, Italy is full of regional ragùs, but Bologna's remains king. An official recipe for tagliatelle al ragú Bolognese was even registered by the Italian Academy of Cuisine at Bologna's Chamber of Commerce in 1982. This does not stop the constant bickering between home cooks, matriarchs and Michelin chefs about the dish's precise methods and ingredients. But there are some rules on which (almost) everyone agrees.

For a start, the main ingredients. These should include fatty and flavoursome meat, usually beef and/or pork, plus pancetta too. There must be finely chopped onion, carrot and celery, caramelised for maximum flavour. Tomatoes are now key, though there's dispute over whether tinned are ever allowed. And wine is a must – ideally a glug of Emilia-Romagna's lightly fruity pignoletto. Then salt, possibly pepper, maybe bay leaves, occasionally nutmeg. No other herbs. Never, ever garlic.

One key thing: it is never served on spaghetti. The correct pasta is tagliatelle – flatter, wider, ribbon-like strands that better hold the meat. Tagliatelle is an Emilia-Romagna speciality, one of its famed *pasta all'uovo* (egg pastas), made with a ratio of 100g (3½oz) of flour to one large egg. Referred to in the 1570 tome *The Art of Cooking*, tagliatelle has wormed its way into the local consciousness ever since. Generations of Bolognese children were raised being told that if they didn't eat their tagliatelle they wouldn't grow big; girls who couldn't make tagliatelle were warned they would never find a husband. The phrase *'Conti corti e tagliatelle lunghe'* ('May you have short bills and long tagliatelle') is a common local maxim.

Tagliatelle is traditionally made by hand and should, aficionados say, be worked with a wooden rolling pin, on a wooden surface. The natural grain of the wood creates a texture on the dough that helps sauce adhere to the strands. The Chamber of Commerce recipe even specifies the tagliatelle's perfect width: 8 millimetres (⅜ inches), otherwise expressed as 12,270th the height of Bologna's leaning Torre degli Asinelli. Built in the twelfth century, this 97 metre- (318 foot-) high tower is the symbol of the city. It's possible to climb the 498 steps to the top for one of the best views over Bologna, though you might not want to attempt that climb right after dinner.

Literary

Bath

Where? England
Which? *Northanger Abbey* & *Persuasion* by Jane Austen (1818)
What? Splendid English city, setting for a send-up of Georgian high society

The crescent's honeyed stone glows in the afternoon sunlight, a radiant architectural swoosh between the neat green lawn and cloudless blue sky. A long procession of Ionic columns and sash windows sweeps away in perfect symmetry, while the footsteps of the slowly strolling curious – faces up-turned, mouths agape – slap on worn-smooth slabs. Such splendour! But look behind the flawless facade and this elegant terrace tells a different story. Round the other side it's an untidy irregularity of annexes and add-ons.

A Queen Anne front, a Mary-Anne back. A public face concealing darker truths . . .

'Oh! Who can ever be tired of Bath?' Who indeed. In *Northanger Abbey*, Jane Austen's playful satire on the Gothic novel, heroine Catherine Morland speaks of the allure of the Somerset city in the early nineteenth century – an allure that continues to this day. In England, there is nowhere else quite like it; nowhere as perfectly, homogeneously preserved. To walk along its sweeping crescents and golden streets now is almost to step straight back into Austen's pages, minus the bonnets and breeches.

Bath nestles within a loop of the River Avon, on the southern edge of the rolling-green Cotswold Hills. The city owes its situation and success to its hot springs, unique in Britain, and first developed by the Romans who built an elaborate bathing complex here, which they called *Aquae Sulis*. Though the Roman temple fell into disuse, and was eventually forgotten – until its rediscovery in 1775 – these healing waters continued to be sought after. From the seventeenth century, following a succession of royal visits, Bath became the resort du jour, with society's finest coming here for 'the season' to bathe, drink, see, be seen, gossip and matchmake. Befitting its status, the city was given a stylish Georgian

64   EUROPE

facelift, with father-and-son architects John Wood the Elder (1704–1754) and Younger (1728–1782) remodelling the city, using the local golden limestone. Between them they designed many splendid streets and edifices: Queen Square, the perfect Palladian ring of The Circus, the grand Assembly Rooms, the Royal Crescent's curve of 30 classical townhouses. By the time Jane Austen moved to Bath in 1801, living here until 1806, it was the most coherent and majestic of cityscapes, even if its fashionability was beginning to wane.

Austen herself wasn't especially enamoured with Bath. She was a creature of the countryside and found the city's superficiality and ostentation overbearing. But it provided rich creative pickings. An entire city obsessed with manners and class was a useful backdrop for her brand of quick-witted, acerbic social commentary. Two of her novels, *Northanger Abbey* and *Persuasion*, which were first published in one volume in 1818 shortly after Austen's death, are partly set in the city. They offer not only a picture of Bath, but of English high society during the Regency era.

Balls and parties were an integral part of fashionable life. Jane herself, as well as *Northanger*'s Catherine and *Persuasion*'s Anne Elliot, attended gatherings at Bath's Assembly Rooms, opened in 1771, where four public rooms – the Octagon, Ball Room, Card Room and Tea Room – allowed for all sorts of socialising. The eighteenth-century crystal chandeliers, under which Austen's envoys would have danced and whispered, still dazzle from the soaring ceilings; now the building also houses the Fashion Museum, where you can try on Georgian hats and dresses.

The Pump Room was another must in Austen's time. The beau monde would visit this colonnaded building by Bath Abbey to take either the curative waters or afternoon tea, to listen to the orchestra and to 'parade up and down for an hour, looking at everybody and speaking to no one'. It was during preparatory investigations into the construction of the Pump Room that the remains of the Roman complex were rediscovered. Today, part of this grand meeting place is the excellent Roman Baths museum, where you can descend into an underbelly of ancient pools, temples and hypocausts. However, in the Pump Room's main hall, you can still eat cake and finger sandwiches, and you can still sip the medicinal, if foul-tasting, mineral waters from the King's Spring.

One of the real beauties of Bath is that so much is so unchanged. And not just the landmark buildings but the layout of the streets themselves. For instance, Austen has her players shopping on lively Milsom Street, still one of the city's premier retail rows; look up above the modern shop fronts to the tops of the buildings and you're transported back in

66   EUROPE

time. Austen's characters also promenade Great Pulteney Street – still the city's most impressive Georgian avenue – and take carriages up to the 'lofty, dignified situation' of Camden Place, a little-touristed terrace affording excellent views if you can bear the stiff walk up.

Northanger's Catherine hastens to the Royal Crescent 'to breathe the fresh air of better company' (today many go to visit No. 1, now a museum furnished in eighteenth-century style). Meanwhile, at the close of *Persuasion,* Anne and her Captain Wentworth reconcile along the tree-lined Gravel Walk, which still connects the Royal Crescent with Queen Square.

Bath has become synonymous with Austen. Despite the destructive Bath Blitz of April 1942 and the so-called 'Sack of Bath' in the 1960s, when ill-thought urban development saw some heritage lost, the Georgian spirit of the city remains. It's easy to envisage the streets filled with ladies in their white gloves and empire-line dresses, and gents in their tailcoats and cravats. Come during the annual autumn Jane Austen Festival and you don't even need to imagine, as Catherine Morland and Anne Elliot-alikes really do flood the streets, their slippers and gauze gowns grazing the cobbles – Austen's creations come to life.

Guernica

Where? Spain
Which? *Guernica* (1937) by Pablo Picasso
What? Spanish town symbolising peace

On 26 April 1937, German bombers appeared over the blue skies of Guernica – or Gernika, in Basque – a peaceful market town in the province of Biscay, and launched the first aerial bombing raid of the Spanish Civil War. The defenceless town was razed to the ground by the Nazis, who were allies of General Francisco Franco, the fascist dictator who took control of Spain in 1939 until his death in 1975. The bombing shocked the world, turning Guernica into an everlasting symbol of the atrocity of war – a tragedy that was immortalised in the famous, monumental painting by Pablo Picasso (1881–1973).

Built on the intersection of the roads from Bermeo to Durango, and from Bilbao to Elantxobe and Lekeitio, Guernica was established in the fourteenth century. On a hillside in the town is an oak tree, Gernikako Arbola, where for centuries, locals have held assemblies to discuss matters affecting the community, laws have been drawn up and generations of Basque leaders and Spanish kings have sworn to respect the region. Behind Gernikako Arbola is the Assembly Hall or Meeting House, its elegant Neoclassical columns echoing the straight oak's trunk, and behind these is the Peace Park, a relaxing oasis that was created after the 1937 bombing, and where nowadays families and couples picnic, and children play, all around a large, semi-abstract sculpture by English sculptor Henry Moore.

Far removed from the horrors of the 1930s now, Guernica is once again a peaceful, thriving town, set in lush hills dotted with old farmhouses, all within sight of the sparkling azure Atlantic Ocean. The local area includes Mundaka, a small seaside resort where surfers gather throughout the seasons and whitewashed houses cluster, dominated by a Romanesque church that stands proudly by the sea. Outside the church walls, locals play the Basque racket game of pelota. Further west along the coast is the busy fishing port of Bermeo, with a large

ARTISTIC 69

dry dock and a clutch of colourful houses, connected by narrow streets. Historically, this little port has seen plenty of action since the fourteenth century, when whalers left to travel as far as Newfoundland for their quarry. Close by is the small hamlet of Elantxobe, where more colourful and whitewashed houses spread, seemingly clinging to the sheer cliff face, and steep alleyways lead down to a tiny harbour.

Then there's the town of Guernica itself. During the Spanish Civil War, Guernica was the northern stronghold of the Republican resistance movement and the heart of Basque culture. Even today, evidence of that April day can be seen in the pockmarks of bullet holes in the stone arcades of the old marketplace. It was market day when the bombing occurred, and women and children were out enjoying the spring sunshine. Then the pounding started, lasting for more than three hours. At the time, Picasso was living in France, and had been commissioned by the Spanish Republican government to create a mural for that summer's Paris Exhibition. He was working on ideas for it when he read a newspaper account of the bombing. Immediately, he abandoned the original idea he had been working on and began painting Guernica in black, white and grey, to reflect that he had learned of the atrocity through newsprint. The painting became Picasso's most powerful political statement, and one of the world's most renowned images of the tragedies of war and the individual suffering it inflicts. Soon after it was completed, the painting was taken around the world on a brief tour, where it became internationally acclaimed and drew attention to the Spanish Civil War. This was not what the Spanish Republican government had intended when they commissioned Picasso.

Picasso had not been back home to Spain for several years when the Nazis bombed Guernica and he vowed that neither he nor the painting would ever return to Spain while Franco remained in power. He began painting the vast work using the distorted approach he had become known for, which created a stronger expression of emotion than realism. He included a bull to symbolise Spain and suggest brutality, next to a sobbing woman holding a dead child. The bull's tail represents a flame or curl of smoke from the bombing. Behind it, a dove holds an olive branch as a sign of peace. A light bulb blazes from the ceiling, its jagged edge suggesting an explosion – or perhaps an all-seeing eye, or the sun, again, a symbol of hope. Although Picasso rarely explained his work, he said that the contorted horse stands for the people. Next to the horse's head, a terrified woman holds a candle. In traditional Christian iconography, a flame is a sign of the Holy Spirit or implies hope. There are two 'hidden' or subliminal images in the horse's body. One is a human skull symbolising death, while a second is below the body; another bull's head, its horn goring the horse's breast. Under the horse is a dead, dismembered soldier with a severed arm that still grasps a shattered sword from which a flower grows. In the soldier's open palm is a stigmata, a symbol of martyrdom from Christ's crucifixion. Of his famous work, Picasso said: 'In the panel on which I am working, which I shall call Guernica . . . I clearly express my abhorrence of the military caste which has sunk Spain in an ocean of pain and death.'

Some 43 years after the bombing, Guernica was rebuilt and declared a global symbol of peace, with its own peace museum, the Museo de la Paz de Gernika, and park. The church bells that once pealed as the first warning that aircraft had been spotted now chime sweetly for weddings and baptisms, celebrating and honouring new beginnings. Visitors of any faith, gender, age or ethnicity will be touched by the serenity and history of this special, reflective place.

Literary

Nordland

Where? Norway
Which? Growth of the Soil by Knut Hamsun (1917)
What? Spectacular Norwegian wilderness where quiet heroes might prevail

A sip of water from a purling stream. A handful of bilberries. A lichen-crusted log on which to briefly rest. The ripe soil below nurtures the spruce and pine, the tiny ferns and cow mushrooms, the paint-splatter of wildflowers. A hare bounds across the grass, a grouse sputters from the heathers, the forest gently soughs, but otherwise all is quiet. This place is now. But it could be then. Or – with hope, with care – tomorrow. A timeless place of simplicity and awe . . .

The county of Nordland encompasses more than a third of Norway, but only around five per cent of its people. Even today, this feels like pioneer country. A landscape of coastal mountains, narrow fjords and pine, birch and aspen; a region of Sami people, old superstitions, northern lights and midnight sun. The world that shaped Knut Hamsun.

Hamsun was born in 1859 to peasant farmers in central Norway. But his childhood was spent in Hamarøy, north of the Arctic Circle, where he worked on his uncle's farm. He didn't go to school until he was nine years old. The land was his early education. And the land is the lead character in his masterpiece, *Markens Grøde – Growth of the Soil*.

This 1917 novel follows the quietly courageous endeavours of Isak, a strong, monosyllabic farmer-settler, and his wife Inger, a woman with a harelip and 'good, heavy hands'. To begin, Isak sets out alone, seeking 'a place, a patch of ground'. On his chosen plot he chops, hoes and sows, building a home with nought but sweat and brawn – an understated hero. With the passing of the seasons, he meets Inger, has children, lives a life of 'little happenings and big, all in their turn'. There are some black moments – not least infanticide – but there is also an evocation of rural life in all its uncomplicated beauty.

Growth of the Soil was a hit. In 1920, Hamsun was awarded the Nobel Prize for Literature, chiefly for this saga of strife and struggle.

It encapsulated the life of pioneering Norwegian homesteaders at the beginning of the twentieth century. Norway only gained full independence in 1905; Hamsun's tale of a man claiming his place was nation-building fiction from an author with a love of agrarian society, homeland and blood-and-soil nature.

These beliefs had a darker consequence. They chimed closely with the ethos of Nazi Germany, and Hamsun became an outspoken supporter of Adolf Hitler and National Union Party leader Vidkun Quisling, who collaborated with the Nazis after they occupied Norway in 1940. Hamsun even gifted his Nobel medal to Joseph Goebbels. This has muddied the author's legacy. Some scholars laud him as the best of a generation, even the 'father of modern literature', but, no matter how great the work, many cannot forgive his wartime stance.

Because of this, it wasn't until 2009 – on the 150th anniversary of his birth – that one of Norway's greatest novelists was commemorated in a significant way. The striking Knut Hamsun Centre, which draws architectural inspiration from the region's stave churches, sod roofs and rugged mountains, sits in the village of Presteid in Hamarøy, on the banks of the Glimma River. It's not without controversy. But it offers an exploration of both the writer's words and world views. And the view from the tower, over the countryside that inspired the writer, is undeniably splendid.

Also, there's nothing controversial about the soul of Norway's Nordland – the land itself, the soil of Isak and Inger. Exploring its hills, fjords and forests lies outside politics. Indeed, it's pleasingly democratic: the Norwegian law of *allemannsrett* (Everyman's right) grants any individual permission to hike, camp and forage on another's land, as long as they do so respectfully. So you can head into the wilderness and claim, for one night at least, a land of your own.

LITERARY   73

Foodie

Copenhagen

Where? Zealand, Denmark
Why? Be blown away in the capital of New Nordic cuisine

Is it food? Or a new way of thinking? The creations being placed on the table run from the sublime to the whimsical, the weird and even to the inedible. There's beer brewed from birch sap; fairy gardens of fungi and moss; roast turbot drifting in mushroom tea; razor clams on horseradish snow; Christmas doughnuts stuffed with fried fish; asparagus spears furred with mould; reindeer genitals; brains; live ants sprinkled like pepper; fjord shrimp served still swimming. It's disorientating, confusing, challenging, fabulous. It's the culinary catalyst that's transformed an entire region . . .

Historically, the Danish diet was pretty simple. Before the Industrial Revolution most people here lived off the land, subsisting on what they could grow, nurture, catch or forage. Staples included root vegetables, brassicas and, later, potatoes; dark, wholegrain rye bread and porridge of millet, barley or oats; forest fruits and berries; a little meat; and plenty of fish – Denmark's coastline is 7,000 kilometres (4,350 miles) long, after all. Diets would adjust to the seasons. Long winters necessitated expertise in salting, smoking and pickling.

Fast forward to today and, in many ways, nothing – yet everything – has changed. The hub of Denmark's food revolution is the country's effervescent capital, Copenhagen (København). What began life as an unexceptional hamlet on the edge of the Øresund strait became, from the twelfth century, a fortified stronghold, a herring-fishing hub, a royal seat, a trading centre and, more latterly, one of the world's most liveable cities: colourful, clean, stylish, sustainability-focused, enviably cool.

Still, at the close of the twentieth century, it wasn't much thought of for its food. At this time Copenhagen had no real gastronomic identity. Eating here would likely be traditional, probably unremarkable. Fried pork with parsley sauce and pan-fried *frikadeller* (pork meatballs) were restaurant mainstays – the Danes love pork. Fancier places leant towards an imported French style. More fun were the informal

FOODIE   75

joints, like the street-side *pølsevogne* (hot dog wagons) grilling chunky sausages slathered in sweet mustard, crispy onions, pickled cucumbers and curried remoulade. Or the cafés serving smorgasbords of *smørrebrød*, the country's classic open sandwiches: neat rectangles of thin-sliced rye topped with everything from pickled herring to beef tartare, veal tongue, boiled eggs, potato salad and smoked eel.

Then 2004 arrived. Led by Danish food activist, cook and entrepreneur Claus Meyer, a group of 12 chefs from across the region convened in Copenhagen that year to discuss and create a manifesto for *Det Nye Nordiske Køkken* – New Nordic Cuisine. This would be a different way of thinking about the culinary offering of this northern European fraternity. A declaration with the lofty but commendable goal of transforming the Nordic countries – Denmark, Finland, Iceland, Norway, Sweden – into one of the world's greatest hubs for food.

The manifesto had ten points. It stated that New Nordic food should 'express the purity, freshness, simplicity and ethics' of the region. It should reflect changing seasons and local landscapes. It should promote Nordic products, producers and culinary traditions while developing new applications of traditional foods and combining them with the best ideas from overseas. As well as striving for good taste, it should be conscious of health and wellbeing, animal welfare and environmental sustainability. It wasn't a revolution to be confined to fine-dining establishments but a call to stir every farmer, fisher, cheesemonger, shopkeeper, wholesaler, coffee-grinder and home cook. It was about shifting mindsets and extolling the benefits of improving Nordic food culture for everyone.

The apogee of New Nordic is Noma, the Copenhagen phenomenon set up by Claus Meyer and chef René Redzepi in 2003. Frequent winner of 'Best Restaurant in the World' titles, Noma – an abbreviation of *nordisk* (Nordic) and *mad* (food) – is the movement's most headline-grabbing extreme. It is dedicated to extracting the full, hitherto unrecognised flavour possibilities of what lies on the city's doorstep via scientific experimentation and unbridled creativity. That means smoked carrots served on hay, hours-caramelised celeriac that slices like shawarma and delicate crab meat served in flatbreads that are cut and fried to look like, well, crabs.

But at its heart, New Nordic isn't a niche cuisine. And it's catching. Noma will close its doors in 2024 but its influence will continue to reverberate, because for 20 years the pioneering restaurant has been a talisman, helping to give Denmark a culinary identity and to revitalise the Copenhagen food scene. In that time it has inspired other restaurants to do better, so now the city is full of menus focused on bringing out the finest flavours of the region, places where local ingredients and ideas are permitted to shine.

And small-scale producers have been encouraged too, now seeing a market for their heritage fruits and grains, organic cheeses, sustainably farmed oysters or foreshore-foraged sea herbs. Carlsberg, the goliath of Danish grog-making, which started brewing in Copenhagen in 1847, is being countered by innovative newcomers like Mikkeller, founded in 2005 and the pioneer of Denmark's craft-brew movement.

New Nordic has upturned dining in Copenhagen. This former gastronomic wasteland is now one of the most delicious cities in the world, from the Michelin-starred places following in Noma's wake to the corner shops now stocking sea buckthorn on their shelves. The food here is daring and innovative but, for all its headline-grabbing oddities, also fresh and simple. It's recalling those historic Danish principles of eating local and seasonal, foraging and preserving, but with a new take. It's forward-thinking food made by going back to the roots.

Davos

Literary

Where? Switzerland
Which? The Magic Mountain by Thomas Mann (1924)
What? Timeless Swiss alpine idyll almost removed from the real world

The view from the hotel terrace is like a tonic; like sinking into a beautiful ice bath, thrillingly, rejuvenatingly fresh. Snow blankets everything; the rocks, hollows, tree boughs and high peaks have been cloaked, plumped and softened. Everything sparkles too, winter sun scattering diamonds across the powdery slopes. Up in the magical mountains, the real world seems far, far away. Who wouldn't feel better after spending a week, or even years, here . . . ?

The Magic Mountain by Thomas Mann is the tale of young and naïve Hans Castorp who goes to visit a tubercular cousin at a Swiss sanatorium – and doesn't leave. Instead, Castorp sinks rather happily into the insularity and decadence of sanatorium life. And while doctors try to improve his physical health, conversations with fellow patients end up expanding his mind.

A bit like Thomas Mann. An ardent patriot during the First World War, the German author revised his outlook in the conflict's dark aftermath. By 1924, when *The Magic Mountain* was published, he was leaning leftwards towards democracy and liberalism. But this is not the sole ideology of the novel: it doesn't propose any one answer; it makes clear that there are many contradictory ways to understand the world.

The Magic Mountain is also a meditation on the nature of time, which passes differently in the rarified air and seclusion of Davos' Berghof sanatorium. Here, shielded from external cares, the hours, days, months, years are a ceaselessness of extravagant meals, proscribed rest, woodland walks, intellectual discussion. To the latter end, an international cast – Russian, Italian, Asian, Polish; the planet in microcosm – is assembled in safe, neutral Switzerland to debate culture and philosophy. But as the patients in the sanatorium seek a cure, Europe beyond is sick. The novel begins in the first decade of the

78   EUROPE

twentieth century, the continent on the brink of war. When Castorp eventually leaves his alpine bubble seven years later, it's for the trenches. The final pages leave him limping across the mud, bombs falling, alive but with 'prospects poor'.

The hellish trenches are certainly a far cry from Mann's bewitched Swiss valley setting, where 'the towering statues of snow-clad Alps' can awaken 'feelings of the sublime and holy'. The high mountain town of Davos, in the canton of Graubünden, is now best known for hosting the annual World Economic Forum. But, from the mid-nineteenth century, it was a popular spot for the sick. Many doctors believed the town's alpine air and microclimate were ideal for combatting illnesses, in particular tuberculosis. Some two dozen sanatoriums opened here, and patients spent hours sitting on terraces, wrapped in blankets, soaking up the sunshine; they'd take constitutionals, drink creamy milk and wine and breathe in deep lungfuls of the crisp, clear air.

Though not a precise version of Thomas Mann's fictional Berghof, the Schatzalp is a good approximation. Floating high on the mountainside above Davos, it opened as a luxury clinic in 1900. The funicular train, which conveyed patients up in minutes, is still the only way to get there, other than on foot. Being higher up the valley, the Schatzalp receives more sunshine than the town below, and the sanatorium was built facing south to optimise exposure to natural light. Its long, wind-sheltered verandas allowed patients to recline on deckchairs in the sun, enjoying the very best views.

The Schatzalp was converted into a hotel in the 1950s, when innovations such as penicillin killed the sanatorium industry. It has retained much belle époque charm, from its stained glass and painted peacocks to the hundred-year-old plumbing. There are also nods to its medicinal history – the lightbox panels above the bar reveal that this used to be the X-ray room.

A Thomas Mann Way walking path, dotted with quotations from *The Magic Mountain*, now connects the Schatzalp to Davos, via the Waldhotel – formerly the Woodland Sanatorium. This is where Katia Mann was recuperating from a lung complaint when her husband, Thomas, came to visit in spring 1912 and decided that this could be the setting for a good story . . .

Lake Attersee

Where? Austria
Which? Lake Attersee (1900) by Gustav Klimt
What? Ethereal, glass-like tranquil lake

Cool and still, the air hangs over the waters of Lake Attersee at the edge of the Austrian Alps. The glass-like surface is surrounded by soft green hills and blue-grey mountains, and depending on the sky and where you are standing, the crystal water changes colour throughout the day, from turquoise to sapphire, to cobalt and indigo. In the beautiful Salzkammergut region, Attersee is the largest lake in Austria, and popular for boating, bathing, walking, hiking and picnicking. Although the shores of the lake have been populated since Neolithic times by various settlers, including Romans and the bourgeoisie of the early nineteenth century, today it remains peaceful and uncrowded. Since the nineteenth century, paddle steamers, boats and ships have propelled across the water, ferrying people and goods to the many villages located around the shores – or simply for pleasure. Boats are often helped by the easterly *Rosenwind* (breeze of roses), a soft wind that carries the scent of roses from a castle garden across the lake. It was here in the summer of 1900 that the artist Gustav Klimt (1862–1918) first visited, escaping the heat of the city, after writing to a friend, 'It's terrible, awful here in Vienna. Everything parched, hot, dreadful.'

After his first visit, Klimt stayed in Lake Attersee for 15 more summers, creating more than 45 of his 50 landscape paintings there, in the tiny lakefront towns of Seewalchen, Litzlberg and Weissenbach. He always stayed with his close companion, Emilie Flöge, initially in the Flöge family villa, and later in Villa Oleander. Klimt and Emilie first met in 1892, when she was 18 and he was 30. Emilie's sister Helene was married to Klimt's brother Ernst, who died aged just 28 in 1892, and from then on, Klimt supported Helene and her daughter and became exceptionally close to Emilie. It is not known whether they were lovers, but she became his muse and they often wrote to each other several times a day – disjointed, secret messages between two people who knew each other extremely well. Their friendship lasted 20 years and when Klimt suffered a stroke in 1918, his first words were: *'Emilie soll kommen'* ('Emilie, come').

One of the most important founders of the Vienna Secession – an art and design movement, similar to and concurrent with Art Nouveau – in 1897, Klimt was 38 when he first visited Attersee. There he relaxed, replacing his city clothing with floor-length robes, and abandoning his society portraits for often square landscapes of his summer paradise. He believed this square shape created a sense of tranquillity. Inspired by the presence of Emilie and the breathtaking scenery, Klimt's landscapes were unlike any other painted at the time. They did not explore skies or light or atmospheric views, but they resembled richly embellished or embroidered textiles, combining vivid colour, interesting shapes and flowing rhythms.

In his earliest visits to Attersee, Klimt rowed on the lake to paint, but after a few years he bought a stylish motorboat, which he used as a floating studio, often painting directly onto his canvases from the water. For his painting *Lake Attersee* (1900), which he executed during his first summer there, he worked from the jetty of a small boathouse by the Flöge residence. With most of the square composition filled with the lake, he focused on the surface of the water, applying short, broken, modulated brushstrokes in harmonious, luminous colours – with the palette he used only at Attersee. He reduced the scene to almost an abstraction, eliminating all detail and evoking the sheer expanse of still, calm, blue-green lake. Fascinated by the water, Klimt could spend hours staring at the lake, watching the changing patterns of light and colour.

The Attersee became his favourite lake, and on what would have been his 150th birthday in July 2012, the Gustav Klimt Centre opened in Kammer-Schörfling along Schloss Kammer avenue that he once also painted. Today, with the Klimt Centre and the stunning lake and surroundings that have barely changed since Klimt was there, you can follow in the artist's footsteps. In particular, you can walk along the Klimt Artist Trail, where you can retrace his and Emilie's steps and witness the breathtaking scenery for yourself.

Cinematic

Belchite & the Sierra de Guadarrama

Where? Spain
Which? *Pan's Labyrinth* (Guillermo del Toro, 2006)
What? Poignant ghost town and mountains haunted by the horrors of the past

The spirits of hundreds haunt this village, those hills. They pass through the crumbling walls and drift along the shattered streets; they whisper in the forest clearings and sink into the roots of the twisted trees. Places soaked in blood have stories to tell that, when real life becomes too much, might just run into fantastical realms . . .

In *Pan's Labyrinth*, writer-director Guillermo del Toro proffers two worlds entwined: the savagery of fascist Spain and the ripe imagination of a young girl. This nightmarish phantasmagoria of a film follows Ofelia (Ivana Baquero), the girl in question, as she's taken to a remote military base in the forest with her pregnant mother to live with her merciless stepfather, Falangist Captain Vidal (Sergi López). Rendered powerless in this hermetic, barbarous outpost, Ofelia is quickly drawn into a mythical land and proceeds to face monsters both magical and human. It seems like an escape ('The world isn't like your fairytales,' she is told, 'the world is a cruel place'), although the events unfolding in her imagination are just as brutal as those happening outside it.

Pan's Labyrinth may be part fantasy but its setting couldn't be more grounded in reality, at a more precise moment in time. It is 1944. The Spanish Civil War ended five years previously, with Franco's Nationalist regime triumphant. But in the pine-cloaked hills, pockets of Republican resistance continued to hold out; they were known as the Maquis, after the dense shrubland in which it is easy to hide.

In the movie those hills are the Sierra de Guadarrama. A designated national park, with peaks soaring over 2,000m (6,500ft), wildlife-filled forests of pine, oak, juniper and broom, and numerous hiking and cycling trails, it is a spectacular sweep of Iberian nature, only an hour's drive north of the Spanish capital, Madrid. The first battle in the Spanish Civil War took place here, in summer 1936; in this instance the Republicans came out on top, preventing the Nationalist troops from crossing the mountains. However, by the time of *Pan's Labyrinth*, the tables are very much turned. Captain Vidal is in charge, hunting down the guerrillas with sadistic pleasure.

The old stone mill in which the captain is based was constructed for the film, as were all the magnificent visual flights of fancy: the twisted fig tree (inside which Ofelia wrests a key from a giant toad); the banquet hall of the ghoulish, child-eating Pale Man (who represents, says del Toro, the Catholic Church); the old stone labyrinth itself. However, one fleeting, stirring sequence is all too real. At the beginning of the film, the camera roams over the remains of a bomb-blitzed ghost town, more falling than standing. This is Belchite, in Aragón, 350 kilometres (217 miles) east of the Guadarrama mountains, which became one of the Civil War's bloodiest battle grounds.

The Confraternity of Belchite was founded in 1122 by the King of Aragón to defend the border between Arab and Christian Spain. Centuries later, Belchite found itself on the front line again, as Nationalist and Republican forces clashed here during the war. In 1937, during a two-week siege, thousands of people were massacred and Belchite was virtually destroyed. But not quite. Rather than demolish the shattered remains, Franco left them to stand as a symbol of Nationalist might. Now, however, they remain as a monument to the futility of war.

It's possible to tour the eerie site – by day or night – with descendants of its former residents. They lead visitors amid piles of rubble that were once homes, around the broken clock tower and into the bullet-scarred Church of San Martín de Tours, telling stories of the past. New chapters are being added, too: in late 2021 excavations at Belchite's cemetery uncovered two graves containing dozens more Civil War victims. It's estimated that, across Spain, 130,000 people are still buried in unidentified mass graves, 90,000 of whom were killed during the war and 40,000 in the years after. Truly hellish facts, more tragic than Ofelia's tale. For while the movie sees its villain punished, in reality, for many, there was no magical escape.

Literary

Paris

Where? France
Which? Les Misérables by Victor Hugo (1862)
What? French City of Light, squalor, revolution, *égalité* and Enlightenment

Do you hear the people sing? The angry men, demanding to be heard? Once, before these elegant boulevards ploughed through the congested slums, this city screamed with revolution; tight-packed, disease-festered alleys clogged with barricades and voices yearning for *liberté, égalité, fraternité*. Now, the avenues are wide, bright, brimming with bonhomie; the noise is of coffee cups chinking on enamel tabletops, breezes rattling the neat plane trees. These streets are elegance and amour incarnate. But once they flowed with blood . . .

By the 1850s – when Victor Hugo was writing *Les Misérables* – Paris was quite literally the City of Light. Around 15,000 newly installed gaslights illuminated the French capital. Night-times became safer; citizens were drawn to the streets at all hours – a pavement culture that endures today. But just a few decades before, when *Les Misérables* is set, the city was a far darker place. Paris may have birthed the eighteenth-century's intellectual Enlightenment but, for the impoverished majority, it was still rife with inequality and despair. As Hugo once wrote, 'He who contemplates the depths of Paris is seized with vertigo. Nothing is more fantastic. Nothing is more tragic. Nothing is more sublime.'

Les Misérables contains all of those qualities. One of the longest novels ever written, it charts the travails of Jean Valjean, beginning in 1815, as he's paroled after nearly two decades in prison for stealing a loaf of bread, and finishing in the aftermath of the 1832 Paris Uprising, when Valjean finds redemption on his deathbed.

During this period, the city was still the 'old Paris' that Hugo loved, a labyrinth of narrow, intertwining streets, courtyards and crannies where characters could slip easily into the shadows. However, the city was also overcrowded, unhealthy and increasingly disillusioned: despite the world-upending 1789 Revolution, France seemed to be sinking back

LITERARY   89

into aristocratic ways. Hence the Uprising. On 5 June 1832 around 3,000 Republican insurgents briefly controlled eastern and central Paris, an area spanning from the Châtelet to the Île de la Cité and Faubourg Saint-Antoine; barricades rose in the streets off rue Saint-Denis. But by 6 June the reinforced National Guard had stamped out the rebellion. Around 800 people were killed or wounded.

Hugo himself witnessed the riots. He was writing in the Tuileries Garden when he heard gunshots from the direction of Les Halles, the traditional market area with its warren of alleys (now replaced by a shopping mall). He followed the noise north, but was forced to shelter in passage du Saumon (now passage Ben-Aïad – closed to the public), while bullets whizzed past.

The city has changed immeasurably since. Between 1853 and 1870, urban planner Baron Haussmann razed much of the medieval city, replacing its ancient chaos with modern order: broad, straight boulevards, open intersections, public parks, harmonious terraces of mansard-roofed mansions. Avenues were made wide enough for carriages; they were also made too wide for effective barricades. The result was a city more homogenous, more hygienic, arguably more handsome but stripped of centuries of history.

Haussmann has certainly made it more difficult to follow in the footsteps of Valjean, his ward Cosette, her suitor Marius and the rest of Hugo's revolutionaries, vagabonds, gendarmes and whores. But echoes of his Paris remain. Most evocative is the Marais (the marsh), where there are more intact medieval buildings than anywhere else in the city. This neighbourhood on the Right Bank of the Seine survived Haussmannisation; it's still a maze of tight-knit cobbled lanes, easy to get lost in, and now jam-packed with bookshops, boutiques, bars and cafés. It's in the Marais that you'll find the Places des Vosges, a perfect, tree-lined square framed by arcaded seventeenth-century houses, one of which is Hugo's former home (now a museum). At the heart of the Marais is the baroque Jesuit church of Saint-Paul-Saint-Louis, where Marius and Cosette are wed; it's also home to two shell-shaped fonts that Hugo donated to the church after his own daughter married there.

The area to the west, the Latin Quarter, is another remnant of medieval streets. The Sorbonne, France's first university, was founded here in 1257, establishing this area as a studenty haven of intellectual thought and no-frills bistros. This is where Marius and his fellow revolutionaries would have spent their days discussing a new tomorrow.

Nearby is the Jardin du Luxembourg, Paris' second-largest park, and a leafy setting for love. Amid the Jardin's sparrow-twittering chestnut trees, Marius and Cosette first catch each other's eye. You can still walk the gravel paths, among the centuries-old pear trees and the statues of poets and politicians. One sculpture, *Le Marchand de Masques* (1883), depicts a boy hawking masks of famous people; the mask in his raised hand is the face of Hugo.

However, the best way to sense the plight of Hugo's *misérables* is to descend into the sewers. For Hugo, they were 'another Paris under herself', a dank, foul-smelling facsimile with its own streets and alleyways. It's by descending to this abyss that Valjean rescues the wounded Marius – salvation via hell. Haussmann improved the sewage system but still, a visit to Musée des Égouts de Paris (the Paris Sewer Museum), following the raised walkways above the effluent, brings to mind – and nose – the Paris of Valjean.

Valjean dies at peace, and is buried beneath a blank slab in an untended corner of a Paris cemetery. On his deathbed in 1885, Hugo asked to be buried in a pauper's coffin, but was first processed up the Champs-Élysées and laid in state under the Arc de Triomphe, before being put in the crypt of the Panthéon, alongside Dumas and Zola. In death, raised to hero; on the page, striving with the common man.

Foodie

Nuremberg

Where? Bavaria, Germany
Why? Nibble a festive treat in its rightful home

Lebkuchen aren't biscuits. They're the baked essence of a German Christmas. Dark, dense, chewy, sweet, soft, spicy; they taste of ginger and cinnamon, cloves and nutmeg. But also of snow-cloaked fir trees and stockings left out for St Nick, roaring hearths and advent candles, fairy lights flickering over old cobbled streets, choirs singing 'O Tannenbaum', crisp winter air and festive *gemütlichkeit* (good cheer). And there's no better place than this to take a bite . . .

Bavaria's second city, Nuremberg (Nürnberg) has seen it all. From 1050 to 1571 it was the de facto capital of the Holy Roman Empire, with a colossal castle that once housed the empire's crown jewels. But it is also where, in the 1930s, the Nazi party held its most frenzied, most bone-chilling rallies – and where, post-war, Nazi leaders were tried and executed. Glory and ignominy; a complicated past.

Lebkuchen stem from the glory years. Located at the intersection of ancient trading routes, Nuremberg was one of the great commercial centres of Europe; along with Constantinople (Istanbul) and Venice, it was a hub for spice: cinnamon, cloves, cardamom, nutmeg, aniseed and ginger fragranced the city. And some of these made it to the local Franconian monks.

Monastery bakeries had long made cakes using honey, which was known for its healing powers. But as new spices poured in from the East, the monks began adding them to the mix too.

These were considered medicinal and the resulting *pfefferkuchen* (pepper cakes – pepper being a catch-all term for any spice) were made to ease digestive ailments. Eventually the name changed: the word 'lebkuchen' first appeared in Nuremberg in 1395.

This new type of gingerbread thrived in Nuremberg, thanks not only to the spice trade but also to the ready supply of honey. The Lorenzer Reichswald, a swathe of birch, oak, pine and heather southeast of the city, had such vast wild swarms it was known as 'the Holy Roman

92   EUROPE

Empire's Bee Garden'. Here, designated *Zeidler* (beekeepers), sporting distinctive green outfits and pointy hats, were tasked with harvesting the precious nectar.

These days you'll find lebkuchen all over Germany. But Nürnberger Lebkuchen is a cut above, granted Protected Geographical Indication (PGI) status in 1996. The crème de la crème of the lebkuchen world is *Elisenlebkuchen*. According to legend, these are named after Elisabeth, the daughter of a master Nuremberg Lebzelter (gingerbread-maker). His beloved daughter fell ill, and the doctors could not help her so, in his despair, the baker made her a specially spiced lebkuchen, using no flour and only the finest ingredients, including a fragrant mix of cinnamon, vanilla, cloves, coriander, allspice, nutmeg, ginger and cardamom. It worked. Elisabeth recovered, and now the premium lebkuchen bears her name. To be considered authentic, *Elisenlebkuchen* can contain no more than 10 per cent flour and must have at least 25 per cent nuts, sometimes up to 45 per cent. Often decorated with almonds and lemon peel, it is baked on an *oblaten*, the circular communion wafers used by the early Franconian monks to stop the biscuits sticking in the oven.

Today, Nuremberg embraces all aspects of its past. There are moving museums marking its Nazi-era history. And, although the *Aldstadt* was decimated by Allied bombs in 1945, much of the medieval old town, including alleys of half-timbered houses and the enormous castle, have been painstakingly reconstructed. The city also maintains its magical Christkindlesmarkt, one of the world's oldest Christmas markets, which dates back to the sixteenth century. From late November until 24 December, the Aldstadt's main Hauptmarkt square transforms into a festive flurry of glühwein and bratwurst, brass oompah bands and angelic church choirs, bauble-strung trees and stalls populated with 'prune people', the city's traditional, dressed-up dolls made from pieces of dried fruit.

Nowadays you can eat lebkuchen all year round, and you can eat it anywhere – of the 70 million produced in Nuremberg annually, the majority are exported. But there's no better time or place than at Christmas, right here.

London

Where? England
Which? Paddington (Paul King, 2014)
What? City of bright lights, big sights and ancient history, where the whole world rubs along

Colossal spans of steel and glass curve way above, seemingly high as the sky; ornate tracery etches the ironwork, light floods in. This cathedral of transportation – a grande dame of a railway station – was built not only for practical purpose but for visual oomph. Below this dizzying roof, tens of thousands of people rush daily, soles clacking on the polished limestone floors, dashing to and fro between trains that shuttle them out, or deliver them home. An interesting place, then, for a little bear – dwarfed by Victorian engineering and a city of nine million – to be looking for a home of his own . . .

Paddington Station was built as the showpiece London terminus of Isambard Kingdom Brunel's Great Western Railway. The biggest train shed in the world when it opened in 1854 – the largest of its three roof spans measuring 31m (102ft) across – its design was inspired by the shimmering Crystal Palace that had hosted the Great Exhibition in Hyde Park three years earlier. In the intervening years, the station has remained one of the UK capital's major stations, and has also lent its name to one of London's most endearing (if fictional) adopted sons.

Writer Michael Bond created the character of Paddington, a bear from 'darkest Peru' taken in by the Brown family, in 1958. In 2014 a movie version brought Bond's beloved bear – and the London he inhabits – to life. It provides a charming tour of the city's icons, including everything from Big Ben and Beefeaters to red phone boxes and Tube stations. But it's also a fable about immigration, xenophobia and the treatment of strangers – which is nowhere more appropriate than here, in this twenty-first-century melting pot: these days more than one-third of Londoners are foreign born, comprising 270-plus nationalities.

'If you ever make it to London you can be sure of a warm welcome.' So says explorer Montgomery Clyde to Aunt Lucy and Uncle Pastuzo

CINEMATIC   95

when he meets these intelligent bears in Peru in the film's opening scenes (filmed, incidentally, in Costa Rica). When Paddington does first land on British shores, it's at Tilbury Docks on the River Thames in Essex. Long the principal port for London, it was here that the HMT *Empire Windrush* arrived from Jamaica in 1948, bringing West Indian immigrants looking for new opportunities. One of the passengers was Trinbagonian calypso artist Aldwyn Roberts (better known by the stage name 'Lord Kitchener'), whose satire-heavy song 'London Is the Place for Me' resounds as Paddington takes a circuitous black cab ride to the Brown's home, wide-eyed at the city's sparkling sights: the London Eye, Tower Bridge, St Paul's Cathedral. The rain is chucking it down, but can't diminish the city's vim.

Before that cab ride, of course, comes the moment when the little bear acquires his English name, having been dropped by a post van at Paddington Station and, eventually, encountering the Browns. While nearby Marylebone stood in for the station's exterior, the interior shots were filmed in Paddington itself. The station was refurbished in the 1990s, with the glass in Brunel's original roof replaced with polycarbonate glazing and the ornamental tracing restored to its former glory. A bronze statue of Paddington sitting on his suitcase, with an evacuee-style label around his neck ('Please look after this bear. Thank you'), can be found under the clock on Platform 1.

The Browns live in an unspecified West London location, at '32 Windsor Gardens'. In the film, this is portrayed by Grade II-listed Chalcot Crescent, in posh Primrose Hill, a serpentine sweep of baby-blue, lemon-yellow and candy-pink Victorian townhouses, with handsome Doric porticoes and cast-iron balconies. It's an exclusive address indeed – in 2021, the average price of its properties stood at just over £2.5 million.

Back in real-life West London, you can find Mr Gruber's antique shop exactly where it's claimed to be: on Notting Hill's similarly colourful Portobello Road. Paddington goes to the bric-a-brac-packed emporium, run by the Hungarian refugee, to seek advice about the origins of his trademark hat. The red-fronted store, at number 86, is actually Alice's Antiques, one of many such businesses: the street, where over 1,000 dealers trade, is the world's largest antiques market. Notting Hill has long been a diverse, multicultural, creative neighbourhood. When it was first developed from farmland in the nineteenth century, it was close to central London but much cheaper, therefore attracting artistic types and, later, poorer immigrants – many Windrushers settled here, a factor leading to the race riots of 1958 and, more happily, the vibrant Notting Hill Carnival, founded in 1966 and still going strong today.

The climax of the movie plays out at the Natural History Museum. This is where taxidermist Millicent Clyde (Nicole Kidman) attempts to stuff poor Paddington, before the Browns come to his rescue. The South Kensington building is unmistakable. Opened in 1881, it was designed by Alfred Waterhouse in a Romanesque style and made entirely of terracotta, to better resist London's sooty air. It's decorated with a flamboyant menagerie, extinct species on the east wing, living species on the west, including gargoyles in the shapes of lions and pterodactyls and carvings of monkeys, ammonites and dodos. In the film, Paddington runs along the spine of a Diplodocus in the museum's great Hintze Hall. 'Dippy' was replaced by the skeleton of a blue whale in 2017, which is still worth visiting. Look up too: the hall's vaulted ceiling is adorned with 162 exquisite panels illustrated with plants from across the globe.

Indeed, the museum, like London itself, houses all sorts. As Paddington optimistically notes, 'In London everyone is different. But that means everyone can fit in.'

Brussels

Where? Belgium
Which? The Empire of Light (1953–54) by René Magritte
What? Belgian region of innovative architecture that inspired a surreal image

With its mild climate, Brussels is perfectly designed for walking. There's so much to see: parks, buildings and squares such as Grand Place; a beautiful central square surrounded by Gothic-style buildings, including the Town Hall and the King's House; open-air antique markets, bars and cafés that spill on to the streets, and the elegant street where the Surrealist painter René Magritte (1898–1967) lived for nearly 30 years. Visitors today can soak up the atmosphere so familiar to Magritte in Greenwich café, Rue des Chartreux, where his paintings were once rejected and where he often met friends and sometimes played chess, at least once with Marcel Duchamp.

Known for its culinary specialities, including artisan beers, velvety hot chocolate and hot, sweet waffles, Brussels is a region like no other, comprising 19 municipalities, with 2 native languages spoken: Dutch/Flemish and French, and English, spoken by nearly a third of the population. The city's artistic tradition goes back to the Middle Ages, when it became notable for its innovative artists. These included Rogier van der Weyden, one of the most influential painters of the northern Renaissance, famed for his expressive, naturalistic images; Jan Brueghel the Elder, who worked alongside Peter Paul Rubens; and the Expressionist James Ensor, who, in 1888, painted a scene of Christ entering Brussels in a rather unnerving Mardi Gras parade. Long known as a meeting place for artists, writers and intellectuals travelling across Europe, today, Brussels continues to attract a vibrant community of artists.

Located in the north-central part of Belgium, about 110 kilometres (68 miles) from the coast, Brussels has many different architectural styles standing adjacently, including Art Deco, Gothic and Baroque. Some examples to look out for include the steel-and-glass Art Nouveau

Musical Instrument Museum, the opulent La Monnaie opera house, the Gothic church of Notre Dame du Sablon and the Baroque Eglise Saint-Jean-Baptiste au Béguinage. The city is also famous for its Art Nouveau townhouses designed in the 1890s by the innovative architect Victor Horta, who, although born almost 40 years before René Magritte, was similarly inventive, as is apparent with his use of iron and glass.

From its beginnings in the Stone Age as a small rural settlement on the river Senne, Brussels rose to a prominent position in Europe by the second half of the twentieth century. German forces occupied it during the two world wars, and René Magritte lived through both. At the end of the First World War in 1918, he graduated from Brussels' Royal Academy of Fine Arts, four years later, he married his childhood sweetheart Georgette Berger, and he lived in ten different places in the capital. Apart from a brief period living in Paris – where he became part of the Surrealist group – Brussels remained a constant in Magritte's life. His home in Jette at 137 rue Esseghem – now the René Magritte Museum – became his artistic headquarters, and he and Georgette lived there for 24 years.

Magritte made almost half of his entire output of work while living in Jette and many of his paintings were executed there at his easel in his living room. Everywhere in and around the apartment you can see his inspirations – from the windows to the fireplace, the garden aviary to the staircase. From outside the house, you can picture his mysterious paintings *The Empire of Light* (1953–54) that present an unexpected juxtaposition. He painted several versions, all depicting a dark street at night, showing his own house in shadows, but illuminated brightly from the inside and from the outside by a single street light. Above is a pale daytime sky with scudding clouds. The disconcerting paradox of day and night together deliberately confuses our understandings about time and existence. The painting explores Magritte's fascination with the workings of the mind, showing that the inexplicable can be found in even the most conventional of places. In a radio interview in 1956, he explained, 'This evocation of night and day seems to me to have the power to surprise and delight us. I call this power: poetry.' Standing across the street and looking back at his house, you can visualise Magritte's *The Empire of Light* and contemplate this poetry.

Galway

Where? West of Ireland
Why? Lively hub of Irish trad in a country made of music

The story of Ireland doesn't belong in a textbook. It should be told in a song. In the beat of a bodhrán. The twiddle of a fiddle. The sweet wheeze of the uilleann pipes. History not in dates and details, but notes and melodies, because music has shaped the Irish identity. It is so integral, in fact, that the national symbol is the Celtic harp – Ireland is the only country to have a musical instrument as its emblem. Yes, music is a language here, a means of communicating the struggles, the joys, the roots and the resilience of the people, and the most potent way in which Ireland is heard across the world . . .

Music has been central to the idea of Irishness since the Celts first arrived with their harps in around 500 BCE. When St Patrick brought Christianity to Ireland in the fifth century, new sounds developed, pagan melodies blending with Christian hymns, and wandering bards adapting holy psalms to secular tunes. From the Middle Ages the skirl of war pipes led armies into battle. Later, harps became the soundtrack of courtly life then, following their prohibition by the English Crown, a symbol of resistance.

Indeed, in the toughest times – from colonial oppression to the devastating Great Famine – music was a lifeline. Ballads emerged, passed from generation to generation, reflecting hardship, kinship, rebellion, solidarity and the yearning for freedom. These songs became powerful symbols of Irish identity and were spread far and wide by waves of emigrants seeking better lives elsewhere.

Today, there are more places to hear trad music than there are places in Ireland, such is the international diaspora. But sticking to the Emerald Isle itself, the west-coast city of Galway (Gaillimh) is one of the liveliest choices. A former fishing village, between the waters of Lough Corrib and the Atlantic Ocean, Galway was founded by the Anglo-Normans in the twelfth century, and quickly grew into a bustling trade hub. It weathered plenty of political turmoil, including clashes between the

MUSICAL 101

ruling Anglo-Norman elite and the indigenous Gaelic population; for many centuries it was effectively controlled by 14 merchant families, earning it the nickname the 'City of Tribes'. Despite enduring sieges, rebellions and economic fluctuations, it's now an affable and artsy hub of around 80,000 people – with, it seems, a ditty for every one of them. Galway isn't a city to look at so much as one to soak in: its seagulls and sea breezes, its energy, its creativity, its thriving music scene.

Galway is known as *Croí Cultúrtha na hÉireann* (Ireland's Cultural Heart). An Irish-speaking stronghold, it has rich musical roots. For instance, De Dannan, one of the most revered traditional Irish groups of past decades (named for Tuatha Dé Danann, a supernatural race in pre-Christian Irish mythology) hailed from here, and the city is a-thrum with live performance. The centre, with its remnants of medieval walls, winding old lanes and brightly-painted buildings, remains Galway's beating heart – and its literal beat. Outside, on the street corners, buskers strum guitars, excite fiddles, toot tin whistles. Inside, atmospheric old pubs are a-thump with sound – maybe a folk group or ballad band, maybe a trad *seisiún* (session), when a gathering of skilled musicians results in a knees-up. The fluid and organic nature of Irish traditional music, the way it varies from place to place, player to player, means no two nights will ever be the same.

So, follow your ears around Galway. Let them lead you to Tigh Chóilí, a cosy spot right in the thick of things, with live music twice daily, year-round; performers squash into the front bar, playing to locals, incomers and walls of framed photos of those who've strummed and fiddled here before. Or try Tigh Neachtain, a royal-blue boozer, founded in 1894. There are logs crackling on the fire, vintage whiskies behind the bar, famed Galway oysters on the menu and – on occasion – trad tunes spilling out the door. Or head along the Sea Road to the Crane, a two-storey corner bar and perhaps the best trad spot in town. Upstairs, a small stage hosts some of Ireland's finest folk musicians, while downstairs is more spontaneous, a drop-in of players and punters crammed in together, candles flickering, toes tapping, letting the Irish rhythms flow.

Cinematic

Fårö

Where? Sweden
Which? Persona (Ingmar Bergman, 1966)
What? Desolate Baltic Sea isle, as rocky and lonely as the human soul

Relentless gusts off the inky sea, lashing rain, a shore that's fringed with razor-sharp rocks. But also flower-flecked meadows, pine-backed sand, sunshine and wild strawberries. The island is both. A barren beauty. Harsh yet soft; dark yet light. A place of two faces, impossible to pull apart . . .

Persona (mask in Latin) is writer-director Ingmar Bergman's minimalist masterpiece, and one of the most striking cinematic probes into the fractured human mind. In it, stage actress Elisabet Vogler (Liv Ullmann) stops speaking one night, mid-performance, for reasons unknown. She is put in a psychiatric hospital but remains resolutely mute, so Elisabet's doctor suggests that her patient spend the summer at her beach house, attended by young nurse Alma (Bibi Andersson), in the hope it will do Elisabet good. But the island environment they enter is intense – severe, insular, remote – and, as Alma talks and Elisabet listens, the two women begin to merge, locked in an intimacy that becomes a joust, a seduction, a synthesis.

The idea is that the island will be restorative; that it will be a haven of salt-spritzed air and simple Swedish pleasures: coffee fresh-brewed, mushrooms foraged, lazing in near-endless hours of sun. And at first it seems to work. Elisabet writes that, 'I'd always like to live like this. This silence, living cut off – this feeling of the battered soul finally beginning to straighten out.' But it's a utopia that doesn't last. In fact, the island's extreme isolation has the opposite effect – it becomes the physical incarnation of the women's inner states.

That island is Fårö, a small scrap of wind-swept limestone sitting just off the top of Gotland, Sweden's largest isle. Far-flung from the mainland, halfway to Estonia, out in the Baltic Sea, it's a singular place. The terrain is flat and craggy, with pockets of pasture sneaking in among the bogs, scrubland and pine groves; strange stack-like rock formations – called rauks – guard the shores; there are old hamlets of thatch-and-tar huts, a nineteenth-century lighthouse and a medieval church.

Fårö has been settled since the Stone Age, occupied by the Vikings and even has its own dialect, an ancient variant of Old Norse called Faroymal, claimed to be the oldest language in Sweden – apt for a movie where speaking (or not speaking) is key. Farming and fishing were once the mainstays but these days it's tourism that sustains the resident population of 600-or-so souls – though, due to the presence of a military base, it was actually off-limits to non-Swedes until the 1990s. There's no bank, no post office, no police. But it is indelibly linked to Sweden's greatest auteur.

Bergman filmed several movies and documentaries here. On his first visit, seeking locations for *Through a Glass Darkly* (1961) he realised Fårö was his perfect match: 'If one wished to be solemn, it could be said that I had found my landscape, my real home', he said. 'If one wished to be funny, one could talk about love at first sight.' The island was his natural film set; it gave him forms, proportions, silences, simplicity, breath. And when he discovered the stony beach at Hammars while filming *Persona*, he built a house there and lived in it, on and off, for 40 years.

Elisabet and Alma are no longer clambering around on Fårö's rocks, but the legacy of Bergman is easy to find, island-wide. The Bergman Center, next to the Fårö Museum, hosts exhibitions, screens films and runs a 'Bergman safari', which explores the director's filming locations, most notably the striking rocky seascapes where his characters endured so much psychological strife.

Fårö is also Bergman's final resting place. He is buried, with his last wife Ingrid, in a quiet corner of the graveyard at Fårö Church, forever sunk into its soil, the master and his geographical muse eternally merging as one.

Venice

Where? Italy
Which? The Entrance to the Grand Canal, Venice (c.1730) by Canaletto
What? Magical jewel-box city, steeped in history

How many feet have tramped this magical, floating masterpiece? Romantic, ancient and enchanted, Venice is unequalled; a glittering city of canals, gondolas, jewel-box architecture, endless waterways and domed cathedrals. Sail a little further and you reach the colourful towns of Murano and Burano or the peaceful, laid-back Giudecca. Nothing could be grander than the Grand Canal that mirrors the splendours of centuries of Venetian pride and power, while rising up all along the canal, glittering in marble and glass, are decadent palaces and churches that hold the secrets of time.

As well as churches and palaces, Venice is home to several remarkable art collections, including the Peggy Guggenheim Collection, the Galleria dell Accademia, Museo Correr and the Punta della Dogana. Everywhere are works of architecture that resemble decorative pieces of wedding cake, such as the Bridge of Sighs, a white limestone masterpiece that connects the interrogation rooms of Doge's Palace to the prison, or the Rialto Bridge, an ornate structure that crosses the Grand Canal, connecting San Polo to the *sestiere* (district) of San Marco. In the narrow back streets, even the tiniest churches are filled with breathtaking paintings by Venetian natives, such as Veronese, Titian, Jacopo, Gentile and Giovanni Bellini, and Tiepolo and Andrea Mantegna, as well as magnificent statues and dazzling stained-glass windows that sparkle like gemstones, making this city a treasure trove for aesthetes. Many artists have captured its beauty with great success, such as Claude Monet and John Singer Sargent, who both captured its special atmosphere in their own individual ways.

But one artist above all is synonymous with this dazzling city. If you're facing west, you might be lucky enough to catch one of Venice's spectacular red–gold sunsets. Made famous by Giovanni Antonio Canal

(1697–1768), known as Canaletto, Venetian sunsets are known the world over. Canaletto also made many other views of Venice renowned. During the eighteenth century, long before postcards or photographs existed, Canaletto's skill at capturing the atmosphere of Venice gained him great success among tourists, many of whom were young aristocrats on their Grand Tour – an educational journey through Europe.

These wealthy young things purchased Canaletto's paintings as mementos of their travels, of the theatricality and feast for the senses that Venice has always been. At the time, Canaletto became the ultimate postcard painter on a huge scale. To achieve accuracy, he perfected his skill of painting with almost photographic likenesses by using a tool called a camera obscura. Despite the exacting likenesses, he often moved some elements within his paintings to create harmonious compositions. Taking home a painting from this most esteemed local artist was a prestigious memento, and in time, almost every British aristocrat had a Canaletto on their walls. Over his career, Canaletto produced more than 1,000 paintings and drawings in total, but although he travelled elsewhere, his depictions of Venice were his most popular.

Art is not the only draw here – with its tantalising traces of ancient spice routes, Venetian cuisine is inventive while retaining the elements of traditional Italian fare. Pop into any one of the warm and welcoming bars at happy hour and find lavish spreads of *cicchetti* (Venetian tapas), or go to Harry's Bar to sample the original Bellini – prosecco and peach purée, invented sometime between 1934 and 1948 by Giuseppe Cipriani, who named it Bellini because its pale pink colour reminded him of the toga of a saint in a painting by Giovanni Bellini. Make sure you leave room to also sample the lagoon seafood at any of the canal-side bistros – washed down with Veneto's signature bubbly prosecco.

Venice became established in around 400 CE, when the Roman Empire collapsed and refugees settled there after escaping successive waves of barbarian invaders in their original homes in Roman cities such as Padua, Aquileia, Treviso and Altino. By the Byzantine, Renaissance and Baroque eras, Venice had become a major city, with some of the most opulent architecture along its waterways and in the central Piazza San Marco. Here, you can discover sumptuous Byzantine mosaics, elegant statues, the splendid Gothic Doge's Palace, lively cafés and bars, the towering red-brick Campanile and, of course, spectacular St Mark's Basilica itself, one of the best-known examples of Byzantine architecture in Europe.

Architectural shapes are unmistakably Venetian. For instance, in the Dorsoduro sestiere of the city between the Grand Canal and the

Giudecca Canal, is Baldassare Longhena's magnificent basilica, Santa Maria della Salute, its white stones and high domes gleamingly visible from Piazza San Marco. Yet before building could even begin on this landmark, at least 100,000 pylons had to be driven deep into the *barene* (mudbanks) to shore up the tip of Dorsoduro. Distinctive and uniquely Venetian, the architecture draws on several influences, including Greco–Roman pagan temples and Jewish Kabbalah diagrams.

Few cities can claim such a priceless artistic and historical heritage. Built on mud, sand, slime and continuous water, the city itself was formed on a group of 118 small islands in a shallow lagoon. Separated by canals that are now linked by over 400 bridges, this city, in the Veneto region of north-eastern Italy, remains a miraculous testament to creativity, human endeavour and genius architectural engineering. With his innovative technique, strong colours and atmospheric effects, Canaletto's landscapes captured this city's famed originality, and even today, three centuries later, when travelling down the Grand Canal, it is like stepping into a Canaletto painting.

Literary

Yorkshire Moors

Where? England
Which? *Wuthering Heights* by Emily Brontë (1847)
What? Wild, windswept English landscape, as savage as Heathcliff himself

The landscape is brooding. A gunmetal sky hangs low over the barren, boundless moor, muting its palette to olive greens, tarnished golds, bruise purples. Its apparent emptiness belies secret treachery. This is nature as obstacle course: a hidden gauntlet of engulfing marshes, dangerous roots, deep hollows and dark swamps. The weather is wild too. A north wind whips over the rise by the old stone ruin, quivering the heather, distorting the lone fir tree, making it cower in fright. Or maybe it's not wind at all that's blowing but the spirits that haunt this moor, as tempestuous in death as they were in life . . .

When describing *Wuthering Heights*, painter-poet Dante Gabriel Rossetti called it 'a fiend of a book' where 'the action is laid in hell'. That 'hell' is the Yorkshire Moors, a swathe of rolling hills, dales and heather-cloaked heath in northern England, bleakly beautiful. But the moors are more than the setting for Emily Brontë's only novel, a strange, savage tale of love and revenge. They are the actor-director – stealing scenes, shaping characters, influencing action, defining mood.

The moors of *Wuthering Heights* are far removed from the rest of the world. As well as being geographically isolated, they seem to exist outside of the rules of man. Few niceties are observed here; rather, life is lived at the whim of Mother Nature. At times the moors are nurturing and benign, full of gurgling streams, singing larks, humming bees and harebells. They offer star-crossed lovers Catherine and Heathcliff liberation from domestic violence and social constraints. However, more often the moors are brutal, a Hades howling with gales and ghosts.

It was a landscape Emily Brontë knew well. From 1820, the Brontë family (including Emily's novelist sisters, Charlotte and Anne) lived in the parsonage at Haworth, a hard-working Pennine village producing worsted yarn and cloth. At the time, industrialisation was rebalancing

LITERARY 111

England, from a mainly rural to a mostly urban society. Haworth – not so far from the powerhouses of Leeds and Manchester – was both: a crowded, polluted centre set high on the moors' edge, open country just beyond. Emily Brontë would often escape into that hinterland, and it suffused her writing; Charlotte called her 'a nursling of the moors'. Emily found inspiration in the rocks, crags and waterfalls, and understood nature as both a destructive and soothing force.

The novel's two main locations, Wuthering Heights (the Earnshaw home) and Thrushcross Grange (home of the well-to-do Lintons), are just 6.5 kilometres (4 miles) apart but distinct in personality – like their fictional owners. The former sits high on the tops, chill and gloomy; the latter nestles in the valley, more civilised and refined.

Wuthering Heights is believed to be based on Top Withens, a long-abandoned sixteenth-century farmhouse a few miles southwest of Haworth. Its structure doesn't match Emily's creation, but its remote, windswept position fits the bill. Walk across the moor from Haworth parsonage – now the Brontë Museum – to reach the exposed stone ruin and it's easy to think yourself into the pages of a Gothic romance.

Architecturally, a more likely candidate for Wuthering Heights is Ponden Hall, a manorial farmhouse near Haworth, which suits in size and style, if not situation. Actually Ponden is more usually cited as the model for Thrushcross Grange. Built largely in 1634, and extensively rebuilt in 1801 (the year in which the novel begins), Ponden did have a long, tree-lined drive like Thrushcross, but it lacks the grandeur and grounds that Emily describes. However, the Brontës visited regularly, and Emily would read in the extensive library.

Ponden Hall is currently a B&B. Now anyone can book the 'Earnshaw Room' to sleep in its eighteenth-century-style box bed and peep out of the tiny window in the thick stone wall. Though be warned that your dreams might meander the wind-raged moors, and you might hear the ghosts demanding to be let in . . .

Foodie

Lisbon

Where? Portugal
Why? Trace the story of nuns and navigators to taste the original Portuguese pastry

Sweet on the nose, warm to the touch; scrumptious little packages that fit into the palm of the hand. They're pleasingly messy: caramelised singes smear their golden tops like fingerprints – no two quite the same. But the bite is bliss. Layers of buttery, crisp pastry just about keeping hold of the creamy custard inside, a delicate gloop that oozes slightly, softly, but doesn't drip. An indulgent treat. But also the taste of ingenuity, exploration and centuries of tradition . . .

Pastéis de nata may be known worldwide, but they are baked into the bones of Lisbon. These egg-custard tarts brighten the counters of every street-corner *pastelaria*. For Lisboetas, they're as inevitable as the city's seven hills or wide Tagus River – they seem to have been here forever.

This isn't quite the case. Portugal's prodigious baking culture began in earnest in the eighth century, when the Moors occupied the Iberian Peninsula and brought with them their repertoire of desserts. After the reconquest, Catholic nuns took up the mantle. Using egg whites for all manner of things, including the starching of their habits, they found themselves with large quantities of leftover yolks, which it would have been quite ungodly to waste. When sugar arrived from overseas colonies in the fifteenth century, the nuns began combining these ingredients in various ways. They sold the resultant sweets from their cloisters, to raise money for their good works. When dignitaries visited, the nuns would try to impress them with especially intricate creations.

With every convent kitchen cooking up its own specialities, a large canon of conventual sweets – and a new national culinary culture – emerged. Sugary deliciousness was served up in an array of forms and flavours. Tens, maybe hundreds, of concoctions were made, such as *papos de anjo* (angels' chins), glistening dollops of whipped yolk baked and then boiled in sugar syrup; *toucinho do céu* (bacon from heaven), an almond cake made using lard; *barrigas de freira* (nuns' bellies), a sort of

FOODIE   115

Portuguese bread pudding; and *bolo podre* (rotten cake), flavoured with olive oil and cinnamon. Then there were *pastéis de nata*.

The *pastéis de Belém*, as the originals were called, can be traced back to Lisbon's Jerónimos Monastery. This magnificent Manueline masterpiece rises like a wedding cake in the riverside suburb of Belém, the Atlantic port from which Portugal's great explorers embarked during the age of discovery. The monastery and nearby tower – equally frilly and flamboyant – were commissioned to celebrate Vasco da Gama's 1497–99 voyage, on which he found the sea route to India; da Gama is buried inside.

Pastéis were made here using a closely guarded recipe, until 1834, when the end of the Portuguese Civil War saw the dissolution of monasteries across the country. Some enterprising nuns and monks, now at a loose end and seeking to earn a living somehow, began selling their bakes and recipes. In 1837, the Antiga Confeitaria de Belém, a small shop attached to a sugar refinery near Jerónimos, started producing the monastery's signature sweet. It continues to do so today, still making each pastel by hand, the secret recipe unchanged. It's said only three master confectioners know the precise details.

The first hungry visitors came from downtown Lisbon to Belém by steamboat. There's a tram these days, or you can walk along the waterfront from the eighteenth-century Praça do Comércio square – it takes around 90 minutes. The confeitaria makes up to 20,000 (sometimes 50,000) perfect *pastéis de Belém* every day. The queue is always long, both for the vintage counter, where you can buy takeaway tarts in cardboard tubes, and for the azulejo-tiled café, where you can sit and enjoy them with a dusting of icing sugar or cinnamon (optional) and a *bica* (espresso). Though similar to the ubiquitous *pastéis de nata*, the Belém version has especially light, crisp pastry while the egg-custard filling is slightly less sweet, making it all the easier to eat more than one.

Bern

Where? Switzerland
Which? Mount Niesen, Egyptian Night (1915) by Paul Klee
What? Ephemeral city surrounded by snow-capped mountains

Everywhere is cool and crisp. Glistening, snow-capped mountains of the Bernese Alps encircle the city, creating a calming, almost mystical presence. On clear days, from certain vantage points, you can see across the panorama of the city and all the way to the Eiger, Mönch and Jungfrau mountains. Although Bern is one of Europe's smallest capitals, its heart is anything but diminutive. Here, among many other things, you will find superlative art galleries, first-class urban swimming and the smoothest chocolate in the world.

All around Bern, the clear mountain air glitters in the sunshine. Powdery white distant peaks are the source of the meltwater that flows down to the astonishingly blue River Aare, where hardy swimmers gather daily for a bracing dip.

At one of four Gelateria di Berna across the city, you can tempt your tastebuds with homemade Swiss gelati, in delicate flavours such as lavender, hibiscus flower or moreish raspberry and ginger. Popular among local workers is the Turnhalle café and bar in the centre of the city – which is also frequented by artists and designers who rent studios in ProGR (the attached cultural centre). Sip a steaming coffee, nibble on a melt-in-the-mouth pastry and browse for books at Apfelgold, then buy hunks of chocolate at Läderach, where every flavour you can imagine is displayed in huge slabs on the counter and sold by weight. Or you can visit two especially famous landmarks, the thirteenth-century clock tower (Zytglogge) and the cathedral with its 100-metre (328-foot) spire.

Elsewhere in this sparkling city are some of the most mesmerising, world-class art galleries and museums, including the Kunstmuseum Bern, with its permanent collection of over 50,000 masterpieces, covering 800 years of art history. On the outskirts of the city is the Zentrum Paul Klee that houses some of the finest works by Bern's most famous artist, as well as hosting regular international exhibitions. Although he spent much of his life in Germany, Paul Klee was born in Bern in 1879, and died there in 1940, having been forced out of Germany by the Nazis. Klee's Swiss mother and German father spent most of their lives in Bern too, and it was largely at their home that Klee developed his highly innovative style, influenced by several avant-garde art movements as well as his fascination with colour, his dry humour, his love of animals, his outstanding musical talents and his natural draughtsmanship.

Approximately 60 kilometres (37 miles) from the city, overlooking Lake Thun in the Bernese Oberland region, is Mount Niesen, which forms the northern end of a ridge stretching north from the Albristhorn and Mannliflue mountains, and separates the Simmental and Kandertal valleys. Although the translation of the German word niesen is 'sneeze', the shape of the mountain has traditionally earned it the nickname 'The Swiss Pyramid'. This famous pyramid shape has captured the eye of numerous artists but most notably, it was painted several times by Paul Klee – usually depicted as a triangle or pyramid and often linked to ancient Egypt, as in his 1915 painting Mount Niesen, Egyptian Night. Variously associated with Expressionism, Cubism, Futurism, Surrealism and Abstraction, Klee's art cannot be categorised, so it remains elusive, but through his original interpretations, his use of different media, his extensive writing and lecturing about his inventive methods, and his theories, he became exceptionally influential to other artists and designers. Take the funicular railway – the red Niesenbahn train – from Mülenen to the summit of Mount Niesen, or, if you prefer, take the 11,674 steps that flank the funicular, the longest stairway in the world. However you get there, the spectacular views at the peak over the Bernese Alps will not fail to inspire you, just as they did in the early twentieth century for Paul Klee.

Salzburg

Where? Austria
Which? *The Sound of Music* (Robert Wise, 1965)
What? Fairytale city of joyous song, living hills and uplifting endings

Fresh air – snow-crisp, pine-scented – seems to float out of the screen as the majesty of the Alps unfurls. Clouds billow. Valleys rise, dip, fold and swell. Grasses quiver in the breeze. Yes, the voice is right: the hills ARE alive; they are vital, elemental, quietly euphoric. Up here, perhaps that little bit closer to God, is freedom and beauty; a place where the life force of nature can make the spirit soar, even in darkening times . . .

Bright as a copper kettle, sweet as apple strudel, *The Sound of Music* is an enduring favourite thing – and one of the most successful movies ever made. It was the first to earn more than $100 million at the box office, and remains in the top ten-grossing films of all time. And some credit for that must go to Salzburg. Unusually for a big 1960s musical, much of *The Sound of Music* was filmed on location. Those aren't idealised mountains daubed onto an LA sound stage; this is the actual Salzkammergut, shot in all its heart-fluttering glory.

The opening scene – an aerial sweep over rolling summits and a twirling Maria (Julie Andrews) – sets the tone and underlines the importance of this specific locale: we are in 1930s Austria, on the brink of Anschluss, the country about to be occupied by the Nazis. In fact, that first sequence was filmed in Germany, just over the border from Salzburg, on Bavaria's Mehlweg meadow; somewhere amid the Alpine splendour in the background is the Obersalzberg, site of the Berghof mountain base where Hitler and the Nazi top brass spent much of their time. But, in the film, that's where the Führer stays – in the background. Somehow *The Sound of Music* manages the tricky feat of mixing the rise of the Third Reich with a frothy, ebullient story of faith, love and family, eased along, of course, by Academy-award-winning tunes.

Founded in 696 CE, Salzburg has long been a city of music – it is, after all, the birthplace of Mozart. It's also an exceptionally handsome place.

The UNESCO-listed Altstadt (Old Town) is a perfectly preserved baroque fairytale of maze-like alleys and flamboyant domes and spires rising around the Salzach River against a backdrop of magnificent mountains.

While the movie takes liberties with the facts, it's based on a true story. The naval commander and widower Georg von Trapp did live in Salzburg – his actual home, the modest Von Trapp Villa, was not featured in the movie but is now a hotel and a *Sound of Music* museum. And Georg did marry Maria Augusta Kutschera, a would-be nun who came to tutor one of his seven children. They did form a singing troupe and they did flee the country after Nazi occupation, though they left by train rather than on foot. (Indeed, the finale shows the family hiking out of Salzburg over the Untersberg, which would, in reality, have taken them into Germany and right towards Hitler's Berghof.)

Yet although there are holes to pick, *The Sound of Music* is authentically Salzburg. The city and its surrounds are frequently centre stage and many of the locations can be easily visited.

For instance, it is to Salzberg's Nonnberg Abbey that Maria sprints after her hill-top trilling – the same convent (established around 715 CE) where real-life Maria was a postulant, and where you can still hear the nuns' Gregorian chanting each morning. The Hollywood crew built sets for the interiors but Nonnberg's Gothic walls appear on film.

After Maria has been told she must go and be a governess, she leaves the abbey through its creaking iron gates, looks out across the city's rooftops (though this view is from the Winkler Terrace) and, before long, strides through elegant Residenzplatz, defiantly flicking water at the snorting horses of the square's huge fountain.

Maria then travels down the Hellbrunner Allee, a die-straight, tree-flanked boulevard, built in the seventeenth century to connect the city with Schloss Hellbrunn. Along here lies Frohnburg Palace (now a music academy) whose imposing metal gates and yellow façade stood in for the front of the von Trapp home. The back was played by Leopoldskron Palace, a wedding cake of a building by the Leopoldskroner lake; here, steps lead from the parterre terrace, through horse-flanked gates, to the water – this is where Maria and the children tumbled in, dressed in clothes made of curtains. Leopoldskron Palace is now a hotel, and guests can wander the gardens and peep into the Venetian Room – its mirrored and gilded interior inspired the movie's ballroom, which was constructed in Hollywood.

Most fun is a 'Do-Re-Mi' pilgrimage. This musical number begins high on a flower-flecked alpine meadow – the Gschwandtanger Wiesn, above the village of Werfen, south of Salzburg; in 2015, the village created an official *Sound of Music* hike to the spot. This is pure Salzkammergut splendour, with High Werfen Castle visible behind. From here, the sequence moves back to Salzberg, with Maria and the children belting out the notes to sing from atop the Mönchsberg (Monk's Hill) on Winkler Terrace, continuing by carriage from St Erhard Kirche, along Nonntaler Hauptstrasse, and finishing in the gardens of Mirabell Palace. They head through the vine tunnel and Dwarf Garden (a gaggle of mini-grotesques, sculpted in the eighteenth century), under the Greek fencing statutes, around the Pegasus Fountain and up-down-up the North Terrace steps. The choreography is specifically designed around Salzburg's fine features, a perfect melding of picture and place.

Berlin

Where? Germany
Which? *Berlin Alexanderplatz* by Alfred Döblin (1929)
What? Indefatigable German capital with a dark and dazzling past

Life swarms around the square. S-Bahn trains and electric trams disgorge an endless stream of people, hurried feet weaving around the wide, paved plaza, eyes scanning the department stores and advertising boards, mouths wrapped around Ketwurst hot dogs and multifarious conversations. Each person has their own trials and triumphs: bankers, builders, adulterers, crooks, cabaret stars – who knows? Each writing their own story in this great metropolis . . .

For author Alfred Döblin, Berlin wasn't just a city – it was *the* city. He grew up in the German capital, worked as a doctor in one of its slum neighbourhoods and once called himself a 'Berliner with vague notions of other cities and regions'. He only moved away under duress – after the 1933 Reichstag fire, the city was a dangerous place for a left-leaning Jew. But before Döblin went into exile, before the country was in full thrall to the mania of Hitler, he wrote his masterpiece: *Berlin Alexanderplatz.*

The novel, published in 1929 during the years of the Weimar Republic, follows convicted murderer Franz Biberkopf as he's released from prison. Biberkopf is determined to go straight but can't quite free himself from the city's seedy underbelly. He falls in with a gang, commits robbery, loses an arm, finds solace with a prostitute, gets framed for her murder and slowly loses his mind. But while the book is Biberkopf's story, Döblin makes clear that his miserable anti-hero is just one of many souls surviving in this heaving city – at the time, the third-largest in the world. *Berlin Alexanderplatz* is an evocation of Berlin itself, capturing it at one of its headiest and darkest moments.

Via an expressionist collage of newspaper reports, biblical stories, drinking songs and urban slang, Döblin brings the city to life, from the sewers up, recording its cacophony, machinery, mundanity, enormity. By the turn of the last page, Berlin has been heard, breathed, imbibed.

The novel's backdrop is rife with violence, struggle and sin. The action plays out in the turbulent late 1920s, when Germany was clawing itself out of the First World War doldrums; a period of economic hardship and political unrest but also unprecedented cultural vitality, creativity and liberalism, as people sought respite from the recent horrors. *Berlin Alexanderplatz* snapshots this complex moment, when architecture, art and literature thrived, the nouveau riche were leading decadent lives but the proletariat were starving – in 1928, around 133,000 Berliners were unemployed. There's a sense of foreboding too. Hitler made his first public speech in Berlin in 1928, the year before the novel's publication; the rise of Nazism is imminent.

The working-class Alexanderplatz district is the ideal setting for Döblin's urban portrait. 'Alex' lies in Mitte, the heart of Berlin, both geographically and culturally. A transport hub since the Middle Ages, in the nineteenth century the district's main square was used as a cattle market and parade ground, but by the 1920s it was one of the city's raciest spots, a hotbed of nightclubs, burlesque shows, prostitutes, cocaine dealers, high hemlines and homosexuality.

Today, Alex is transformed. Alexanderplatz itself was largely flattened by Allied bombs during the Second World War but was rebuilt in the 1960s, when it was the centre of East Berlin. At this time, the square was pedestrianised and flanked with the dull, concrete Plattenbau-style architecture favoured by the DDR. Also, more notable landmarks were erected: the huge Centrum department store (now the Galeria Kaufhof mall); the *Weltzeituhr* (world clock), which shows the time in 148 cities; and the copper bowls of the *Brunnen der Völkerfreundschaft* (Fountain of International Friendship). Lording over everything is the 368 metre- (1,207 foot-) high *Fernsehturm* (TV tower), completed in 1969 to provide a strident symbol of Communist power. It's still Germany's tallest building. Lifts – or 986 steps – lead up to the tower's sphere, where a visitor platform and rotating restaurant offer sweeping views. Quite the eyrie from which to look down on Döblin's much-changed but indomitable city.

LITERARY   125

Wells

Where? England
Which? Hot Fuzz (Edgar Wright, 2007)
What? Sleepy Somerset town whose ancient alleys make an unlikely venue for bullet-spraying action

Welcome to the country's best-kept village! (Or so it likes to think.) A picture of civic neatness – it's quaint enough to please any seeker of ye olde England, with its honeystone church, cobbled streets, wood-beamed pubs serving pints of warm ale, flower-filled hanging baskets and swans gliding elegantly along a medieval moat. Yet, just as those surface-smooth swans are actually paddling like crazy, there's a more turbulent tale unfolding underneath . . .

The setting of *Hot Fuzz* – the fictional town of 'Sandford' – couldn't be more English. But the action is 100 per cent Hollywood. And therein lies its exquisite absurdity, and anti-cinematic cinematic-ness. The car chases, gunfights, gore and explosions of a big-budget buddy-cop blow-em-up are brought to the un-mean streets of the West Country, where, when super-cop Nicholas Angel (Simon Pegg) first arrives from London, it seems the locals' biggest concerns are a few oiks spraying graffiti, an irritating living statue and whether they'll be able to win Village of the Year. The movie is a homage to action classics – all the tropes, lovingly pastiched – and a rollicking satire on little Britain.

Sleepy and seemingly crime-free Sandford is really Wells in Somerset, the country's smallest city and hometown of director Edgar Wright. It sits to the south of the limestone Mendip Hills, with Glastonbury and the fabled Somerset Levels spreading to the south and west. There was a settlement here in Roman times, centred on the three purportedly curative wells that give the town its name. In the early eighth century, Saxon King Ine of Wessex chose Wells as the site of a minster church and, from then on, its ecclesiastical importance grew, resulting in this relatively tiny place possessing one of England's most remarkable medieval cathedrals. So remarkable, in fact, that it was digitally removed from the movie to retain Sandford's small-town feel.

Yet even with its immense Gothic monument erased, Wells remains recognisably present throughout *Hot Fuzz*. As Sergeant Angel and puppy-like, action-movie-obsessed constable Danny Butterman (Nick Frost) go about their daily patrols, they cover all corners of Wells, with its humdrum corner shops and lanes becoming backdrops to high-octane, blood-and-guns carnage.

It's possible to join a *Hot Fuzz* walking tour of the town, which will reveal every nook and cranny that appeared on screen. However, much of the action plays out along and around the High Street and Market Square – not least the climactic shoot-out. It's here you'll find City News (the place to buy a Cornetto, Danny's snack of choice), the site of the now-defunct Somerfield supermarket run by oily Simon Skinner (Timothy Dalton), the ornate Bishop's Eye arch (where missing swans are discussed) and the eighteenth-century Market Cross and Fountain itself. The Crown pub, where Angel and Danny often go for a beer/cranberry juice, is here too – although the interior of the fifteenth-century inn wasn't used. However, the Crown's links to law enforcement date back to at least 1695, when William Penn – a Quaker and later founder of Pennsylvania – preached to 3,000 people from an upper-floor window, but was stopped by a constable with a warrant to arrest him for unlawful assembly. Plaques here commemorate the visits of both Penn and the *Hot Fuzz* cast.

Elsewhere, you can check in to the Swan Hotel, where Angel (along with many of the cast) stayed. You can go to St Vincent's – aka St Cuthbert's, Somerset's largest parish church – where Sandford's fete is held and a journalist is split asunder by a falling finial. And you can visit the thirteenth-century Bishop's Palace, where the dastardly Neighbourhood Watch Alliance convene and where swans can be found in the moat, having been taught, since the 1850s, to ring the Gatehouse bell for food. Sometimes fact is stranger than fiction.

CINEMATIC 129

Musical

Vienna

Where? North-east Austria
Why? The wonderful waltzing ground of classical greats

Vienna has visual onomatopoeia. The city looks just like it sounds: opulent, harmonious, refined. Indeed, the world-changing music that has been composed here over the centuries seems to echo the resplendence of the royal palaces, the grandeur of the Ringstrasse, the spin of Prater park's historic Ferris Wheel, the intoxication lying in wait in the surrounding vine-cloaked hills, the graceful flow of the blue Danube. In Vienna, it's as if architecture is orchestra, Mother Nature conducting, each elegant element playing its part . . .

Vienna is often called simply the 'City of Music' – no other has made such a mark on the classical stage. Capital of Austria, it lies on the Danube, Europe's second-longest river, between the foothills of the Alps and the Carpathian Mountains, fringed by the Vienna Woods. It's a setting that attracted the Romans, who developed a garrison town here. But the city's big transformation occurred under the powerful Habsburg dynasty, who ruled ever-shifting swathes of central Europe from 1282 for around 600 years, and made Vienna its de facto capital.

Many Habsburg emperors were avid music lovers, and, from the seventeenth century, Vienna became an artistic epicentre. Baroque music – and building styles – flourished, and the city's location, at the heart of Europe, made it a cultural crossroads; talent flooded in from across the continent, filling Vienna with bright minds and new ideas.

However, it was the so-called 'First Viennese School', which emerged in the eighteenth and nineteenth centuries, that came to define what 'classical music' really is. The patronage of the wealthy and influential allowed creativity to thrive, shaking up the music scene. At the school's core, three musical heavyweights: Joseph Haydn (1732–1809), Wolfgang Amadeus Mozart (1756–91) and Ludwig van Beethoven (1770–1827). This uber-talented trio were all drawn to Vienna. It was here that Haydn, the 'Father of the Symphony', laid the groundwork for the new classical style. It's where Mozart employed his supreme mastery of melody,

MUSICAL   131

using obbligato instrumentals – complimentary parts no less vital than the main line – to create concertos of profound expression. It's where Beethoven pushed the boundaries of symphonic structure, producing works of rich emotional depth and complexity. At this time, under these men, there was a surge in secular music – composition distanced from religion, art for art's sake – and the traditional symphony orchestra expanded. It was fervent, thrilling, game-changing.

Later came the rise of the Viennese waltz, epitomised by Johann Strauss (1825–99), then Johannes Brahms (1833–97), Gustav Mahler (1860–1911), Richard Strauss (1894–1949) from the Romantic era, who all found inspiration here. Later, the Second Viennese School shook things up again, challenging listeners with their avant-garde compositions.

And so it remains: Vienna is still a vital musical centre. It's reckoned that, on any given night, 10,000 people are listening to live classical music in the city. This might be within landmark institutions such as the grand Vienna State Opera, the Art Nouveau Konzerthaus or the Musikverein, founded by the Society of Friends of Music. Or it might be at a concert inside St Stephen's Cathedral, waltzing at one of the city's 450-odd balls during the winter ball season or at a more intimate piano recital at a chandelier-hung café. The Viennese love them all. Locals here have long had a philosophy of *Lebenskunst* – 'the art of living well', of appreciating beauty in all things, all sounds. It's no surprise, then, that this city of green parks, palaces and handsome boulevards of bars, bookshops and theatres is often voted the most liveable in the world.

One way to seek out Vienna's musical heritage is to be guided by one of its musicians. A tour in the footsteps of Beethoven, for instance, who, having settled in Vienna, spent most of his life here. On Mölkerbastei, in the Inner City, is the Pasqualatihaus, where Ludwig lived for eight years – it's possible to step inside and gaze out at the same inspirational view. His former residence in Probusgasse, is now the Beethoven Museum, where some of his most important works were written. A commanding bronze of the man himself broods over Beethovenplatz, while a vast Klimt wall painting honouring the composer lies inside the striking Secession art gallery. Beethoven is buried, alongside other luminaries – Schubert, Brahms, Johann Strauss II – in the grand Vienna Central Cemetery. A worthy place to pay respects, but in the knowledge that music in Vienna is still very much alive.

Foodie

Tusheti

Where? Caucasus, Georgia
Why? Make for the wild mountains, where a national dish might have been born

According to Russian poet Alexander Pushkin, 'Every Georgian dish is a poem'. This is a nation where food is not just sustenance but story; each recipe a hearty serving of flavour, artistry, emotion and centuries of cultural exchange. This country on the cusp of Europe and Asia has always been a crossroads, absorbing and adapting influences over millennia of invasions, colonisations and trade. So, a 'Georgian speciality' is necessarily the outcome of centuries of to and fro . . .

That's the case with *khinkali*. These giant soup dumplings – fist-sized knobs of twisted dough, swollen with a spiced meat broth – are considered one of the country's national dishes. The patriotic legend is that khinkali were created in Tusheti, Georgia's final frontier, an untamed enclave of the Greater Caucasus, 200 kilometres (125 miles) north of the capital Tbilisi, right by the Russian border. Here, the peaks reach 4,500 metres (14,700 feet) and winter temperatures plunge well below zero. Sheep herding is the main occupation, and soup dumplings – piping-hot parcels of fat and protein that feed both belly and soul – are the ideal comfort food.

Most likely, though, khinkali originated far beyond these mountains. Dumplings were first steamed up in southwest China; it's probable that Genghis Khan's marauding hordes spread Chinese *jiaozi* to all corners of the Mongol Empire, where they took on multiple new identities, from Russian *pelmeni* to Korean *mandu*.

Still, *khinkali* are now a Georgian staple, and Tushetian *khinkali* are considered the best. The dumplings found here are made of a particularly thick, stiff dough, packed with a simple filling: chopped lamb or mutton, or occasionally beef, with a dash of caraway, possibly other herbs. In Tusheti, *khinkali* never contain pork – pig meat, believed to bring bad luck, is forbidden here. Each one is made by hand, the dough expertly folded and cinched around a generous ooze of spiced meat. They are orb-shaped in honour of the sun, a nod to the mishmash of animist, pagan and Christian beliefs that form the region's unique religious code.

Once made, *khinkali* are boiled and then served immediately. And there's a knack to the eating. First, grab them by their top knot. Then take a tiny bite to pierce the skin and suck down the salty, steaming liquid inside. Once that's done, you can eat the rest, discarding the dough handle on your plate. You could eat it, but it's considered a waste of stomach space when there are more delicious dumplings to be consumed. Besides, how many you can eat is a badge of honour, and the knots are a good way to keep count. Dispatching more than ten in a sitting is considered the mark of a man. Mastering the art of dumpling making – perfecting the accordion-like folding of the dough – is, so they say, the sign a woman is ready to be wed.

Getting to Tusheti is not easy. Only one unpaved, perilous road penetrates this wilderness, via the 2,900m (9,500ft) Abano Pass. It's only open for a few months of the year, usually from June to early October. Even most Tushetians – numbering around 2,000, spread across 48 isolated, off-grid villages – don't stay here over winter. They bring their animals in to graze the highlands when the snow clears and take them down to the lower pastures at summer's end.

It's certainly a long, arduous journey to make for a plate of dumplings. But fortunately, *khinkali* have made it out of the mountains and onto Tbilisi's cosmopolitan streets. Here, it's common to find them stuffed with a mix of beef and pork, cheese, vegetables or mushrooms, and a range of spices. The proper accompaniment is beer or vodka, or both.

However, the ultimate in Georgian eating is a *supra* – named for the tablecloth (supra) on which this traditional feast is spread. Dish upon dish upon dish will be served here, from vegetable salads to barbecued meat, from *khachapuri* (cheese bread) to, of course, *khinkali*, all washed down with innumerable toasts of local wine. A whole anthology of poems on the plate.

Artistic

Oslo

Where? Norway
Which? The Scream (1893) by Edvard Munch
What? Emotive, inspiring Norwegian fjordland

Sitting between dense forests and a glittering fjord, Oslo is unique among capital cities, with one of the lowest carbon footprints in the world, created by efficient public transport, a commitment to sustainable food production, refreshing water that sparkles from the tap and an abundance of open spaces. The air in this energised metropolis feels fresh and clear, and there are beautiful views over the Oslo Fjord and the surrounding mountains, forests, parks, waterways and ski slopes. Bars, cafés and restaurants are bustling but chilled, and it is easy to relax in the unhurried atmosphere beneath the clear sunlight that shines for much of the year, whether in the height of summer or during the crisp, cold winter.

Although Oslo is modern and progressive, aspects of the city date back nearly a thousand years, when it was founded by King Harald Hardrada in around 1050. In approximately 1300, the Akershus Fortress was built by Haakon V. After the town was destroyed by fire in 1624, Christian IV of Denmark–Norway built a new city slightly to the west of the original, under the walls of the Akershus Fortress, and called it Christiania, or Kristiania. It was not until 1925 that its name changed from Kristiania to Oslo. These days, as with most cities, examples of old and new nestle alongside each other; in the architecture of the museums, galleries, university, theatres, concert halls and opera houses.

There is a great diversity of culture to admire, from the Historical Museum and the National Museum of Art, Architecture and Design, to the botanical gardens, the Norwegian Folk Museum and the Viking Ship Museum. More contrasts include the large, airy Frogner Park with its lake and sculptures, the modernist Ekeberg restaurant, the Neoclassical Royal Palace and twin towers of City Hall in the city centre, the Holmenkollen ski slope that rises above the sea to the fjord, the opera house where waves lap around its glass façade, and the Munch Museum, named after acclaimed artist, Edvard Munch (1863–1944), whose 1893 painting *The Scream* turned the city, and especially the fjord, into an icon.

Munch grew up in Oslo, and although he moved away for several years, he began his career there and returned for the last decades of his life. When he was one year old, his family moved to Nedre Slottsgate, a street in the Kvadraturen area of Kristiania. They later moved to Pilestredet and various addresses in the Grünerløkka neighbourhood, east of the River Akerselva. A stroll around this borough gives a good idea of the Oslo that Munch would have known – a former industrial and working-class area; while some gentrification has since taken place, the architecture remains, perhaps surprisingly, much as it was when Munch lived there.

Munch rented his first studio opposite the Parliament building on Karl Johans Gate, Oslo's main street. This lively thoroughfare remains a focal point of the city today, and a leisurely stroll down this street takes you past bustling cafés, restaurants and shops, as well as local street performers, artists and musicians. Munch painted a number of works featuring Karl Johans Gate, such as *Spring Day on Karl Johan Street* in 1890 and *Evening on Karl Johan Street* in 1892. In 1893, he produced four versions of a painting that he initially called *The Scream of Nature*. It has become one of the most recognised paintings in the world. An agitated figure stands in a distorted Oslo landscape against a fiery red sky. Two figures are walking on, unaware of the crisis their friend is experiencing.

Although the image is deliberately exaggerated and misshapen, Munch said he was inspired by the Oslo (Kristiania) Fjord seen from Ekeberg, a neighbourhood within the city. The Ekeberg Park, close to Ekebergparken Sculpture Park, is the spot and is a must-see when you are there to admire the view as Munch once did. Munch was also inspired by the bay of Bjørvika and the Akershus Fortress – seen in the background of the painting and another essential stopping-off point. More than a landscape, however, the painting represents both personal and universal feelings of anxiety and alienation. It was one of the first works of art to explore inner emotions rather than outer appearances.

St Petersburg

Where? Russia
Which? Crime and Punishment by Fyodor Dostoyevsky (1866)
What? Imperial Russian city that can mess with a man's soul

The city in July: humid, suffocating, penetratingly bright. The sun barely sets during these summer 'white nights'; it glitters almost 24/7 on the canals, the baroque domes, the Neoclassical palaces and the Soviet tower blocks. It seems to swing like a spotlight, exposing everything. Or maybe that scrutiny is all in the mind – a hot-bothered brain, addled by issues of penury, morality, faith and murder . . .

Founded by Peter the Great in the early eighteenth century, St Petersburg was planned to be Russia's 'window on the West'. Built on swampland by indentured labourers, the city grew quickly; by the 1860s it was overcrowded, and rife with poverty, crime and disease. This is the city of Fyodor Dostoyevsky. Like Dickens' London, Dostoyevsky's St Petersburg is desperate: there are, he writes, 'few more grim, harsh and strange influences on a man's soul than in Petersburg'.

Dostoyevsky's *Crime and Punishment*, the world's first psychological thriller, follows impoverished ex-student Rodion Raskolnikov who, in desperate need of money, devises a plan to rob and kill an unscrupulous old pawnbroker. Mental torment ensues. It's a tale rooted in time and place. Not only does it exude the stink and suffocation of St Petersburg's streets in July, circa 1866, it delves into the great philosophical debate dividing society at the time: should Russia embrace its place in Europe or return to its folk traditions? Dostoyevsky – conservative, religious, Slavophile – was of the latter school of thinking, and viewed rising western ideas of nihilism, rational egoism and secularism as dangerous to the country's future.

These are the ideas plaguing Raskolnikov, whose inner turmoil is mirrored in his external world. The novel shuns St Petersburg's magnificence and instead roams its squalid back rooms, brothels and spit-sticky inns. The action is centred on Sennaya Ploshchad, the Haymarket district. In the nineteenth century it was a notorious slum area, cramped and chaotic. It's been razed and cleaned up now, though one of the original buildings around the old market remains, the yellow Guardhouse – where Dostoyevsky himself spent two days imprisoned for a censorship violation in 1874.

Raskolnikov measures the footsteps – of which there are 730 – between his rented attic and the home of the pawnbroker, and it's possible to walk to the scene of the crime, just as he did. The anti-hero lived on the corner of Stolyarny and Grazhdansky streets; a plaque now marks the building, its words roughly translating as: 'The tragic fates of the people of this area served as the basis of Dostoyevsky's passionate sermon on good for all humankind.'

When finally fixed on robbing and killing the pawnbroker, Raskolnikov procures an axe and takes a roundabout route, heading slowly south along Stolyarny, which was then an alley of 'unbearable stench', heaving with dingy taverns and drunks. Dostoyevsky himself lived here, at the corner of Kaznacheisky Street, while writing *Crime and Punishment*.

Raskolnikov follows Stolyarny to Kokushkin Bridge – then wooden, now metal-railed – which spans the Griboedov Canal. Pre-revolution, this waterway through the heart of St Petersburg was officially known as Ekaterininsky, after Empress Catherine the Great. However, those who lived within sniffing distance called it *kanava* (ditch) – back then it was an open cesspit. These days it's one of the city's finest thoroughfares, cleaned up and flanked by resplendent buildings.

Although current government advice is to avoid travelling to Russia, we can still explore St Petersburg through Dostoyevsky's words and Raskolnikov's footsteps. From the bridge, Raskolnikov walks via Yusupov Gardens, where he dreams of installing fountains to 'refresh the air'; now it's a public park with a lake. After 20 minutes, he arrives at the pawnbroker's apartment. It's thought to be 104 Griboedov Canal, a private apartment block with exits onto both the canal and a side street – perfect for an escaping felon. For a more intimate encounter with Dostoyevsky, the house where he died, 5/2 Kuznechny Alley, is now a museum, and his tomb is located at Alexander Nevsky Monastery.

Lake Mälaren

Artistic

Where? Sweden
Which? The Ten Largest, No 7 Adulthood (1907) by Hilma af Klint
What? A fusion of nature and spirituality on a Swedish lake

At one time Lake Mälaren was a bay of the Baltic Sea, inviting boats and ships to sail deep into Sweden. Eventually, as the Earth's crust moved, the bay became a lake that now spills across the countryside west of Stockholm. All around the lake's shores, the soft lapping of water, the hum of insects, gentle calls of birds and erratic scurrying of small wild animals can be heard, while the ripe soil nurtures colourful, delicate wildflowers, including cornflower, honeysuckle and blackthorn. The third-largest freshwater lake in Sweden (after Vänern and Vättern), Lake Mälaren is dotted with thousands of islands, including Selaön, Lovön, Munsö, Björkö and Adelsö.

Around the shoreline are wooded areas, deep forests, sandy beaches, pretty little towns with red wooden cottages and often historical remains, particularly Viking evidence, such as at the archaeological site on Björkö island at Birka of a Viking city from the ninth and tenth centuries. In summer, the lake is busy with boats and ships, and each year, these islands witness mystical natural occurrences including spectacular northern lights and midnight sun. It was in this land of the midnight sun, on the island of Adelsö, west of Stockholm, that Hilma af Klint (1862–1944) spent summers with her family at their manor, Hanmora. In these idyllic surroundings, af Klint came into contact with nature, and her close association with natural forms became an inspiration in her work. Later in life, she lived at Villa Furuheim on Munsö, an island next to Adelsö.

Probably the first artist in the West to produce an abstract painting, af Klint was one of the earliest women to receive a higher education at the Royal Academy of Fine Arts in Stockholm.

She graduated with honours, and was awarded a scholarship in the form of a studio owned by the Academy in central Stockholm. At the

ARTISTIC   143

end of the nineteenth century, spiritualist movements were fashionable in the United States and Europe, especially in literary and artistic circles. Scientific developments were radically altering prevailing ideas about the world. Darwin's evolutionary theories, while not yet entirely accepted in academic circles, affected many, and the discovery of such things as radioactivity and X-rays confirmed for spiritualists that there is an invisible realm of existence.

Inspired by the mystical teachings of theosophy and anthroposophy, af Klint tried to understand both the visible world we are all aware of and the spiritual world that we cannot see. In 1896, with four female artist friends, she began a group called *De Fem* (The Five). They held regular séances and experimented with unconscious writing and drawing, and were apparently successful in making contact with six spirit guides. The women documented their experiences in notebooks, collaborating on automatic drawings filled with biomorphic forms inspired by their visions. In 1904, two of the spirits asked the women to convey the spiritual world through painting, and to design a temple to house the resulting works. The other members of the group refused, believing that such a prolonged, intense engagement with the spirit realm could lead to madness. But in January 1906, af Klint promised to undertake this 'great commission'. From 1906, she produced *Paintings for the Temple*, resulting in 193 works on canvas and paper by 1915. Sometimes resembling diagrams, her paintings were a visual representation of complex spiritual ideas, especially ten that each illustrates a different phase of human life, including childhood, youth, maturity and old age. These huge paintings are called collectively *The Ten Largest*, and there are two themed 'Childhood', two themed 'Youth', four themed 'Adulthood' and two themed 'Old Age'. Af Klint wrote, 'The pictures were painted directly . . . without any preliminary drawings . . . I had no idea what the paintings were supposed to depict; nevertheless, I worked swiftly and surely, without changing a single brushstroke.'

With their free-flowing organic forms of different sizes and bright colours, the *Paintings for the Temple* are at once meditative and calm, dynamic and flowing, neatly echoing the artist's botanical studies of the wildflowers around Lake Mälaren.

Foodie

Kraków

Where? Poland
What? Bite into the bread that's become the symbol of a city

The secret is getting up early, as soon as the carts are wheeled out. There will be one of these small blue wagons standing sentry on every street corner in Kraków's Old Town, from the base of the castle-topped Wawel Hill to the edges of the medieval Market Square to the historic Jewish quarter of Kazimierz. And each will have its belly packed with discs of golden-brown bread; crusty quoits fresh-baked each day, which should be eaten while still warm and soft – within hours they'll be stale. But while each individual roll doesn't last long, the recipe has endured for hundreds of years . . .

Kraków is Poland's second city, former capital, artistic hub and crown jewel. Having escaped the Second World War largely intact – unlike most of the country's major hubs – it's a glory of Romanesque, Gothic, Renaissance, Baroque and art nouveau architecture. Indeed, its historic centre was placed on the inaugural UNESCO World Heritage list in 1978. However, for all its grandeur, one of the city's most enduring and beloved symbols is a humble piece of bread.

The *obwarzanek krakowski* is the Kraków equivalent of a bagel or pretzel – though not quite like either. Each roll is made from two or three strands of yeasted wheat dough, twisted together into a spiral and sealed in a round or oval shape with a hole in the middle. These rings are then parboiled, which is where they get their name: *obwarzać* means to dip in steaming water. Finally, they are baked, either plain or sprinkled with poppy seeds, sesame seeds, herbs, spices, onions, cheese or salt from one of the nearby salt mines like ancient Wieliczka. When done, they should lightly glisten and be firm to the touch; the texture should be dense, soft and chewy, the flavour slightly sweet.

The first record of *obwarzanki* appears in royal documents dating back to 1394. It's possible they evolved from the pretzels brought to Poland by German artisans, who were encouraged to migrate here in

146   EUROPE

the fourteenth century. Just like pretzels – which are shaped like two arms raised in prayer – *obwarzanki* were originally associated with Lent. Indeed, their popularity rose when pious Queen Jadwiga – who, in 1384, became the Kingdom of Poland's first female monarch – chose to eschew richer, fancier breads and cakes and eat *obwarzanki* during the 40-day religious fast. Containing no fat or sugar, they were considered the abstemious choice. However, being made from wheat, which was expensive at the time, they were still a treat reserved for queens and nobles. Most Poles had to make do with rough rye bread, if they could afford bread at all.

Even before this, Polish royals held Kraków's bakers in high esteem. Members of the city's bakers' guild were granted numerous privileges, including the right to construct and earn rent from bread stalls, and to choose where their flour was milled. In the late fifteenth century, King Olbracht decreed that no one outside the city limits was permitted to bake *obwarzanek*, or any other white bread. Later, the guild was given the power to decide which Kraków bakers were allowed to sell them. Stalls would open at 6 a.m., with officials performing daily quality checks; any wrongdoing was harshly punished.

In Kraków today, *obwarzanki* are affordable for everyone, available everywhere. But this cheap street food is the product of centuries of experience and tradition. There's even an Obwarzanek Museum, where you can have a go at baking your own. In honour of their heritage and status, the *obwarzanek krakowski* was granted Protected Geographical Indication status in 2010. To be authentic, the bread must be made and baked within the city or surrounding districts. It must adhere to strict measurements – 12–17 centimetres (5–7 inches) in diameter, 80–120 grams (2¾–4½ ounces) in weight, always braided in a ring. And it should be made by hand, not by machine, ensuring every one of the 150,000 *obwarzanek* sold in Kraków every day has a subtly different shape, its own unique identity.

FOODIE 147

Musical

Andalucía

Where? Southern Spain
Why? Hot Iberian passion in guitar and footwork form

Flamenco isn't music. It's a human soul being wrung from a body. Artistry at its most primal: guitar twangs, castanet clacks, finger snaps, hand claps and deep, gut-felt vocals, all emotion laid bare, scrubbed raw, vulnerable and exposed. Tragedy, comedy, grief, joy, sorrow – everything spills from its burning rhythms. Indeed, watch a flamenco dancer move and they do not dance 'nice' – their slow steps, stamps and swirls accelerate into a kind of mania. It's as if they are toys being wound up, and then – *olé!* – exploding in a hot-blooded frenzy of physical poetry, sweat-spray, unbridled passion . . .

Flamenco has become synonymous with the Spanish national identity. Curvaceous female figures flourishing fans in frilled *sevillana* dresses have graced many a come-to-Spain poster. But the origins of this *cante* (song), *baile* (dance) and *toque* (guitar-played) musical style – with plenty of jaleo ('hell-raising') thrown in – reach far further than the Iberian Peninsula.

The roots of the word 'flamenco' date back to the early fifteenth century, when Romani *gitanos* (gypsies) arrived from India, bringing their moves and melodies with them. At the time Andalucía was still under Arab rule – Granada, the last Muslim stronghold, fell in 1492 – so these Romani traditions became part of an existing musical culture.

Following the Catholic Reconquista, all these groups faced persecution, causing many to seek refuge in Andalucía's rural villages and remote mountain reaches. So, it was in this often-unforgiving backcountry of olive groves, vineyards and soaring sierra, that flamenco evolved as an art form of the marginalised, conveying the toughness of existence in this historically poor part of Spain.

In its original form there were no instruments, just the primitive cry of vocal chords and a wooden staff beating out a rhythm. It wasn't music for the ears of kings and courtiers, it was the soundtrack of the gutter, a way for the lowly to articulate their struggles and celebrations;

MUSICAL   149

a music infused with life's daily rituals that reflected the people's spirit and resilience.

Flamenco began to move out of the ghettos in the eighteenth and nineteenth centuries when the Romantic movement became intrigued by the exotic and erotic dances of these mysterious outsiders. It developed quickly, performed in *cafés cantantes* (singing cafés) to audiences enthralled by the dancers' thrusts, the vocalists' unusual tones and the guitar players' virtuosity.

These days flamenco is on UNESCO's Intangible Cultural Heritage list. It is found across Andalucía, and different regions have different styles or *palos*. These range from synchronised *sevillanas*, to fast and joyful *bulerías*, sensual *soleas*, solemn *seguiriyas* and passionate *fandangos*. The essence of them all, though, is *duende*. The term comes from the name of a mischievous goblin in Spanish folklore. However, in the context of flamenco it's the attainment of a heightened emotional state – somewhere between rapture and despair. Transcending technical skill, *duende* can be felt in the guitar's reverberations, the unrestrained wails of the singer, the pounding of the dancer's feet, and imbues flamenco with its intensity and authenticity. It is said to manifest when the artist surrenders absolutely, blurring the boundaries between the physical and spiritual, their performance unfiltered and uninhibited.

Seville is a major centre for flamenco, in particular the namesake *sevillanas* style. Indeed, the capital of Andalucía, full of grand Mudéjar, Gothic and Renaissance buildings, is as flamboyant as flamenco itself. There are many places to imbibe flamenco here, from renowned *tablaos* (flamenco venues, from the word for 'floorboard') to the Flamenco Dance Museum. But the music's heartland is Triana. Historically, this is the neighbourhood of *azulejos* tile-makers, of sailors, of bullfighters – and flamenco. Some of the most authentic performances in the city can be found in Triana's low-lit, late-night joints.

But maybe even better is Jerez de la Frontera, a city further south towards the sea. It has many of the attractions of Seville: magnificent Mudéjar architecture, an impressive cathedral, mouthwatering tapas and sherry bodegas, but on a more intimate scale. And some argue this is the true birthplace of flamenco. Jerez is home to the Centro Andaluz del Flamenco, the art-form's ground zero. There are also plentiful *peñas* (social clubs) and *tabancos* (traditional bars) hosting live music, mostly for free – unreconstructed places with tiled floors, dusty bottles lining the shelves, sherry casks for tables, matador posters on the walls. Follow the crowds and the beat to one you fancy, order a glass of dry *fino* and watch a very Spanish type of magic unfurl.

London

Where? England
Which? Oliver Twist by Charles Dickens (1839)
What? Den of grime and crime, where the tale of an orphan augured British social reform

This city is a still labyrinth; a confusion of hither-thither streets, grunge and clamour, too many people. The pea-soup fog and miasma of desperation have largely lifted, but many a corner still conjures up the past. When the constant din was of horse-clatter, cab-rattle and peddler-patter. When the streets were packed with prostitutes, pickpockets, fraudsters, gangsters, ragamuffins and the piteously poor. When crime was so rife, your handkerchief might be pinched at one end of an alley and hawked back to you at the other. A city writ larger than life; wondrous and wretched in equal measure . . .

All of London is laced with Charles Dickens. It seems there's barely a pub he didn't drink in, a street he didn't stroll. Moreover, he painted so strong a portrait of the UK capital at the beginning of the Victorian age that, while the city has existed for over 2,000 years, 'Dickens' London' is the incarnation that most vividly endures.

Charles Dickens was born in Portsmouth in 1812. When his father was sent to debtors' prison in 1822, young Charles was sent to work at a boot-polish warehouse on Hungerford Steps (now the site of London's Charing Cross Station). The experience left a lasting impression, fermenting his views on socioeconomic reform and the heinous labour conditions borne by the underclasses – a situation that got worse when the 1834 Poor Law Amendment Act stopped virtually all financial aid to the poverty-stricken. At this time, London was the world's biggest city, an imperial and industrial powerhouse. But it was seething with destitution and class division.

Into this arena came *Oliver Twist*. Dickens' second major work, the novel pulled no punches, describing with ruthless satire the levels of crime and depravity rife in the capital. For fictional Oliver – like so many real Londoners – the city's streets were full of 'foul and frowsy dens, where vice is closely packed and lacks the room to turn'. Via the tale of the workhouse orphan who ends up embroiled with Fagin's gang, Dickens shone a gaslight on the horrors of life on the margins in mid-nineteenth-century Britain.

Dickens saw the sordidness first-hand. In 1837 he moved to 48 Doughty Street in Holborn, where he wrote *Oliver Twist*. Dickens was a great wanderer, and the streets he paced seeped into his pages. And the areas around his former home, which is now the Charles Dickens Museum, still whisper of the past.

A little east of Doughty Street lie the alleyways of Clerkenwell. In the early nineteenth century this was one of London's most squalid, crime-ridden neighbourhoods, teeming with thieves and hoodlums. In the 1860s an improvement project cleared the 'rookeries' (slums) and Clerkenwell was transformed. However, you can still walk across Clerkenwell Green, where Oliver watches in horror as the Artful Dodger pickpockets Mr Brownlow. And you can still, like Dodger, 'scud at a rapid pace' along the nearby alleys towards Saffron Hill. Named for the spice that was grown here in the Middle Ages (to mask the taste of rotten meat), in Dickens' time this was the site of an infamous rookery beside the sewage-stinking Fleet Ditch. Saffron Hill is now a nondescript sinew of offices and apartments but there's atmosphere within The One Tun pub. Founded in 1759, but rebuilt in 1875, it's reputed to be the basis for Dickens' Three Cripples, the favourite haunt of murderous villain Bill Sikes. Field Lane, the location of Fagin's lair, was demolished in the clear-up, but probably stood a little south of the pub, near where Saffron Hill meets Charterhouse Street.

Continue further south and you end up before Lady Justice and the Old Bailey, the country's Central Criminal Court. Part of it is built on the site of Newgate Prison, a gaol since the twelfth century, whose 'dreadful walls . . . have hidden so much misery'. Dickens witnessed a public execution here, and sent Fagin to its gallows – in *Oliver Twist*, the bad 'uns get their comeuppance, the good live happily ever after. For Victorian London's real working classes, life was seldom so fair. But through his words, Dickens ensured they were not ignored.

Arles

Where? France
Which? Café Terrace at Night (1888) by Vincent van Gogh
What? Ancient Roman city of swirling skies and artistic legends

Long before Vincent van Gogh (1853–90) produced approximately 300 paintings here, Arles in Provence on the River Rhône was a Greek colony, established in the sixth century BCE. Five centuries later, Julius Caesar occupied Arles, turning it into the flourishing gateway to Roman Gaul, transforming the area into an imposing civilisation and one of Gaul's most venerated cities. Featuring aqueducts, canals, roads, pavements, sewers, latrines, thermal baths, a forum, a hippodrome, a theatre and an arena, from 308–12 CE it became home to Emperor Constantine, who brought Christianity with him. These days, several charming classical antiquities and examples of Romanesque stonework remain, while the rest of the town boasts shady, restful streets and squares, and shuttered houses basking in golden sunlight.

Every Saturday there is a colourful market in Arles, brimming with local produce, clothes, trinkets and household items for sale. Most famous, of course, for the dramatic events and vibrant works of art produced by Van Gogh, Arles is a popular city for tourists, many of whom follow in the artist's footsteps on the Van Gogh Walking Tour. Maps are available from the Visitors Centre on Boulevard des Lices, or in the smaller Visitors Centre at Arles train station, and this free, self-guided tour takes you around the city, exploring all the major sites that Vincent himself saw and painted during his time living there. At each key point, there is a reproduction of the scene that he painted on that spot, so you can fully immerse yourself in Van Gogh's world and see through his eyes.

When Van Gogh arrived in Arles in February 1888, he was yearning for the sunshine and glowing colours of the south of France, so was shocked and disappointed to discover it had recently snowed. But for most of the year – around 300 days – the city and surrounding

ARTISTIC   155

countryside are illuminated by dazzling yellow sunlight or peppered with sparkling silver stars and a glowing moon. So once the snow had melted, he made the most of it. Van Gogh first checked in at the hotel-restaurant Carrel, and later at Café de la Gare. After six months, in early September, he moved into the Yellow House at 2 Place Lamartine, which he had been using as a studio since the beginning of May and where he lived for a time with the artist Paul Gauguin. It was here that Van Gogh severed his own ear in December 1888, allegedly after a row with Gauguin, who had announced he was leaving Arles. Van Gogh ended up in the local hospital, where he was treated by assistant physician Dr Félix Rey, who believed that Van Gogh was suffering from a form of epilepsy brought on partly by too much coffee and alcohol and too little food. A few weeks later, he voluntarily entered an asylum in nearby Saint-Rémy, from where he painted his famous work, The Starry Night, in 1889.

Although the famous Yellow House, which he painted in 1888, was destroyed during the Second World War, many other vistas that Van Gogh painted in Arles, such as *Starry Night Over the Rhône*, *Café Terrace at Night* and *Les Alyscamps* (all painted in 1888) remain remarkably unchanged. The whirling skies really are as Van Gogh painted them; clear and blue by day, deep and velvety by night.

In the first century CE, the Place du Forum, where Van Gogh later painted *Café Terrace at Night*, was the centre of the city. The part that remains today is only a segment of the Roman original, but because of Van Gogh's painting, it is now more associated with him than with its connection to antiquity. Now called the Café Van Gogh, the café still looks as it did when he painted it, and visitors can while away a few hours here, soaking up the atmosphere of a place the artist loved. Nearby, in the restored fifteenth-century Hôtel Léautaud de Donines, the Fondation Vincent van Gogh was established in 2014 to present aspects of his time in Arles and reflect on his impact on art today.

Other features of the Roman settlement in Arles can still be seen today, including the Arles Amphitheatre, constructed during the reign of Emperor Augustus. Built for 20,000 spectators, it once showcased gladiators and chariot racing. Next door is the Théâtre Antique, which also dates from the first century CE and is now used in the summer for dance, film and music performances and festivals. Also remaining is the Thermes de Constantin – the Roman baths of the Emperor Constantine, which were built in the fourth century as part of his palace.

In the Arles Museum of Antiquity, just outside the city centre at Rue du Cirque Romain, among other fascinating objects is the oldest known bust of Julius Caesar that was made during his lifetime, and unearthed in 2008 in the River Rhône. Also found in the River Rhône, having spent 2,000 years under water, is a remarkably well-preserved ancient Roman wooden barge. More history can be uncovered at the Hôtel Nord Pinus, where bull fighters, Pablo Picasso, Ernest Hemingway and Henry James all either socialised or stayed. The building contains two embedded Corinthian pillars from a temple that was once part of the ancient Roman Forum, while the Hôtel Jules-César, that was once a convent, was designed by renowned French fashion designer Christian Lacroix, who was born in Arles.

Meanwhile, just beyond Arles is the mythic Camargue, an astonishingly beautiful area featuring salt flats, small saltwater lakes, lagoons, marshlands and farmland, and roamed by black bulls, white horses and pink flamingos. Not far too, is the Alpilles, a small, rocky mountain range that runs between the Rivers Rhône and Durance. Arles, however, will forever be primarily renowned for its connections with Vincent van Gogh as a place where he was happy – for much of the time – and where he produced some of his brightest works, such as *Wheat Field with Cypresses* (1889), *Pont de Langlois* (1888) and his series of Sunflower paintings (1888–89). Even today, long after he left it, Arles epitomises Van Gogh's vision. So briefly touched by a brush of genius, the town has become iconic.

Cinematic

Montmarte

Where? Paris, France
Which? Amélie (Jean-Pierre Jeunet, 2001)
What? Delightful district of the French capital, where you can live out the Parisian dream

Ah, this vision is *très jolie*. An artist's impression of a charming neighbourhood, where gay shop awnings swing out over cobbled streets and Thonet chairs sit at marble tables topped with petite glasses of cognac and vin rouge. No grit or graffiti, just the sort of nostalgic, Gallic picture that we all long to step inside . . .

Amélie is a romantic comedy set in the most romantic part of the most romantic of cities. A bright flight of fancy, it dances on the screen, dripping with idealised Frenchness. Not the real Paris, maybe, but seen through rose-coloured spectacles; note, its shy but spirited heroine is always dressed in or surrounded by red.

That heroine is Amélie Poulain (Audrey Tautou), a waitress in Montmartre, the hilltop village-like enclave located in the 18th arrondissement, in the north of the city. She's a solitary soul but, following a chance event, decides to dedicate her energy to do-gooding, playing secret fairy godmother to a cast of eccentrics, changing their lives – and, in the end, her own – for the better.

The movie does stray across Paris a little. For instance, we see six-year-old Amélie standing outside Notre-Dame as her mother is killed by a suicidal tourist leaping from the medieval cathedral's roof. But mainly it sticks to Montmartre.

Meaning 'martyr's hill', Montmartre is linked to the legend of St Denis, the first bishop of Paris and patron saint of France. In 250 CE Denis was decapitated by the Romans here but, it's said, picked up his head and walked off, delivering a sermon as he went. Though it became a place of pilgrimage, for centuries Montmartre wasn't part of Paris at all but a rural hamlet where windmills twirled and an abbey of nuns tended orchards and vineyards. However, following the French Revolution in 1789, the abbey was razed and the windmills supplanted by guinguettes, suburban taverns where wine was cheap and gaiety guaranteed – the sort of vibrant atmosphere evoked by Renoir's *Luncheon of the Boating Party* (c. 1880), which Amélie's housebound neighbour paints on repeat. Indeed, Montmartre has attracted many artists – including Monet, Matisse, Toulouse-Lautrec – and this creative spirit remains.

Amélie adds to the canon, painting its own picture of Montmartre, in a vivid palette. Amélie's apartment and the Maison Collignon grocery are on Rue des Trois Frères – the shop is actually known as Chez Ali, but the movie-prop signs still hang above its enticing fruits and legumes. Amélie works nearby at Café des Deux Moulins, a real delight of an art deco brasserie that opened in the early twentieth century and has retained its vintage style: zinc-topped bar, moulded ceiling and neon tube lights. The tobacconist counter seen in the movie has been removed but you can order an Amélie crème brûlée – one of her favourite things, we learn, is to crack the caramelised crust of this classic dessert with the tip of a spoon. The café is at 15 Rue Lepic, a lively old thoroughfare that winds its way up from sex shop-lined Boulevard de Clichy (close to the infamous Moulin Rouge) to Place Jean-Baptiste-Clément; Van Gogh once lived at no. 54.

North of here is Métro Lamarck-Caulaincourt, its handsome entrance flanked by a double staircase. It's to this spot that Amélie leads a blind man in a sensory whirlwind, describing the street's lollipops and sugarplums, smell of melons and the price of ham. It's a scene good enough to eat, and a reminder to notice the little things while wandering Montmartre's alluring streets.

Inevitably that wander will lead to the Sacré-Coeur, the blinding-white Roman–Byzantine-style basilica that sits atop the butte of Montmartre. Here, Amélie devises an elaborate plan involving Nino (Mathieu Kassovitz), the love interest she's too fearful to actually meet, and Nino climbs the steps that weave up from the old-fashioned carousel at the base to the top terrace. From here, the highest point in the city, Paris spreads out below – in all its real and romantic glory.

London

Where? England

Which? Nocturne: Blue and Gold – Old Battersea Bridge
(1872–75) by J.A.M. Whistler

What? Atmospheric scenes on the River Thames

The fog that defined it for centuries has long gone, but parts of London, especially around the River Thames, remain as atmospheric as ever. London continues to be brimming with people – busy, active, enjoying all it has to offer as one of the world's most important cities for business, finance and culture. At approximately 2,000 years old, London is steeped in history, pageantry and culture, and much of this is still in evidence in many parts of this sprawling metropolis, where you'll find Roman remains, Gothic churches, Tudor halls, Georgian palaces and Victorian bridges. Red brick and slate are adjacent to sheet glass, steel and concrete, while cosy pubs, stately houses, opulent theatres, narrow alleyways, luxurious hotels, broad thoroughfares, peaceful parks and lively squares are all in close proximity to each other.

Over the centuries, this city of eclectic layers has been explored and depicted by hundreds of artists and writers who have appreciated its breadth and diversity, its famous landmarks and its lesser-known gems. It's worth walking off the beaten track to discover some of these gems that crop up almost everywhere. London is the biggest city in Western Europe, and the square mile of the City, its financial hub, has long been joined by the many villages that surrounded it, such as Battersea, Camden, Westminster, Chelsea, Kensington and Marylebone. Although now one huge conurbation, each area has its own personality, characteristics and charm. In 1870, the American artist James Abbott McNeill Whistler (1834–1903), who had been born in Massachusetts, was living in London. He had first stayed there in the late 1840s for a year with his half-sister and her husband. In May 1859, he returned permanently, rejecting the hospitality of his half-sister in Sloane Street, Knightsbridge, and instead taking lodgings in Wapping, where he was one of the first artists to appreciate the working-class

ARTISTIC 161

environment of the East End, seeing beauty in the urban landscape and its inhabitants. There he lived near to the dockers, watermen and lightermen who occupied ramshackle dwellings by the riverside. He frequented the pubs where they ate and drank, sketching and capturing the environment in etchings, making a feature of the wooden wharfs, jetties, sheds, warehouses, docks and yards, often including portraits of the characterful men who lived and worked there; characters that his contemporary Charles Dickens also captured, in words. With the demolition and rebuilding that soon took place, much of the architecture and character of Wapping began changing, and Whistler's prints became admired as records of an already vanishing London. Today, Wapping's former docks have been redeveloped with residential apartments filling the converted warehouses, and popular pubs, bars and restaurants appearing all along the river. The bustling St Katharine and Tobacco Docks are also regenerated, now thriving with homes, businesses, bars, restaurants and shops.

By 1867, Whistler had moved further west to Chelsea, and his linear etchings became replaced by evocations of the misty atmosphere that resulted from increasing pollution and smog. He lived for years in Chelsea, beside the River Thames that became an enduring source of inspiration to him. Years later, when far from London, he reminisced: 'I begin rather to wish myself back in my own lovely London fogs! They are lovely those fogs – and I am their painter!' Based on his memory and pencil sketches made from a boat taken along the River Thames, he painted scenes of Chelsea, Battersea and the river, seeking to convey the sense of tranquillity he saw there. He called these atmospheric paintings 'Nocturnes', and *Nocturne: Blue and Gold – Old Battersea Bridge* of 1872– 75 was the fifth in a series, featuring Battersea Bridge as a shadowy arc high in the composition, with Chelsea Church and the lights of the newly built Albert Bridge in the distance. Another of his nocturnes became the centre of the most famous lawsuit in art history when in November 1878, he sued the writer and critic John Ruskin for libel. Not understanding the concept of Whistler's paintings, Ruskin wrote about his 1875 Nocturne in *Black and Gold: The Falling Rocket*: 'I have seen, and heard, much of Cockney impudence before now; but never expected to hear a coxcomb ask two hundred guineas for flinging a pot of paint in the public's face.'

In court, Whistler was asked about the atmospheric, hazy painting that represented sparkling fireworks cascading over a London park at night. He explained that a nocturne 'is an arrangement of line, form and colour first. As to what it represents, that depends on who looks at it. To some persons it may represent all that I intended; to others it may represent nothing.' When the judge asked him if he asked for 200 guineas for the labour of two days for the work, Whistler replied: 'No; I ask it for the knowledge of a lifetime.' He won the case, but received inadequate damages and was forced into bankruptcy.

Nowadays, houseboats of all shapes and sizes are moored along the Chelsea side of the River Thames. Nearby are some of the most desirable residential areas in London. Rows of Georgian houses face the river and preserve the village atmosphere that made Chelsea so popular during the eighteenth and nineteenth centuries. Chelsea Embankment was built in 1871, and before that, much of Battersea's riverside was undrained marshland. Battersea Park was created and opened in 1858.

Early in 1896, two years after Whistler's wife Beatrix had been diagnosed with cancer, they took a suite at the brand new Savoy Hotel on the north bank of the River Thames. Sitting by Beatrix's bedside, Whistler worked on a series of lithographs, mainly depicting the view of the river from the hotel window. Three years later, on his advice, his friend Claude Monet also stayed at the Savoy, and over the next few years painted more than 70 views of Charing Cross and Waterloo Bridges and the Houses of Parliament in changing light and weather conditions. Since opening in 1889, the Savoy Hotel has hosted numerous artists, including Whistler, Monet, Pablo Picasso, Oskar Kokoschka and Andy Warhol. The stunning views of the River Thames that mesmerised them can still be seen from many of its sumptuous bars, restaurants and bedrooms, but you don't have to stay there to experience the charm of London. That can be found almost anywhere in this richly diverse city, and the beautiful flowing river remains an oasis of calm in an ever-bustling metropolis.

Literary

Naples

Where? Italy
Which? My Brilliant Friend by Elena Ferrante (2011)
Why? Southern Italian city of dirt and danger for two young girls coming of age

The close-packed, dirty-white apartment blocks compress the stinking heat. It's a thick fug of frying *panzerotto*, ripening tomatoes, trash and urine, two-stroke engine oil, fish on the turn, neglect. Residents of the windowless ground-floor flats stand on their doorsteps, peeling vegetables, smoking cigarettes and gossiping in an impenetrable, passive-aggressive, sing-song dialect that rattles along with the passing trains. In spit-'n'-sawdust bars, *disperazione* – the hopeless – drink to escape. But somewhere a bell rings and children run from the schoolyard with their friends and their book bags and, perhaps, their minds on a brighter future . . .

A darkness enveloped 1950s Naples. And it wasn't just the ever-present threat of nearby Mount Vesuvius, which had blown rather dramatically in 1944. It was a street-level wretchedness; the ugly stains of poverty and socioeconomic squalor, plus a simmering violence that – like the volcano – could erupt at any time. The southern city had been poor before the Second World War but afterwards lay in tatters: Naples was bombed around 200 times, more than any other Italian city. The rich could buy their way out. But most Neapolitans had to scrape by in the grime left behind.

It's into this sphere of dirt and danger that Elena Ferrante throws Elena 'Lenù' Greco and Lila Cerullo, heroines of the author's four Neapolitan Novels. The first book, *My Brilliant Friend*, follows these two bright young girls as they come of age in the middle of the century, in a dingy city suburb where life prospects are bleak.

Just as pseudonymous Ferrante does not give her real name (the author's identity remains a mystery), nor does she name the 'neighbourhood' at the heart of her novels. But it's widely believed to be the Rione Luzzatti, a working-class area just east of the Centrale station

164 EUROPE

and bordered by the Napoli Poggioreale prison. Still bossed by the *camorra* (Naples mafia), this *rione* has a reputation for grime and crime, and isn't for wandering into alone. But there's a Neapolitan authenticity to these scuffed alleyways of Fascist-era blocks, barred windows and graffiti smears. Indeed, Luzzatti feels little changed from the 1950s, offering the dedicated Ferrante pilgrim a glimpse back into Lenù and Lila's world.

The wide Via Taddeo da Sessa is most likely the novel's infamous *stradone*, the wall-like main road that demarcates the edge of the girls' existence. It can be followed all the way to the murky 'tunnel with three entrances' on Via Gianturco, down which Lenù and Lila make their first attempt at escape, hoping to walk to the coast: despite living in a port city, just a few miles from the sea, they have never seen it for themselves. Within the heart of Rione Luzzatti you can almost conjure the novel's characters: a baker – like Signor Spagnuolo – creating oozy cream puffs and crisp *sfogliatelle*; a modern Enzo selling fruit, not from a cart these days but from the bonnet of his car; a 'mad widow' type, like Melina Capuccio, shrieking over the street-strung laundry.

In counterpoint to this earthy grit is more affluent Naples, specifically the sea-facing Chiaia neighbourhood: shiny, manicured, populated by women who seem to 'breathe a different air'. On occasion Lenù and Lila dip into this rarified realm, which Ferrante maps with far more precision. It's possible to follow the pair – and the wealthy, elegant people – down pedestrianised Via Chiaia, past Via Filangieri's high-end tailors' shops to Piazza dei Martiri's patriotic monument and into the leafy park of Villa Comunale. Walking here was, says Lenù, 'like a border crossing; a dense crowd and a sort of humiliating difference'.

Ending on Via Caracciolo, ahead lies the sea – 'But what a sea!' – with Vesuvius brewing across the water; potentially a whole new world in the distance. And yet. Behind is all of seething, seedy, splendid, seductive Naples, with its power to pull people back.

Foodie

Valencia

Where? Spain
What? Uncover the authentic dish behind the tourist horrors

Which is Spain's best paella? My mother's! No, my father's! No, my mother's father's mother's! Ask a crowd of Valencians about the country's national dish – invented right here – and that's how the debate will play out. The best, they'll argue, is the one cooked on a Sunday afternoon, whole family round the table, fighting over the bits of crusty, caramelised rice – the *socarrat* – stuck to the bottom of the pan like edible gold. The best is the recipe passed down through the generations; the one that has the spirit of this fertile, sun-soaked spot cooked into its every grain . . .

Valencia, now Spain's third-largest city, was founded by the Romans in 138 BCE. But it was the Moorish invasion in the eighth century that shaped its tastes. When they arrived here, on the eastern Mediterranean coast, the Moors discovered a land of flat, fertile floodplains, rivulets and lagoons. They called it L'Albufera, the 'little sea'. Recognising the potential, they laid irrigation channels – still in use today – and transformed this wild wetland into *la huerta*, a mosaic of vegetable gardens, orchards, date palms and citrus groves. And they created extensive paddies to plant their staple starch, *al-ruzz*. The crop flourished and, though the Moors were eventually expelled in 1238, rice – *arroz* in Spanish, derived from the Arabic – remained.

The origins of paella lie firmly in *la huerta*. The first recipes appeared in the seventeenth century, but it began as the food of the fields. Farm labourers would down tools and gather in the campo for lunch, preparing a communal meal over a fire made from the branches of orange trees. Men – it is a dish still traditionally made by men – would use what was readily available in the surrounding countryside. That included rice, ideally a short-grain and pearly variety, better able to absorb liquid, plus tomatoes, *garrafón* (fat butter beans) and *judía ferradura* (flat green beans), live serrano snails, chunks of rabbit or duck

FOODIE 167

(or chicken on special occasions), maybe herbs such as rosemary and, if possible, a little saffron to add colour and flavour.

This al dente mix was traditionally eaten straight from the *paella* – the name of the wide, flat-bottomed pan in which the dish was cooked. These were the perfect vessels: large enough to hold a meal to feed many, shallow enough so ingredients cooked fast. There was no need for separate serving plates – everyone would simply dig into the feast with their own spoon (eating paella with a fork is not the done thing).

So authentic *paella valenciana* is a dish of the land. Over time, the idea spread to the coast, where *paella de mariscos* swapped in seafood such as shrimp, mussels and squid. And there are plenty more rice specialities that hail from the Valencia region, such as pitch-black *arroz negro*, cooked in squid ink, and *arroz al horno*, oven-baked with pork, blood sausage and chickpeas. But the elevation of paella to national treasure status has spawned many culinary abominations. In tourist traps countrywide, frozen peas, broccoli, chorizo, even Frankfurters might be snuck in; seafood and meat often get mixed together; cheap food colouring replaces expensive saffron, turning the golden dish a gaudy yellow.

Fortunately, Wikipaella exists. This organisation was set up by local people to defend Valencia's revered speciality and promote establishments that still serve authentic versions of this special dish. Following its advice means avoiding most of the joints hugging Valencia's big city beach, and diving into the Comunidad Valenciana hinterland instead. It means seeking out the family-run arrocerías (rice restaurants) in otherwise unremarkable villages or out on lagoon edges of L'Albufera. It means sniffing out the places where they're lighting up the orange wood fires, assiduously browning the rabbit and chicken, nurturing the depth of the *sofrito* (tomato sauce), allowing the rice to soak up every last drop of flavour. The places where they're making paella like your mother's father's grandfather would.

Cinematic

Dumfries & Galloway

Where? Scotland

Which? The Wicker Man (Robin Hardy, 1973)

What? Landscape of ancient myth, Christian foundations and oddly exotic nature

Comely cottages, dancing kids, whirling gulls, a silver-smooth sea – but something's not right in this seemingly bonnie spot. There are grotesque sweets in the Post Office window; a jar of foreskins in the pharmacy; couples fornicating outside the pub; and a blustery headland where the sinking sun isn't the only thing set to burn . . .

The Wicker Man is a startlingly strange tale; a fiction built on a bedrock of folk beliefs stretching back centuries, it is rooted in reality, and all the more horrifying for it. The film follows strait-laced Sergeant Howie (Edward Woodward) who, after receiving an anonymous letter about a girl who's vanished on remote Summerisle, travels from the Scottish mainland to investigate. What he finds is a community that not only conspires against him but one that has relinquished the Christian Church. Being on an island, they are disconnected from the rest of the world, able to operate by their own rules. So here, under the leadership of affably evil Lord Summerisle (Christopher Lee), they worship pagan gods, copulate freely, sing bawdily and conduct archaic rituals, culminating in a creepy May Day procession with a fatally fiery end.

Howie, a devout Anglican, arrives on Summerisle by floatplane – flying, in part, over the Isle of Skye's unmistakable Trotternish peninsula and landing in Plockton, on the shores of Loch Carron. However, while *The Wicker Man* was filmed almost entirely on location in Scotland, it was not made on an island at all. Filming largely took place across Dumfries & Galloway, the country's most southwestern region, and specifically the Machars, an offbeat peninsula of fertile farmland, sandy bays, empty beaches and sharp, craggy cliffs smashed by the Irish Sea.

170   EUROPE

As on fictional Summerisle, where ensuring a bountiful harvest is of life-and-death importance, palm trees and fruit orchards are able to grow in Dumfries & Galloway – not due to sun worship and sacrifices but rather the warming Gulf Stream. Scenes of Lord Summerisle's fecund estate were filmed at Logan Botanic Garden where, thanks to its almost subtropical climate, you can walk around the most exotic collection of blooms in Scotland. The lord's home itself is a composite in the movie. The exterior is Culzean Castle, an eighteenth-century cliff-top pile near Ayr, open to the public. Lochinch Castle provided the insides – it isn't visitable but you can roam the adjacent Castle Kennedy Gardens where the procession passed and stand where a Styrofoam Stonehenge-alike was constructed. (For the real ancient deal, Drumtroddan Standing Stones and the Torhouse Stone Circle aren't far away.)

More filming locations can be found in spots such as Kirkcudbright (the Post Office) and Anwoth (the ruined church). Meanwhile, the final scenes were shot on the windswept Burrow Head, at the tip of the Machars – the ideal spot to burn an enormous effigy (though little evidence of the film's eponymous Wicker Man remains).

It is also near here that, ironically, Christianity was first introduced into Scotland, via St Ninian. It's said that Ninian studied in Rome and brought the faith back to south-west Scotland around 397 CE, establishing a monastery known as Candida Casa (from the Latin 'white house') at what is now Whithorn, just inland from Burrow Head. Whithorn became a centre of pilgrimage, with visitors to Ninian's tomb believing in the saint's power to perform miracles; his shrine can still be seen in the remains of twelfth-century Whithorn Priory.

On the peninsula's west coast is St Ninian's Cave, a deep cleft in the rocks above a pebbled beach. Religious hermits long sought solace here. In the movie it is where, at the end of the procession, after a barrel of ale has been gifted to the god of the sea on the beach below, Howie finally finds the missing girl and, he thinks, saves her life. But all is not as it seems. Just as this place of peace, prayer and natural splendour becomes, at the film's horrific ending, a fire-licked hell on earth.

Giverny

Where? France
Which? The Water Lily Pond: Green Harmony (1899)
by Claude Monet
What? Place of abundant flowers and tranquillity

After years of struggling as an artist, Claude Monet (1840–1926) became successful and wealthy. By 1883, he could afford to rent a house and large garden in Giverny; a village in Normandy, northern France, where the Rivers Epte and Seine meet, about 75 kilometres (45 miles) from Paris. Seven years later, he bought the house and garden, along with an adjacent plot of land. He hired six full-time gardeners to landscape the area with arbours, archways, colourful shrubs, flowers and climbing plants. The adjoining plot was almost completely taken up with a huge pond, created from of a tributary of the River Epte. They filled the pond with waterlilies, surrounded it with weeping willows and built an elegant Japanese-style bridge to arc over it. Monet once said: 'I perhaps owe it to flowers for having become a painter.' By catching transitory moments and changing light effects with short, broken brushstrokes and bright colours, Monet abandoned accepted artistic traditions. He spent the rest of his life painting in this way in his garden in Giverny and sometimes also in the neighbouring area.

Monet – often described as the Father of Impressionism – had first seen Giverny when he passed through it by train, some years before. With its country-feel and proximity to Paris, he determined to live there, and once he did, he rarely left. His passion for gardening, as well as for colours and the effects of light, can be seen in his flowers and pond that are an extension of his paintings of art, and visitors to his house and garden can still see these arrangements of blooms and shrubs – including graceful wisterias and flamboyant azaleas – and drink in the atmosphere. Now the Fondation Claude Monet museum, Monet's house and garden are beautifully preserved as he designed and lived in them. You can visualise him everywhere; in the house, the gardens and even the studios that he built on the plot. Stroll around and spot the familiar aspects of the garden and house that you recognise from countless paintings, then walk through the underpass that connects you to the water garden. Once there, you can look for the reflections that Monet saw, take a selfie on the Japanese Bridge, or even better, get someone else to take one for you. The pond – one of Monet's greatest sources of inspiration that he recorded in countless different light effects – is breathtaking. From the end of the nineteenth century until his death, Monet painted views of this pond over and again, from *The Water Lily Pond: Green Harmony* of 1899, to his vast *Grandes Decorations*, which he undertook between 1914 and 1922. The pond became the principal preoccupation of the last 26 years of his life.

Near Monet's house is the Musée des Impressionnismes Giverny, which showcases more of the Impressionist art movement. Giverny is most easily reached from Paris by a 45-minute train that runs from Saint-Lazare station several times a day. Shuttle buses run into the village from the station every 15 minutes – or you can walk it, it's not far. The hills surrounding Giverny are dusted with wildflowers throughout the spring and summer months, creating the perfect setting for walks and rambles. Pick up a Tourist Board route map or follow the old railroad path and, even if you get lost, you can trace your steps back to Vernon. Historical buildings to explore in Vernon include the Old Mill and the church Collégiale Notre-Dame, both of which Monet painted, as well as the Château des Tourelles, a thirteenth-century castle. Although most famous as Monet's home for 43 years, and where he created his home, garden and monumental waterlily paintings, a settlement has existed in Giverny since Neolithic times, recorded in ancient deeds as 'Warnacum'. In around 1887, drawn by Monet's example, several American Impressionists also settled there – staying at the Hôtel Baudy, which is now a convivial and stylish restaurant – and Giverny became something of an artists' colony until the First World War broke out in 1914. Even today the village is home to many contemporary artists who have established their own small private galleries. Monet himself is buried in the place he loved, in the picturesque cemetery of the Romanesque-style Église Sainte-Radegonde.

Bruges

Where? Belgium
Which? In Bruges (Martin McDonagh, 2008)
What? Beautiful Belgian city where the gorgeous and ghastly become intertwined

It is, by almost any measure, a fairytale: a city of winding lanes, romantic bridges and slender towers. The old gabled houses huddle tight; horse hooves clop; swans glide elegantly along the lazy canals, through reflections little changed for centuries. Disney couldn't concoct a more magical kingdom. Only this is the film set for a darker tale, where one man's heaven is another man's hell . . .

Spellbinding Bruges and pitch-black gangster comedy – they seem unlikely bedfellows. Yet Martin McDonagh's first feature film, *In Bruges*, skilfully uses the charm of one to contrast the wickedness of the other to disorientating, devilishly fun and ultimately redemptive effect.

Veteran hitman Ken (Brendan Gleeson) and newbie Ray (Colin Farrell) are hiding out in the Belgian town after Ray accidentally shoots a boy while carrying out his first professional execution. They've been sent there by boss Harry (Ralph Fiennes) who, despite being a bona fide psychopath, has a sentimental attachment to the city he visited once as a child: 'How can all those canals and bridges and cobbled streets and those churches, all that beautiful f*cking fairytale stuff, how can that not be somebody's f*cking thing?'

For Ken, Bruges IS his thing – he's keen to see the culture, the canals, the art, the views. For Ray, a terrible tourist, it's his purgatory, where he must wait in limbo for his sins to be judged.

Most visitors to Belgium's best-preserved medieval city tend to feel more Ken than Ray. Bruges is a treasure; as visually delicious as its many frites stalls, waffle shops and chocolatiers. The historic centre is listed by UNESCO, on account of its maze of old alleys, fine Brick Gothic architecture and network of canals now plied by tourist boats and swans but once used for commerce. The heyday of the Flemish city was between the twelfth and fifteenth centuries, when it sat at a crossroads

176   EUROPE

of key trading routes; all manner of goods, largely cloth but also wax, furs, gold, silver and spices, changed hands here. After that, Bruges' star waned – it became a literal backwater. But having survived the Industrial Revolution and two world wars virtually unscathed, it's now Belgium's biggest tourist attraction.

The whole city becomes a film set in McDonagh's tale as the two main characters respectively marvel at and mope about its wintry streets. They stay at the smart Relais Bourgondisch Cruyce hotel, a half-timbered retreat right by the canal. They drink beer (as one must here) in 't Zwart Huis bar. They take a chilly boat ride. They visit the Basilica of the Holy Blood, with its phial of, allegedly, Christ's own vital fluid (though this scene was shot in the city's Jerusalem Chapel instead). And they pause at the Rozenhoedkaai, a quay where rosaries were once sold and which now affords one of the finest views in the city: the point where the Groenerei and Dijver canals meet, with the off-kilter Belfort (Belfry) tower rising behind.

There are 366 narrow, spiralling steps to the top of the Belfort itself – a climb that Ken makes but Ray doesn't. Directly below is the expansive Grote Markt square, the heart of the Old Town, lined on three sides by gabled buildings, with cafés spilling out onto the pavement, festive lights strung between the lampposts and horse-drawn carriages trotting through. Postcard stuff – until Ken's body lands, kersplat, on the cold, hard cobbles, having thrown himself from the tower top.

At one point Ken and Ray sit on a bench in Jan van Eyck square, near a statue of the eponymous Renaissance painter (who died in Bruges), discussing their ethics and beliefs. It's a conversation inspired by a visit to the Groeninge Museum, a world-class repository of Flemish and Belgian art, where they see Hieronymus Bosch's *The Last Judgement triptych* (c. 1486), which offers a grotesque vision of damnation, full of freakish torture. Though Ray doesn't agree – for him, hell is an eternity spent in Bruges.

Florence

Where? Italy
Which? David (1501–04) by Michelangelo
What? Iconic Renaissance city, home to countless masterpieces

The cradle of the Renaissance, Florence is a beguiling city, bathed in architectural beauty and artistic charm, and steeped in history. Set on either side of the banks of the River Arno in Tuscany in the north-west of Italy, the small city with its cobbled streets lined with medieval and Renaissance palaces and churches has changed little since the sixteenth century. At different times of day, the light changes from pink and gold to blue and silver, and the stone buildings either glow in response or stand in cool silhouette, while from almost every area, Florence Cathedral (Santa Maria del Fiore) can be seen with its striking green, pink and white marble façade, its imposing brick dome designed by Filippo Brunelleschi and the slender, marble-faced campanile designed by Giotto di Bondone. Throughout the day across the terracotta rooftops, church bells ring out, while the Arno snakes along, attached on both sides by a series of bridges, including the Ponte Vecchio with its Vasari Corridor, a long passageway that connects the Uffizi Gallery on the north side to the Pitti Palace on the south.

A treasure chest of art, Florence surprises and delights at every turn, teeming with charming vistas, quiet courtyards, bustling streets and piazzas, while almost everywhere are magnificent works of art, produced by some of the greatest masters, including Giotto, Lorenzo Ghiberti, Donatello, Filippino Lippi and Botticelli. According to UNESCO statistics, 60 per cent of the world's most important art is in Italy and half of that is in Florence. Probably the most famous of all its works of art is the huge marble sculpture of David made by Michelangelo Buonarroti (1475–1564) between 1501 and 1504. Although his frescos in the Sistine Chapel and his *Pietà* in St Peter's Basilica in Rome are as well-known as his statue of David, Michelangelo is linked above all with his beloved city of Florence – which was also his place of burial.

From the Old Testament, David was a courageous young shepherd who with one shot from his sling killed his people's enemy Goliath. For his bravery, strength and spirit, and for being initially overlooked as insignificant, David became the emblem of Florence, and in 1501, Michelangelo was commissioned to make the statue from a block of marble that another sculptor had previously abandoned. When he completed the 5.17-metre (17-feet) high statue, it was deemed too wonderful for its intended destination – a buttress high up on Florence Cathedral. Instead, the Florentines wanted it to stand in the city's main square, in front of the Palazzo Vecchio. It took four days and forty men to move it the half mile from Michelangelo's workshop behind Santa Maria del Fiore to the Piazza della Signoria. An archway had to be pulled down to accommodate it as it was rolled along, strapped upright in a large wooden cart. Today a replica stands in the Piazza della Signoria, with the original in the nearby Galleria dell'Accademia, and another copy in the Piazzale Michelangelo, a hilltop square in the Oltrarno district on the south bank of the Arno. One of Michelangelo's early biographers, Giorgio Vasari, wrote: 'Without any doubt, this figure has put in the shade every other statue, ancient or modern, Greek or Roman . . . anyone who has seen Michelangelo's David has no need to see anything else by any other sculptor, living or dead.'

Over the course of his 88 years, Michelangelo, a sculptor, painter, architect and poet, changed western art beyond compare. At the age of 13, he became an apprentice in the Florentine workshop of the fresco painter Domenico Ghirlandaio, but within a year, he had moved into the house of the ruler of Florence, Lorenzo de' Medici. Using their wealth to govern and commission art, the powerful Medicis helped to shape Renaissance Florence. With its huge cornice, arched doorways and an internal garden perfumed with the scent of orange trees, the Medici palace in Via Cavour was the earliest Renaissance building erected in Florence, and where Michelangelo first saw the Medici collection of ancient Greek and Roman sculpture and mixed with some of the most learned men of the times. Lorenzo had established a school for young sculptors, and there Michelangelo studied the basics and carved several works. Now called the Palazzo Medici Riccardi, the place where Michelangelo began to sculpt is open to visitors.

Michelangelo became one of the first artists to be renowned as a celebrity, nicknamed 'Il Divino' (The Divine One). To view some of his works, start at the Galleria dell'Accademia, where you will see the statue of David and four unfinished marble 'prisoners' that appear to be trapped in the stone; metaphorically conveying the struggle of the soul to free itself. Also in the Accademia is one of Michelangelo's last works, the Pietà di Palestrina, depicting Christ's crucified body being held by the Virgin Mary, Mary Magdalene and Nicodemus, whose face is probably a self-portrait of Michelangelo himself.

As you make your way towards the Arno, stop at the Basilica di San Lorenzo. During the Renaissance, artists also often worked as architects, and Michelangelo designed the Sagrestia Nuova (New Sacristy) as part of the Medici Chapel attached to the Basilica of San Lorenzo. As well as designing the building, he created seven sculptures inside, including four allegories of time: *Day* and *Night* and *Dawn* and *Dusk*. He also designed the adjoining Laurentian Library, one of the first examples of Mannerist architecture. Closer still to the River Arno is the Gallerie degli Uffizi. There you will find Michelangelo's famous painting known as the *Doni Tondo* (1505–06), a Holy Family in a circular, pyramidal composition and one of only three panel paintings known by him.

Once you have left the Uffizi, cross the river to the Oltrarno district, where, in the Basilica di Santo Spirito, you can discover one of the earliest examples of Michelangelo's astonishing anatomical accuracy; in his teenage years, he created a wooden Crucifix – still there – in thanks for being allowed to study human cadavers in the Santo Spirito hospital. Once run down, the Oltrarno neighbourhood now buzzes with craft shops, restaurants, bars and piazzas, including the Piazzale Michelangelo, which can be reached by a steep but picturesque climb, or by bus or car. Once there, you can admire a copy of the statue of David and a magical panorama of Florence.

Foodie

San Sebastian

Where? Basque Country, Spain
Why? Mix it up in the home of both brilliant bar food and haute cuisine

What'll it be? A night in the old town, in the busy, buzzy thick of things, squeezing up to cramped counters for small plates of skewered shrimp, wild mushroom *croquetas* and *montaditos* (mini sandwiches) stuffed with chorizo and cheese? Or a seat at the table – one of the very best tables – reservation permitting, where dishes are more alchemy than cookery: pigs' blood macarons, rice with plankton, *txangurro* (spider crab) served on a frozen tongue. Or maybe both? In San Sebastián, pick bright-lit bar or Michelin-star – both allow the food to shine . . .

Founded in 1180, San Sebastián – Donastia in Basque – has some physical advantages when it comes to food. Arranged spectacularly around a golden inlet on the Bay of Biscay coast, the fruits of the sea lie ahead; behind is a rural interior that rises to the mountains and overflows with fine produce. As such, menus heave with umami-rich anchovies, mackerel, sardines and *kokotxas de merluza* (hake's jaw), with suckling lamb and extreme-aged *txuleta* beef, with nutty Idiazabal cheese, Tolosa black beans, piquant *guindilla* peppers and *xapata* cherries, all washed down with *sagardoa* (cider) and slightly sparkling *txakoli* wine. But it's perhaps the attitude that really raises the culinary bar. There's serious respect for tradition and provenance here but there's also a passion for trying new things.

Reinvention became essential in the early nineteenth century. In 1813, during the Peninsular War, besieged San Sebastián was razed to the ground. Only one street survived, Calle 31 de Agosto – now the town's liveliest artery. The city had to be rebuilt, and the attentions of Queen Isabel II shaped its new identity. From the 1840s, the monarch spent summers here, making the most of the moderate heat and therapeutic sea-bathing – and making San Sebastián the most fashionable of resort towns. The tight alleys of the *Parte Viejo* (Old Town) were enhanced by Haussmann-style boulevards and Belle Époque grandeur; Gustave Eiffel designed the train station roof and the elegant Gran Casino opened (it's now the City Hall). San Sebastián became known as 'little Paris'.

The city's first food revolution wasn't within the realms of regal cuisine, though, it was down on the streets. Tapas may have originated in southern Spain but the idea was elaborated on here. *Pintxos*, as Basque tapas is known, are meals in miniature, small bites of something delicious, sold alongside drinks. The tradition started in San Sebastián in the 1940s. Bars began serving nibbles held together with toothpicks (or *pintxo*) – handy fodder for soaking up the revelry of a Basque *txikiteo* (pub crawl). It's said the very first *pintxo* dates to 1946, when a customer at Casa Vallés – which is still going strong – impaled olives, anchovies and pickled guindilla peppers onto a stick and christened the tangy concoction the gilda, after the latest Rita Hayworth movie. These days, the Basque spirit of experimentation means a San Sebastián *pintxos* session is quite the creative spread, with constant innovation. Alongside gildas, you'll also find seared foie gras, crab tartlets, squid cooked in its own ink, tuna tacos or tender beef cheeks.

However, it was Juan Mari Arzak who took culinary evolution to new levels here. Arzak grew up above the tavern his grandparents built, becoming the third generation to run what was then a traditional San Sebastián *jatetxea* (restaurant). But in the 1970s, with a group of other Spanish chefs, Arzak set off for France to learn about its then-burgeoning nouvelle cuisine. Returning inspired, he spearheaded *nueva cocina vasca*, the transformation of Basque cooking: innovative, lighter, more sophisticated dishes but always grounded in the region's gastronomic heritage. It was the country's culinary game-changer. And San Sebastián was at the heart of it.

Arzak – now headed by Juan Mari's daughter Elena – holds three Michelin stars. The restaurant is one of a superabundance in the area: San Sebastián has the second most Michelin stars per capita of any city in the world. And this stellar reputation filters down throughout the entire city, ensuring gastronomic excellence everywhere, even on the end of a toothpick.

Artistic

East Bergholt

Where? Suffolk, England
Which? Flatford Mill (Scene on a Navigable River) (1816)
by John Constable
What? English countryside with bucolic view

Towards the end of his life, widowed and depressed, the artist John Constable (1776–1837) travelled by train to his summer home in Dedham Vale on the Essex–Suffolk border. Worn down with worries over finances and the pressures of raising seven children on his own, his heart lifted as he caught sight of the countryside that was so familiar to him. A place where he had grown up, he had painted it countless times and he still loved it; the thickets and hedgerows, the open fields and the broad, bright skies. Impulsively, he turned to his fellow passengers and declared, 'It really is rather beautiful here, isn't it?' Glancing up, an elderly gentleman replied, 'But of course it is! This, Sir, is Constable country.'

While Constable was surprised and delighted at his fame (though admired by the French, he had been largely dismissed by his fellow countrymen and women), few have been surprised since, and the landscape of the Essex–Suffolk border remains linked to him. The area was also the inspiration for one of England's other finest rural and horse painters, Sir Alfred James Munnings, who similarly grew up nearby, the son of a mill owner. In 1919, Munnings bought Castle House in Dedham, and lived and worked there for the rest of his life. Before that, during the eighteenth century, one of the founders of the influential British Landscape School, Sir Thomas Gainsborough, lived in Sudbury, less than 24 kilometres (15 miles) from Dedham.

When you arrive in Dedham, it's like stepping straight into a Constable painting. With its rural landscapes and leisurely pace of life, the place epitomises the spirit and nostalgic traditions of the English countryside. This is where Constable was inspired to paint some of his most famous works, including *The Hay Wain* (1821), *The Cornfield* (1826) and *Flatford Mill (Scene on a Navigable River)* of 1816. Although he also painted elsewhere, Constable's favourite location remained the Essex–Suffolk border, around the River Stour.

Flatford Mill (Scene on a Navigable River) depicts a working rural locale during the early nineteenth century, when the Industrial Revolution was changing the face of the countryside. Constable captured a scene that he thought would not last much longer. He prepared the painting with sketches on site and back in his studio, but little did he know that his huge, leafy trees, chattering river, dramatic, cloud-filled sky and East Bergholt itself in the distance would still be virtually the same over two centuries later. Every year, visitors flock there, to walk, picnic, cycle or paint, and to explore such things as the white cottage where Constable's neighbour, the tenant farmer Willy Lott lived; Flatford Mill itself, which was owned by the Constable family, and Bridge Cottage, which now houses a permanent Constable exhibition. Constable walked these same fields as he grew up in the late eighteenth century. His father's successful business was about a mile from the village at Flatford, and it included a watermill on the River Stour near Dedham for grinding corn and a dry dock for building the barges to transport grain. Constable had no idea that his myriad views of the area would become truly iconic for so many, nor that these same scenes would remain recognisable so long after he painted them. His love for the place is apparent in his work.

Charming and quintessentially English, the landscape that so inspired him is still fondly known as Constable Country. You can wander through rolling farmland, meadows and ancient woodlands, next to babbling brooks or under leafy trees. Take a stroll in the sun to nearby Flatford Lock, as umpteen boat trippers meander by on the River Stour. Pass through narrow cobbled lanes or along grassy paths, then amble over the bridge to the old granary building and Flatford Mill, both red-brick structures with gables and overhanging eaves that exude an air of rustic simplicity, capturing a time when craft skills were at the centre of rural life. Much here may at first seem familiar – instantly recognisable from the many Constable prints seen worldwide on merchandise – but some of the beauty is unexpected and as abundant as when Constable first captured it.

Part Two:

North America

Monterey

Where? California, USA
Which? Cannery Row by John Steinbeck (1945)
What? Ocean-side California street where life at its most colourful ebbs and flows

In the early, pearly morning, The Row begins to wake. Gulls start their vigils on corrugated-iron rooftops, waiting for trash to become lunch; sea lions bark like hunting dogs over the heave of the ocean. People stir, feet flip-flapping along the tidy sidewalk. A new cast of human characters thrives here now: trinket-shop keepers, aquarium cleaners, tourist dealers. The whole street spruced up for a huge new shoal: visitors in their millions. But back in the day it was a different troupe – vagrants, artists, idlers – who frequented this industrious neighbourhood by the sea. Like a human rock pool, Cannery Row was flow and vitality, colour and oddity, a discrete ecosystem of humanity striving to stay afloat . . .

Cannery Row, a waterfront avenue in Monterey, California, is one of the most famous streets in America. John Steinbeck was born in Salinas, a little northeast of Monterey, in 1902, and set many of his works in this area of central California where the Coast Ranges and rich agricultural valleys – the 'salad bowl of the States' – meet the Pacific Ocean.

By 1930, Steinbeck had moved to Pacific Grove, close to Ocean View Avenue, aka Cannery Row. It was a street lined with noisy, stinking sardine canneries that processed the spoils of the nutrient-rich water offshore – for a time, one of the most productive fishing grounds in the world. The stock seemed inexhaustible, and huge purse seiners with nets a quarter-mile long ravaged the ocean. This kept workers working during the Great Depression and fed needy mouths during the Second World War. But by the mid-1950s, the sardine supply ran dry. The industry collapsed; the last cannery closed in 1973.

Published in 1945, but set in an indeterminate period before that, Steinbeck's eponymous novel remembers The Row with fond sentiment. Steinbeck penned it for a group of soldiers who asked him to 'write something funny that isn't about the war'.

The resulting book is like a series of vivid portraits, showing life on The Row in all its odoriferous, eccentric, enterprising glory. The plot, such as it is, follows the exploits of Mack and the boys, a band of resourceful bums who doss in an empty fishmeal shack. Mack decides they should do something nice for Doc, the intellectual proprietor of a biological supplies lab, whom everybody loves – and who Steinbeck based on his close friend, marine biologist and philosopher Ed Ricketts.

Ultimately, the party ends in disaster – but that's not really the point. The novel is less about action than atmosphere. And it oozes affection for this ramshackle street and its people. These folks may be a motley crew of down-and-outs and chancers, but they are mostly heart-of-gold.

Today's Cannery Row – as Ocean View Avenue was officially renamed in 1958 – bears little resemblance to Steinbeck's. For him, the street was 'a poem, a stink, a grating noise, a quality of light, a tone, a habit, a nostalgia, a dream'. The light is still right – the golden California sun still flickers off the water and down the wharf, bathing the honking sea lions and the wooden piers. But it's all a lot tidier now. The stench has gone, and the defunct factories have been given new leases of life as fish restaurants, gift shops, candy stores and antiques boutiques.

In Steinbeck Plaza, halfway along The Row, a statue depicts some of the area's characters, including Steinbeck, Ed Ricketts and local brothel madam Flora Woods, who gave food to the poor during the Depression and provided inspiration for the novel's Dora Flood.

Further along the street sit real-life buildings that Steinbeck weaved in. There's Wing Chong Market, which became Lee Chong's Heavenly Flower Grocery where you could buy everything from silk kimonos to Old Tennis Shoes whiskey. There's also Austino's Patisserie, once the site of a bordello on which Steinbeck based his La Ida Café.

At No. 800 is Ed Ricketts' clapboard Pacific Biological Laboratories – inspiration for 'Doc's Lab'. Like Doc, Ricketts preserved marine specimens here. His lab became a gathering place for artists, musicians and writers. These days the building is mostly closed, though free public tours run once a month.

Even if Doc's isn't open, you can see plenty of marine specimens on the site of the former Hovden Cannery. Since 1984, this has been home to the Monterey Bay Aquarium, a groundbreaking, not-for-profit facility dedicated to marine conservation and education, with a focus on the wildlife of Monterey Bay. The aquarium is home to some 550-plus species, from sea turtles to huge shoals of glittering sardines. Millions of paying visitors come each year. So while times may have changed, it's still fish that bring the dollars to Cannery Row.

LITERARY 189

Cinematic

Jamaica

Where? Caribbean
Which? Dr. No (Terence Young, 1962)
What? Caribbean Eden of exoticism, elegance and intrigue

The lilt of calypso, the zing of crickets, trade winds blowing through the coconut palms, cocktails – shaken not stirred – being sipped by the sea. Sounds like heaven. But all's not as it seems on this island idyll. Danger lurks in paradise. And only one man can save the day . . .

There are few locations to which James Bond has not been. The fictional spy has a penchant for globetrotting, collecting as many passport stamps as bedpost notches. But his first cinematic outing features only one exotic location – the one closest to creator Ian Fleming's heart: Jamaica.

In 1946, Fleming bought a plot in the small north-coast banana port of Oracabessa and built a house he called Goldeneye. Crediting the 'peace and wonderful vacuum of days', he wrote all of his Bond novels here – including the sixth, *Dr. No*, set on Jamaica and infused with the white sand, blue sea view outside his windows.

Dr. No hit cinemas in October 1962, just two months after Jamaica gained independence, having been a British colony – some say the most barbaric British slave colony – since 1655. However, the Brits are still the dominant force in the movie, which sees Bond (Sean Connery) fly to the Caribbean to investigate the disappearance of a fellow MI6 agent and, subsequently, infiltrate the base of nefarious *Dr. No* (Joseph Wiseman), who plans to obstruct NASA launches at Cape Canaveral with a nuclear-powered radio beam.

Ian Fleming first wrote *Dr. No* as a possible TV show to help promote Jamaican tourism. Certainly, as an advert for the island, it works well – if you overlook the murders, car chases and metal-handed super-villain. From the moment Bond touches down at Kingston's Palisadoes Airport – still in operation, though since renamed Norman Manley International after the statesman who negotiated independence – the audience is transported to a warm, vibrant world far away from drab post-war

190　NORTH AMERICA

Blighty. The template for every future Bond is set: cool spy, beautiful women, exotic surrounds and potential for peril.

In the sixties, Jamaica was a hotspot for the rich and famous – the likes of Errol Flynn, Elizabeth Taylor, Richard Burton and Truman Capote were frequent visitors. Befittingly, *Dr. No's* glamorousness is established with a nice local touch: the photographer snapping 007 in airport arrivals was played by Marguerite LeWars, Miss Jamaica 1961.

Bond is driven from the airport in a nippy convertible down the cactus-fringed Norman Manley Highway to 'Government House', actually Kingston's palatial King's House, still the official residence of the island's Governor-General.

Later, he heads to Morgan's Harbour, near Port Royal, at the western tip of the Palisadoes spit, where he seeks out boatman Quarrel (John Kitzmiller) and has a punch-up at a waterfront bar, amid boxes of Red Stripe, the country's lager of choice. Though now run down, Port Royal – founded in 1494 – was once the largest city in the Caribbean, a hub of commerce, privateering and debauchery. Just the spot for 007.

For the movie's most memorable scenes, the crew crossed the island's lush interior to reach the north coast. Laughing Waters, a little west of Fleming's real-life lair, is a secretive spot where a river wriggles through a shallow ravine and into the sea at a golden beach. It was here that white-bikini-clad Honey Ryder (Ursula Andress) emerged from the waves and into cinematic history. Public access is restricted, but it can be hired or seen by boat; locals sneak in too. Bond and Ryder also frolic in nearby Dunn's River, where water tumbles spectacularly over the smooth, travertine rocks into the ocean – much more easily accessible, much more touristy.

The ultimate Bond pilgrimage, though, is to check in at Goldeneye itself, which is now a luxury resort. Stroll past the mango tree planted by 007 alumnus Pierce Brosnan, or even stay in Fleming's original cliff-perched villa, where the walls echo with the swish of the sea and the whisper of spies . . .

CINEMATIC 191

Brooklyn

Where? New York, USA
Which? Do the Right Thing (Spike Lee, 1989)
What? Hot city block in an increasingly cool neighbourhood

It's hot, HOT, HOT on the street. Folks amble along chalk-doodled sidewalks and sit on their stoops, shooting the breeze. Hip-hop blares from an outsized boombox, juiced-up old-timers slug from brown paper bags, aunties sit on the sills of handsome brownstones like elderly Cassandras who see it all. But as the day gets hotter still, the city block broils, a community slow-cooking until it blows . . .

Writer-director Spike Lee grew up in Brooklyn, and the New York borough has been the setting of many of his films. In summer 1988, Lee's crew took over a block in northern Brooklyn's predominantly Black Bedford-Stuyvesant neighbourhood to make his third feature film, *Do the Right Thing*. The film, shot in bright, popping colours, is set on the hottest day of the summer, fierce enough to make skin sweat, hair frizz and tempers flare. Lee had heard a stat: that, above 35°C (95°F), the murder rate goes up. So what happens on his super-heated street?

The day starts smoothly enough, following the comings and goings of the neighbourhood. American–Italian Sal (Danny Aiello) opens his family-run pizzeria, where Mookie (Spike Lee) works; we meet the block's larger-than-life Black characters, including wise old matriarch Mother Sister (Ruby Lee), drunken Da Mayor (Ossie Davis) and boombox-toting Radio Raheem (Bill Nunn). But gradually the simmering racial tensions erupt and, by nightfall, there's a skirmish, a white cop kills Radio Raheem, a riot ensues, the pizzeria is set ablaze. Lee was inspired by the multiple Black victims of white violence in 1980s New York; more than 30 years later, these issues remain largely unresolved.

Filming on the ground, rather than a Hollywood lot, enhances the movie's realism; *Do the Right Thing* was to be about the racial and political climate of the times, which Lee felt was only possible to capture in situ. And nowhere was more 'real' at that time than

Bed-Stuy. Originally Native American Lenape territory, then a Dutch farming town, in the early 1800s the area was home to one of the first free Black communities in the country. Later, as transport links to Manhattan improved, leafy streets of grand masonry row houses were built, attracting the upper middle classes – to this day Bed-Stuy has the country's greatest number of intact Victorian buildings, around 8,800 built before 1900. But, following the Great Depression, African-Americans started pouring in. By the 1980s, when hip-hop culture was rising and racial tensions were high, it was the second-biggest Black neighbourhood in NYC. There was a strong sense of community with the motto 'Bed-Stuy Do or Die' – but the area was rife with drugs and violence. Before filming started, security teams were enlisted to shut down crack houses and keep the set safe.

The movie was made on the stretch of Stuyvesant Avenue between Lexington and Quincy, which in 2015 was granted a second name: 'Do the Right Thing Way'. At the southern end is no. 173, a classic two-storey-and-basement brownstone where Mookie lives; a few doors down, at no. 167, is the window where Mother Sister sits, observing it all. Sal's Famous Pizzeria and, opposite, the film's Korean grocery store were built from scratch (and subsequently removed) on facing empty lots at the avenue's north end. A Do the Right Thing mural now brightens one of the walls.

In the decades since Lee's movie, Bed-Stuy has changed again. As young professionals priced out of 'better' NYC postcodes seek to snap up its heritage terraces, the area is gentrifying – it frequently features on 'coolest neighbourhood' lists, with a goodly number of vegan cafés and vintage stores. This is altering the ethnic mix: in 2000, three-quarters of residents identified as Black or African-American, yet in 2015 only half did. But Bed-Stuy's grit, fight, historic identity, political activism and community spirit haven't gone yet. And on a hot, hot day, you'll still find neighbours sitting out on their front steps, chewing the fat, as they have for years.

CINEMATIC   195

New Mexico

Where? USA

Which? *My Front Yard, Summer* (1941) by Georgia O'Keeffe

What? Faraway otherworldliness in the New Mexican desert

As the amber sun turns to vivid orange and lowers behind the mountains, the rocks turn an even more spectacular red and the distant mesas glow purple. With its sharp light, expansive skies and ethereal rock formations, the tiny village of Abiquiú was the starting point of the pioneering trade route of the Old Spanish Trail that connected the northern settlements of New Mexico with California. In the Tewa language, Abiquiú means 'wild chokecherry place', and in 1742, 24 Tewa Pueblo families were the first settlers there, led by a Roman Catholic priest as part of the strategy by the Spanish to defend New Mexico's borders against Native American tribes.

Almost 200 years later, New Mexico captivated the artist Georgia O'Keeffe (1887–1986) when she first stayed at Taos in 1929. Instantly enchanted by the rugged, open scenery and the spiritual atmosphere, she began painting the undulating, multi-coloured landscape in her smooth, semi-abstract style. Over the following years, she travelled back and forth to New Mexico several times from her home in New York and gradually stayed for longer periods on a 21,000-acre dude – or guest – ranch, among the colourful bluffs of Abiquiú, called Ghost Ranch. 'As soon as I saw it, I knew I must have it,' she later wrote about the place.

O'Keeffe also described her feelings about the entire location: 'When I got to New Mexico, that was mine. As soon as I saw it, that was my country. I'd never seen anything like it before, but it fitted to me exactly. It's something that's in the air, it's just different.' Eventually, she moved into the house at Ghost Ranch and lived there for the last 40 years of her life, first of all for part of the year and then from 1949, permanently. Blending in with the surroundings, the walls of Ghost Ranch house are punctuated by wide picture windows that open on to majestic vistas. A hand-carved wooden ladder leads to the roof where O'Keeffe often slept under the stars. She lived modestly, collecting rocks, bones and gnarled branches from the desert, and she painted them and the landscape constantly, emphasising the curving forms and bright sunlight. In 1942, she wrote to her friend, fellow artist Arthur Dove: 'I wish you could see what I see out the window; the earth pink and yellow cliffs to the north, the full pale moon about to go down in an early morning lavender sky … pink and purple hills in front and the scrubby fine dull cedars and a feeling of much space – it is a very beautiful world.'

A year before writing that letter, O'Keeffe painted *My Front Yard, Summer* (1941), capturing the panoramic view from her front window. The predominant motif is what she called her 'private mountain', and she captured its shifting colours, sensuous contours and harmonious shape, conveying her deep connection with nature. It is an abbreviated, semi-abstract image, in which she distils what she saw in front of her to its essence, conveying the image and her own emotional reaction to it. By minimising details, she reduces the view to areas of light, shadow and pattern. One aspect she particularly admired about New Mexico was that she could see clearly and expansively over vast distances.

Eleven years after her death, in 1997, the Georgia O'Keeffe Museum opened in Santa Fe. With over 3,000 works, including 140 of her oil paintings, nearly 700 drawings and hundreds of other works, the museum offers insights into her creative processes, as well as the light and land that inspired her. The O'Keeffe Museum also maintains her home and studio in the village of Abiquiú, 95 kilometres (60 miles) north-west of Santa Fe, along the Chama River. Ghost Ranch, O'Keeffe's first home in New Mexico, is now run by the Presbyterian Church and is around 48 kilometres (30 miles) north-west of Abiquiú. You can book a tour through the O'Keeffe Museum. Limited to 12 people, it lasts an hour and takes you on a scenic ride on a shuttle bus to many of O'Keeffe's most inspirational sites, including the dramatic 21,000-acre landscape around Ghost Ranch. According to the Pueblo people, the unique landscape here is suffused with spirits of the past, including, presumably, one of the world's greatest artists who so loved the ancient, sacred place, and made it her home for nearly half a century.

Montréal

Foodie

Where? Québec, Canada
Why? Sample the city through its beloved Jewish dishes

Mouth-watering Montréal, *c'est délicieux!* This is where France and North America mix most appetisingly, accompanied by an array of ethnic sides, from Chinese to Caribbean. Cultured and creative, it's a diverse metropolis that's *un petit peu de Paris*, a touch neighbourhood-style New York but, ultimately, its own invention . . .

Founded by the French in 1642 on an island in the St Lawrence River, Montréal is Canada's second most populous city. And you can eat well and eat widely here. It has among the highest number of restaurants per capita of anywhere in North America; you can gorge on French *patisserie*, Greek gyros, Haitian *griot*, Italian spaghetti, Afghan *kabob* and, of course, *poutine*, the distinctly Québécois moreish mess of fries, gravy and cheese curds. But many of the city's most defining dishes are found in the delis, smokehouses and bakeries of its Jewish community.

Jews began arriving here from the 1760s, settling in what's now Vieux-Montréal, the oldest part of the city. Canada's first synagogue, the Spanish and Portuguese, was established here in 1768 and is still going today. Facing discrimination elsewhere, these incomers were seeking a more accepting society – and largely found it. In 1832, an act was passed that made Québec the first place in the British Empire to grant equal rights to Jews. Waves of immigration from the end of the nineteenth century, and again after the Second World War, saw the community boom. Today there are around 90,000 Jews in Montréal.

The historic Jewish Quarter was along Boulevard St-Laurent ('the Main') between McGill University and Mile End. With the city's Anglophone contingent settling to the west and the Francophone to the east, Jews – and other minorities – gathered along this boulevard between them. In the early twentieth century, many Jews worked in the area's garment factories. And they needed to be fed.

Using techniques remembered from their homelands, Eastern European Jewish immigrants began selling kosher smoked meat.

Hunks of beef brisket – a cheap cut, from the cow's chest – were cured for almost two weeks in peppercorns, herbs and spices, then smoked overnight and steamed for several hours. Thick-sliced by hand, layers of the hot, tender, falling-apart, finger-licking flesh were then heaped onto light rye, with a good slathering of mustard.

There are several classic places to try this staple – Lester's, Dunn's, Snowdon Deli – but Schwartz's, on Boulevard St-Laurent, is a Montréal institution. It's been house-smoking on site and serving hungry patrons since Reuben Schwartz first opened the place in 1928; it even continued after Reuben's gambling and philandering ways forced him to sell. Neither the unpretentious interior nor the secret blend of spices has changed in decades. Expect red-leather-topped stools at the counter, paper placemats on the tables, smoke-scented air, the tang of pickles, a queue wiggling out of the door.

If Montréalers care about their meat, they are tribal about their bagels. The classic roll-with-a-hole, also brought to North America by Jews from Eastern Europe, is given a unique spin here. The dough is poached in honey water and baked in a wood-fired oven, resulting in denser, sweeter bagels, with a caramelised, crisp exterior and light, chewy insides. Two Mile End bakeries, only a few blocks apart, both open daily, 24/7, have perfected the Montréal method over the years: St-Viateur and Fairmount Bagel. Although direct rivals, they can both trace their genesis to the first Montréal Bagel Bakery, opened in 1919. In Montréal, you pledge allegiance to one or the other.

Whichever you choose, it's hypnotic watching the bakers at work, hand-rolling the rings at lightning speed, dunking them in sweetened water, delivering them into the fiery oven on long, well-used paddles, then seeing them taken out again and tossed into steaming piles of doughy deliciousness. They're best eaten plain and hot from the bag, smothered in sesame or poppy seeds. Each one a taste of *heimishe* – the distinctly Jewish notion of comfort and homeliness – in every bite.

Mississippi River

Literary

Where? Missouri, USA

Which? Adventures of Huckleberry Finn by Mark Twain (1884)

What? Mighty waterway through the heart of America, brimming with adventure and social significance

Sometimes this river seems wide as an ocean. A great blue-grey expanse, slipping ever southwards from glacial lakes and tallgrass prairie to the sultry subtropics. It makes a massive, meandering journey, but is a place for simple pleasures; where you can float away from your troubles. It's a place for lazing back, trailing a toe in the flow, and listening to the somnolent trickle. For eating mushmelon and corn dodgers, talking aimless flapdoodle. For gliding to the hum of mosquitoes. For gazing at a sky a-flicker with stars. The ancient river: an invitation to drift, an opportunity to escape . . .

Ol' Man River, Big Muddy, Father of Waters. The Mississippi, a leviathan of many names, flows through the heart of America. It once served as the country's western border, and has long been key for trade and transportation. During the American Civil War (1861–1865), the river's capture by Union forces signalled a turn towards victory. In short, the Mississippi looms large in America's history, culture and consciousness. And it's central to Mark Twain's *Adventures of Huckleberry Finn*.

Samuel Langhorne Clemens – pen name Mark Twain – was born in Florida, Missouri, in 1835 but moved to nearby Hannibal, on the Mississippi's west bank, in 1839. He was raised in antebellum America, a time of growth and expansion, thriving plantations and goods-laden steamboats; as a young man, Twain even worked as a riverboat pilot, gaining intimacy with the Mississippi's many twists, turns and eddies.

This was also a time of slavery. Unlike Illinois, across the river, Missouri was not a free state; by the mid-nineteenth century, a quarter of Hannibal County's population were slaves. While *Adventures of Huckleberry Finn* was published two decades after the 1865 Thirteenth

LITERARY 203

Amendment abolished slavery, the novel is set in the 1840s. And Twain's novel – at first glance, a simple boys' own adventure – is a blistering examination of American attitudes to race at the time.

The novel follows the exploits of teenage vagabond Huck Finn and Jim, a Black adult slave. Both live in the Missouri town of St Petersburg and both want to escape incarceration. Huck is running from his abusive, alcoholic Pap and the constraints of 'sivilized' society – the hand-washin', meal times and starchy britches that have been inflicted on him. Jim is fleeing slavery. So the pair strike out together, intending to raft to the free state of Illinois. Their drifting comes at a cost – they lose their raft, witness a massacre, encounter burglars and murderers. But despite all this, the wandering river provides the ultimate prize: freedom. Unlike life ashore, it's not 'cramped up and smothery'. Once they're sliding down the Mississippi, it's as if they exist beyond society's normal rules. On the water, a white boy and a Black man can float together, talking as equals.

Academics argue over Twain's stance on race. Some see the novel as a scathing attack on prejudice; others feel it stereotypes Black people. But it remains one of the most important works of American literature, as well as a rich evocation of the mid-nineteenth-century Midwest.

To get a taste of Twain's Americana, head to his one-time hometown of Hannibal, on which fictional St Petersburg is heavily based. The heart of the riverside town remains largely intact, its gridded historic centre lined with old-fashioned drugstores and taverns, as well as the old Clemens' house, now the Mark Twain Boyhood Home & Museum. You can also soak up the scenery that inspired Huck's adventures – the sandbanks, the old mansions, the lazy river views – and board a replica paddle steamer for a journey on the Mississippi.

A few miles south of Hannibal is Jackson's Island, where Huck and Jim meet up and forge one of the most monumental friendships in American literature – a mixed-race mate-ship in an era when this was rare indeed. The narrow, wooded island is still uninhabited, aside from the muskrats, turtles and beavers. And it's still an ideal spot to play, hide, lark, tumble and watch the timeless river glide by.

Artistic

New York

Where? USA
Which? Per Capita (1981) by Jean-Michel Basquiat
What? Multicultural, diverse city of opportunity

Teeming with cabs, buses, shoppers, workers and visitors, New York famously never sleeps. Art Deco skyscrapers, glass-fronted hotels, concrete and steel offices, loft apartments, vast stores, museums, restaurants, bars, booksellers, delis and diners all crowd into the networks of streets and avenues. The most densely populated city in the United States, New York is divided into five boroughs: Brooklyn, Queens, Manhattan, The Bronx and Staten Island. These were consolidated into a single city in 1898, and today, as many as 800 languages are spoken there, making it the most linguistically diverse city in the world. With its ideals of liberty and peace, New York continues to attract people from disparate backgrounds and cultures. And that just about sums up Jean-Michel Basquiat (1960–88): culturally diverse and daring.

Drawing inspiration from his mixed Haitian and Puerto Rican heritage, Basquiat played a crucial role in bringing graffiti into the established art world. His artistic interests were encouraged by his parents, especially his mother who regularly took him to some of New York's greatest art museums, including The Met, MoMA, the Guggenheim and Brooklyn Museum – where he became a member at six years of age. With no formal art training, in the 1970s, he and his friend Al Diaz began creating graffiti in and around Lower Manhattan, adding the tag SAMO© – an abbreviation of Same Old Shit. Their spray-painted graffiti included politically-oriented poems, rhymes and phrases, and it was soon noticed by contemporary artists and journalists. Spray-painting on walls and in subways, the art soon became part of the fabric of the city. Art critic Jeffrey Deitch remembered that, 'Back in the late seventies, you couldn't go anywhere interesting in Lower Manhattan without noticing that someone named SAMO had been there first.' Nowadays, however, no confirmed SAMO© works survive.

After Basquiat and Diaz fell out in 1979, Basquiat wrote 'SAMO© IS DEAD' on buildings around Lower Manhattan. Then in 1980, he exhibited paintings in The Times Square show, held in an abandoned building on the corner of 41st Street and 7th Avenue. Along with Basquiat, exhibitors included established artists such as Keith Haring, Nan Goldin and Jenny Holzer, and it was hailed as 'the first radical art show of the 1980s' by *The Village Voice*. From that time, Basquiat was 'discovered' as a fine artist, and in less than 10 years, he produced over 1,000 paintings and more than 2,000 drawings. Borrowing imagery from African, Caribbean, Aztec and Hispanic cultures, his childlike style conveyed complex ideas and he worked with all kinds of media, including pastels, pencils, charcoal, watercolours, oil sticks, spray paint and the end of his paintbrush, as well as with more traditional brushstrokes.

Basquiat first met Pop artist Andy Warhol in a chance encounter when selling postcards of his work. Two years later, Warhol and Basquiat met properly at Warhol's studio, the Factory. The two became great friends; Warhol mentored Basquiat and Basquiat helped to revitalise Warhol's career. Suddenly famous at 20 years old, Basquiat was soon frequenting the unique nightclub Studio 54, socialising with Warhol's outrageous friends. From 1983, Basquiat lived and worked in NoHo at 57 Great Jones Street, an East Village loft owned by Warhol. He had become one of the world's most sought-after artists; but his drug addiction was severe. In 1988, at just 27, Basquiat died of an overdose.

Despite his short life, Basquiat made a massive impact on hip-hop, post-punk and street art with work that appropriated poetry, drawing and painting to draw attention to the gulf between poverty and wealth, segregation and integration, and his artistic legacy is huge. Basquiat was buried at Green-Wood Cemetery in Brooklyn, close to where he was born; his life and legacy forever linked with the city that influenced and inspired him.

Cuba

Where? Caribbean

Why? Distinctive island sounds that have sailed and shimmied far across the seas

Cuba dances to its own rhythm, sways to its own beat. The island is blessed by the same superb sunshine, beaches and sea breezes as the rest of the Caribbean region but is unlike any other part of it. In Cuba, palm trees rub along with vintage cars, fat cigars, revolutionary zeal and an absorbing soundscape, composed from centuries of cultural blending and creativity. It's soulful, spirited and irresistible, tinged with nostalgia, full of passion; music to make your feet shift, hips shake, limbs twist and swing. The island has a whole playbook of syncopated, sensuous beats. They are the stories of what makes it tick . . .

Cuba is a country of around 11 million people, and it feels as if each one of them knows how to dance. Music permeates every aspect of life on the island, from religious ceremonies and political rallies to social gatherings and street corners. On warm evenings (which is most evenings), sultry melodies seem to drift from every open window.

It was ever thus. The indigenous Arawak, Taíno and Ciboney cultures of pre-Columbian Cuba had a rich musical tradition, utilising percussive instruments such as maracas and drums. Spanish colonisation, from the late fifteenth century, introduced European influences such as classical guitar and harp that blended with African rhythms brought by enslaved peoples. By the nineteenth and early twentieth centuries, African elements had coalesced with Spanish melodies and harmonies. The influential *habanera* emerged and *charanga* ensembles filled the air with elegant *danzones*. Slow-tempo bolero emanated from Santiago de Cuba, improvised rumba from Havana dockers. Soon son arrived, with its infectious rhythms and anticipated bass, laying the groundwork for modern salsa. Cuban music began to fuse with jazz, particularly in Havana. Lively mambo joined playful cha-cha-chá.

Curiously, the Cuban Revolution (1953–1959) was a time of incredibly vibrant creativity – in the late 1950s, during the fiercest years of the

MUSICAL   209

conflict, the island's musical development reached its peak. It seemed the repression and fear encouraged joyful expression, music and dance, offering a sanctuary from social concerns. In the aftermath, Fidel Castro's government promoted some forms of Cuban music as symbols of national identity, while also limiting exposure to western influences.

Despite this government control, local musicians continued to experiment, incorporating elements of rock, funk and jazz into traditional Cuban styles, leading to the birth of *nueva trova* and Afro-Cuban jazz. The 1990s saw a resurgence of interest in Cuban music on the international stage, with artists like the legendary ensemble Buena Vista Social Club gaining widespread acclaim, showcasing traditional son and bolero styles to global audiences.

However, Cuban music today isn't all sepia-tinged Buena Vista nostalgia; the island continues to influence and innovate. There is nowhere else in Latin America that's had a greater effect on the world's sound stage. While there is music across the island, the capital, Havana, and the south-eastern city of Santiago de Cuba are official UNESCO Cities of Music. Habana Vieja (Old Havana) is the place to begin. Founded by the Spanish in 1519, it's showing its age, but in the most artfully crumbling of fashions. The old city is a tumbledown of cobbled plazas and decaying, pastel-painted mansions. Down its old alleys, neighbours holler between wrought-iron balconies, señoras sit on stoops in bright headscarves, torcedores roll tobacco, people dance on a whim. The whole city thrums, with music pumping out from an array of one-room hang-outs, retro bars, jumping clubs and halls. Havana is also a great place to take a salsa lesson – the Cuban style involves simple footwork, liberal hip action and lots of shoulder shimmying. A shot of Havana Club rum beforehand should loosen limbs and inhibitions.

Then move on to the spirited city of Santiago de Cuba, which rests up against the wild Sierra Maestra mountains, the hinterland where Castro hid during the revolution. Indeed, the city has something of a rebellious air, as well as music pumping through its veins. Not only is Santiago the original home of Bacardi, it's also the birthplace of virtually every type of Cuban musical genre, from lively *son* to African-influenced *folklórico*. Music is all-pervasive here. The Casa de la Trova, just off the main square, provides an excellent introduction. This hallowed hall is the epicentre of Cuban musical heritage and has hosted all the greatest musicians; these days both locals and travellers flock in to watch expert performers play. But there's no need to actually go inside . . . anywhere. In Santiago, music has the habit of spilling out onto the pavements, setting up on street corners, blowing through the palm trees. This is a place with music running through its tropical veins.

210   NORTH AMERICA

Cinematic

Philadelphia

Where? USA
Which? Rocky (John G. Avildsen, 1976)
What? Underdog city of grit, heart, art and fighting spirit

The steps – all 72 of them, a wide sweep of golden limestone – seem to rise forever; the top never getting any nearer. They're certainly a stern challenge: up, up, up they go, a 1920s Beaux-Arts Stair Master, testing strength, leading to glory. But when you do reach the top, thrust both arms in the air and gaze at the city skyline spreading beyond, you feel you might be ready to go a few more rounds with the world . . .

Rocky is the American Dream writ large. Its script penned in just three-and-half days by its star, Sylvester Stallone, it's the rags-to-riches tale of Rocky Balboa, an unschooled but good-natured working-class Italian–American from Philadelphia's meaner streets. Rocky scratches a living by collecting debts for a loan shark and by fighting minor-league bouts in two-bit clubs. Then, one day, he gets a chance to enter the ring with reigning world heavyweight champion Apollo Creed (Carl Weathers) for a shot at the title.

It's a no-frills, blood-and-sweat fairytale, and a very Philadelphia story. The 'City of Brotherly Love' – one-time US capital, where the Founding Fathers signed the Declaration of Independence in 1776 – relishes its reputation as something of an ornery underdog; a tough us-against-the-rest place that gets back up no matter how many times it's knocked down. Stallone has been quoted as saying that Rocky could only be of this city.

Much of the filming was done – on a limited budget – in Philly itself, and much of it in Kensington, a once thriving, now scruffy blue-collar neighbourhood. Rocky's red-brick apartment is here, at 1818 Tusculum Street, with the same steps to its door, the El train still clattering away above. It's not far from the three-storey building that appeared as Mighty Mick's Gym (only the façade was used), the exterior of the dingy Lucky Seven Tavern (now destroyed) and the site of the pet shop where his beloved Adrian (Talia Shire) worked, which is also no more.

However, one of the best ways to see more of this historic, spirited city is to follow Rocky's training runs. To ape his journey, plodding through pre-dawn streets, via junk piles, train tracks and belching factory chimneys. Past the enormous marble-and-limestone pile that is Philadelphia City Hall, the country's largest municipal building, completed in 1894. And along the banks of the Schuylkill River, where the stone arches of the Pennsylvania Railroad, Connecting Railway Bridge are visible behind.

Rocky also jogs through the middle of the Italian Market. Stretching ten blocks of Ninth Street, it's one of the oldest and biggest open-air markets in the country, the commercial hub of the city's Italian community and the place to pick up a pizza slice. Ninth Street is also, incidentally, home of Pat's King of Steaks, founded in 1930 by the co-creators of the classic Philly cheesesteak (thin-sliced beef and melted cheese in a long hoagie roll) and a local institution; make like Rocky and stop here for a quick bite.

His most famous run is up the East Entrance steps (re-christened the 'Rocky Steps') of the Philadelphia Museum of Art. Completed in 1928, and fresh from a striking renovation by Frank Gehry in 2021, the museum contains extensive collections of world-class Renaissance, American and Impressionist art. However, many visitors come simply to recreate Rocky's triumphal sprint, to stand on the bronze sneaker footprints bearing his name and to punch their arms aloft, looking back along the Benjamin Franklin Parkway to the downtown skyline – the ultimate Philly must-do. You'll also want to pay homage to the man himself: a statue of the boxer, used as a prop in sequel *Rocky III*, sits at the bottom of the stairs, fake art meeting real art. Philly's fictional underdog – the fighter who never quits – immortalised like a true legend.

Foodie

New Orleans

Where? Louisiana, USA
Why? Devour the mixed-up, multicultural stewpots of the Deep South

Stiflingly hot but always cool. Glamorous and grimy. Battered but never defeated. A bit devilish, a bit divine. No, the multifaceted 'Big Easy' is not easily summed up. In 1877, the writer Lafcadio Hearn, who spent a decade living in New Orleans, said that it 'resembles no other city upon the face of the earth, yet it recalls vague memories of a hundred cities'. A century and a half later, this remains true. New Orleans is a cauldron peppered with pinches of this-and-that: French and Spanish, Creole and Cajun, African American, Native American, Italian, Latino, Vietnamese; carnivals, Catholicism and cocktails, voodoo, zydeco and jazz. It's the metropolitan embodiment of its own signature dish: a rich, deep, spicy gumbo of a city . . .

New Orleans wallows between Lake Pontchartrain's southern shore and the curling Mississippi River; beyond, the river soon fizzles into the Gulf of Mexico in a sodden morass of bayous, marsh and swamp. The city itself barely peeps above sea level – in fact, much of it sits below – and is vulnerable to the water all around. In hindsight, it's not a fit place for almost 400,000 people to live. But live they do, with some panache, despite setbacks and disasters. From the pavement buskers to the tarot card readers, the brass band players to the Mardi Gras divas, this is a city of colour and soul.

Here first were a diverse array of indigenous tribes, who came to trade along the Mississippi and gave rise to the area's pre-colonial name: Bulbancha, Choctaw for 'place of many tongues'. That sense of diversity hasn't changed.

La Nouvelle-Orléans was officially founded by the French in 1718, who brought both their culinary know-how and their West African slaves. The city, which grew rapidly, becoming the gateway to the Atlantic, was handed to the Spanish in the 1760s and then became briefly French again in 1801 before Napoleon sold it to the United States as part of the

FOODIE 215

1803 Louisiana Purchase. This mixed-up genesis, plus two subsequent centuries of immigration, have created a unique city and arguably the country's most distinctive regional menu, full of the Cajun recipes of the Acadian French, Euro New World Creole dishes and plenty more besides.

King of NOLA cuisine is gumbo, the ultimate Creole comfort food. With no one obvious precursor – it's an evolution of dishes such as Provençal *bouillabaisse*, Senegalese *soupou kandia* and Choctaw soups – gumbo is essentially a well-seasoned stew, made gloopy by some form of thickener. The West African way, and probably the most traditional, is to thicken it with okra; the dish's name may come from *ngombo*, a Bantu word for okra. The Native American method employs filé, the dried, powdered leaves of the sassafras plant, which the Choctaw called *kombo*. The French technique, imported from the kitchens of the Gallic motherland, is to use a roux, made by browning flour in fat.

These thickeners are stirred in with celery, onion and bell peppers, plus any combination of chicken, duck, rabbit, turkey, alligator, crab meat, crab claws, crawfish, shrimp and oysters. A good way to use up leftovers. Another common ingredient is andouille, a fat, smoked, coarse-ground sausage introduced by early French settlers. The addition of tomatoes is a source of great debate. Gumbo z'herbes, a vegetarian version packed with an array of leafy vegetables such as collard greens, mustard greens, turnip tops and spinach, was traditionally cooked during Lent, when Catholics abstained from eating meat. For all of these, rice is the usual accompaniment.

But despite all the choices and variations, regardless of the fact that no two are ever the same, gumbo is the taste of Louisiana. It's a dish that belongs to all races, cultures and classes, that's scooped out of big, steaming pans everywhere from the restaurants of New Orleans to the stilt-shacks of the backwaters.

The close cousin of gumbo is the equally cross-bred jambalaya. This hodgepodge is a medley of many of the same ingredients – the bell pepper, onion and celery, the eclectic mix of seafood and meats – but is a drier, rice-based dish. It's born from the colonial Spanish settlers' pining for their native paella and the city's people of colour recreating their traditional jollof rice, with goodly helpings of Caribbean spice. Like gumbo, there's no one true recipe. But there is a cultural divide. The Creole version, the type found mostly in New Orleans, is 'red jambalaya', which includes tomatoes. Cajun 'brown jambalaya', more common outside the city, is tomato-free.

These two dishes are, of course, just the beginning. Take your appetite on a walk below the old French Quarter's filigree balconies, out to the historic African American faubourg of Tremé or on a ride aboard a rattling streetcar to seek out more NOLA flavours. That might be a platter of chargrilled oysters – a real New Orleans thing. Or a bag of sugar-dusted beignets, the city's airy doughnuts, introduced by the French. Perhaps pick up a po' boy, crusty baguettes filled with anything from roast beef to fried shrimp, created in 1929 to, so they say, feed poor striking streetcar workers. Or take on a muffuletta, another fat NOLA sandwich, this time layered with cold cuts, cheese and olives, dreamed up in the early twentieth century so Italian immigrants could get all their deli favourites to go. After all this, you'll be full to bursting. But you won't regret a single bite, because you can't eat quite like this anywhere else.

Literary

New York

Where? USA
Which? *The Catcher in the Rye* by J.D. Salinger (1951)
What? Big, brash backdrop for the classic American tale of disaffected youth

This city – the most iconic of cities – is a mass of humanity. A seething megapolis of taxi cabs, dive bars, movie stars, uptowners, out-of-towners, priests, pimps, players and phonies. Everyone squeezed in; everything possible. But it can also be the loneliest place in the world, an anonymising anthill of concrete and steel. New York: where you can choose to ride the carousel or step off the kerb into oblivion. Just the place, then, for a troubled teen on the cusp of adulthood to get drunk, laid, lost or saved . . .

Holden Caulfield, angsty anti-hero of J.D. Salinger's *The Catcher in the Rye*, spoke to a generation. The book contains little action: posh kid gets expelled and spends a few days bumming around New York. But this 16-year-old wise-ass became the poster boy for disaffected youth, beloved for his delicious rebelliousness, his rage against the machine.

And what better setting for this coming-of-age tale than mid-century Manhattan? In 1950, New York was also finding its place, emerging as the biggest and most important city on the planet. It had Wall Street and Broadway, the tallest skyscrapers and the new United Nations. Yet post-war confusion was palpable; hope tinged with fear. *The Catcher in the Rye* is a kind of unorthodox guidebook to the city at a certain moment.

Holden isn't just in New York, he is of it. He was raised on the Upper East Side and, when he's kicked out of his fancy Pennsylvania boarding school, he runs not for the hills but for home. Despite his tender years, he moves effortlessly through the urban clutter of seedy hotels and heaving avenues; he knows where to score a drink. New York overwhelms and repulses him too but, love or hate it, the city is intrinsic to who he is.

It's late one night, just before Christmas, when Holden arrives by train. Today's Penn Station is a rather perfunctory terminus, not a patch

218   NORTH AMERICA

on the ornate beaux arts edifice that was pulled down in the 1960s. But still, exiting the station is to be spewed into mid-town Manhattan, straight into the melee. Stop for a moment in the sea of souls and immediately you get it: the sensation of feeling utterly alienated while surrounded by thousands of people.

Over the next couple of days, Holden moves around the city, a journey of experience and innocence. He checks in to the Edmont Hotel, with its prostitutes and perverts, and he takes a 'vomity' cab to Ernie's Jazz Bar, which is full 'phonies'. Neither establishment ever existed, though there are still basement jazz clubs in Greenwich Village where you can drink Scotch and soda in a dark corner into the small hours.

Holden hits plenty of real-life Manhattan haunts, too. He stows his Gladstone at Grand Central, still a striking terminus – though the left-luggage service has since been discontinued for security reasons. He jostles with the masses on 'mobbed and messy' Broadway; he takes his date ice skating at the Rockefeller Center rink (still open every winter); he watches a show at Radio City Music Hall, a vast venue narrowly saved from closure in the 1970s and now an official City Landmark. The book is set in December and, then as now, Fifth Avenue is a-sparkle with Christmas lights – which might incite festive cheer or an anti-consumerist rant, depending on your perspective.

Central Park is the book's principal location, and you can follow Holden's trail through this great green lung, first opened to provide escape for urbanites in 1858. The vintage carousel, like the one on which Holden watches his sister, is still spinning. Sea lions still swim at the zoo. The parkside Natural History and Met museums that Holden recalls so fondly remain relatively unchanged.

However, Holden's main preoccupation is with the ducks on the lagoon near Central Park South: when it freezes over, where do they go? The answer is nowhere. Wander around, wrapped against the chill, and you might see them, huddled in different parts of the park, adapting to survive. Just as Holden must adapt. Just as this great, glorious, notorious, intoxicating, indefatigable city has had to, too.

Alberta

Where? Canada
Which? The Revenant (Alejandro González Iñárritu, 2015)
What? Wild frontier of breathtaking mountains, rampant nature and human strife and blood

Flawless light – the ethereal glow only possible at dusk – shafts through the straight-backed spruce, which rustle in the wind, whispering their wisdom. Mist hangs low above the jet-black stream, tickles the trees, twists around the antlers of a ruminating moose. A pair of birds circle in an enormous twilight sky. And the mountains give everything the cold shoulder, icily impervious to the drama played out in their shadows: the story of how the West was won but lost, and of how hard a man will fight to survive . . .

The Revenant is a tale of tragedy, adversity, vengeance and endurance played out in the unforgiving Rocky Mountains. It's simplistic and primitive; a creation in which words mean nothing compared to silences, and where the beauty and the wrath of nature – captured via roving camerawork and the interplay of landscape and ever-changing light – are the ultimate stars. It's no surprise that cinematographer Emmanuel Lubezki won an Oscar for his work.

The film is based on the true life story of Philadelphia-born fur-trapper Hugh Glass who, in 1823, was severely mauled by a grizzly bear and subsequently left for dead by his companions. Glass, barely alive, unable to walk, somehow dragged himself around 200 miles, facing manifold dangers – wild animals, rival gangs, frigid rivers, Native American arrows – hell-bent on survival and revenge.

In real life, Glass' ordeal occurred on the Missouri River in South Dakota. This was the era of the mountain men, tough, savvy-or-dead adventurers who set off to make their fortunes in untamed lands. They were hanging on the coattails of explorers Lewis and Clark who, in 1804, having been tasked with surveying the Missouri, made it all the way to the Pacific coast and back, and essentially opened up the American West – as well as marking the beginning of the end for the indigenous peoples' traditional ways. However, Iñárritu chose the wilds of southern Alberta for his Hugh Glass (Leonardo DiCaprio), throwing him into the icy frontierland where the Rockies begin to rise, rivers snake and churn and the landscape feels fittingly untouched. The location might not be geographically accurate but it feels spiritually so.

And the feel is all important. The movie, shot using only natural light, in real, remote locations, using the minimum of special effects, conveys the essence of the wild; the visceral, unforgiving hardship of life at the edge of the then-known world. Nature red in tooth and claw; humankind redder still, in the voracious quest to grab and conquer. The dirt, grime, sweat and phlegm; the creaking trees, crunching snow, raging white-water and flowing blood.

The movie's opening sees the men of the Rocky Mountain Fur Trade Company ambushed by bow-shooting Arikara Native Americans (or Ree, as the trappers call them). But this scene of carnage, played out in flooded woodlands on the banks of a sweeping river, was shot in the territory of the Stoney Nakoda, at their reserve just west of Calgary; around 100 members of the community appeared as background characters. The Stoney Nakoda, the original 'people of the mountains', have long been careful custodians of this land – one reason why the area was so easily able to conjure the pristine, pre-industrial American West.

Many more scenes were filmed in neighbouring Kananaskis Country, in the foothills and front ranges of the Rockies. It's an area of formidable protected reserves – such as the Bow Valley Wildland and Spray Valley Provincial Parks – hemmed in by spectacular summits, coniferous forests, dazzling lakes and wildflower meadows flush with harebells, Indian paintbrush, fireweed and northern bedstraw. It's also a place of extreme winters, with short days and temperatures often dipping to -25°C (-13°F).

The trappers' base in the movie, Fort Kiowa, was constructed near the K-Country village of Dead Man's Flats, in the Bow Valley. Based on a real 1820s Missouri River fur trade establishment, the crew collected old lumber discarded by the parks departments to build the fort's authentically rustic dorms, office, hostelry and outfitters; nothing remains. Scenes were also shot 2,500m (8,400ft) up, in the thick snow near Fortress Mountain Resort; down the Elbow River Canyon and above the cascades at Elbow Falls; and on the ghostly frozen surface of Lower Kananaskis Lake, flanked by peaks including Mount Fox and Mount Indefatigable.

The crew did leave Kananaskis. At one point a meteor is seen racing across the sky above the Badlands of Drumheller, northeast of Calgary, home to the largest deposits of dinosaur bones in the world. The movie's most striking scene – Glass being attacked by the defensive mama bear – was filmed over the border in British Columbia: Derringer Forest, in the Squamish Valley, is over towards the Pacific coast, near Vancouver. The old-growth rainforest here, fuzzed with mosses, ferns and old man's beard, is indeed prime grizzly country – though, of course, no real bears were involved.

The Revenant is a movie of scale and intensity that shines its beautiful but unflinching light not only on Glass' journey but on the wider issues of cultural genocide and humankind's raping of the natural world. While it might have been Alberta's warm chinook winds that caused the snow to melt overnight, forcing the crew to film the movie's final scenes in Tierra del Fuego, far-south Argentina, it must have appeared that this was climate change up close. That the land was telling a story of its own.

CINEMATIC   225

Monroeville

Where? Alabama, USA

Which? To Kill a Mockingbird by Harper Lee (1960)

What? Deep South US town that inspired a simple tale of racial heroism

No one's in a hurry in this tired old town. Maybe it's the heat – the Alabama summer is stultifying, sticky as molasses. It would be swell to swing on a porch all afternoon with an icy Coca-Cola. But this bench under the main square's live oaks and magnolias will do just fine. Folk pass by, strolling between the Christian bookshop, the thrift store and the fine old County Courthouse. No case has been tried here for decades; and in fact its most famous case wasn't tried here at all. But it remains a potent symbol of justice all the same . . .

Harper Lee's classic, *To Kill a Mockingbird*, delivered the right message in the right tone at the right moment. A simple tale of prejudice, unjustness and morality, it was published in 1960, just as the American South faced its biggest social shift since the Civil War. The equality movement was gaining momentum; deeply entrenched attitudes to race and class were being challenged. Alabama saw some of the highest-profile acts. It was in Montgomery in 1955 that Rosa Parks refused to surrender her bus seat to a white passenger. In 1956, anti-integration riots erupted when Autherine Lucy and Polly Myers became the first African-American students to be admitted to the state's university.

Though set in 1930s Alabama, during the Great Depression, *To Kill a Mockingbird* matched the mood of the sixties, and gave voice to the fears and frustrations of this transitional period. It showed the country it needed a conscience and offered an unimpeachable hero: Atticus Finch – single parent, lawyer, 'the bravest man who ever lived'. Atticus, the father of child narrator Scout, defends Tom Robinson, an innocent Black man, against charges of raping a white woman. Atticus knows he is destined to fail, but he proceeds with the case nonetheless.

The Finch family live in Maycomb, technically a fictional place but so modelled on the author's home of Monroeville that the two inevitably merge – the footsteps of Harper Lee and Atticus Finch lead the same way. Maycomb is an isolated, insular, hard-scrabble town, steeped in Southern values. Monroeville is similarly out on a limb, similarly Southern-hospitable, similarly facing testing times. Its former clay streets – 'red slop' in the rain – have been paved but the population is low and falling (currently 6,000 or so) and there's a slight air of decrepitude around the old square, where many businesses have closed. However, its cultural impact has not faded.

Monroeville's literal and literary heart is the County Courthouse. Completed in 1904, this Romanesque clock-towered seat of justice was used until 1963. Attorney A.C. Lee fought many cases here, with daughter Nelle Harper Lee watching from the balcony. In the 1970s the building was almost demolished. But it was surreptitiously placed on the National Register of Historic Places and saved. Restored to its 1930s glory, the Courthouse is now a museum where you can sit in the judge's chair, climb to the 'coloreds' balcony' and, each spring, watch the Mockingbird play, which recreates the novel's action in situ.

A circuit of the square passes the two-storey Monroe County Bank Building (inside which A.C. Lee once practised law) and the tiny jailhouse – 'a miniature Gothic joke' – where the likes of Tom Robinson were once interred; it's now an annexe to the Sheriff's Department. Alabama Avenue leads from the square's southeast corner. A little way down, past the car parks and uninspiring office buildings, is Mel's Dairy Dream, a small retro drive-thru selling burgers and shakes. This was the site of Lee's childhood home, torn down in 1953. Next door, a low brick wall is all that's left of the Faulk house, where a young Truman Capote would stay while visiting his Monroeville cousins, and where Truman and Nelle Harper became lifelong friends.

According to Atticus, 'You never really understand a person until you consider things from his point of view . . . Until you climb inside of his skin and walk around in it.' Visiting Monroeville lets you walk a little with Harper Lee.

Cinematic

Dead Horse Point State Park

Where? Utah, USA
Which? *Thelma & Louise* (Ridley Scott, 1991)
What? Scorched-rock landscape of vast canyons, huge horizons and freedom

Top down, engine gunning, dust clouds spewing into vast desert skies. Ahead lies the open road. Behind the wheel are two women, red hair tousled by the wind, fuelled by Wild Turkey and feminist rage. Two women flooring the accelerator through red-raw canyons who've tossed off their old lives and vow, together: let's keep going . . .

Thelma & Louise ruffled feathers on its release in 1991. Part buddy film, part on-the-road epic, part girl-power parable, it had the audacity to be a movie about two women – downtrodden housewife Thelma (Geena Davis) and her sparky best friend Louise (Susan Sarandon) – who accidentally become outlaws when one shoots the man she catches in the act of raping the other. On the run, driving west across the US, they become ever more felonious, ever more themselves. Increasingly refusing to cooperate with the patriarchy, they instead do what they must in order to be free.

The movie purports to travel from Arkansas through Oklahoma and New Mexico to Arizona, where the women and their metallic-green convertible 1966 Ford Thunderbird make their final, suicidal, triumphal plunge – 'I think,' says Louise, wondering where they are 'it's the goddamn Grand Canyon'. In fact, it's not. Many of the locations used were actually close to Los Angeles, California, while Utah – which director Ridley Scott called his 'third character' – provided most of the dramatic desert scenes.

For instance, the lonely road featured in the opening credits is winding through the mighty La Sal Mountains, which rise on the Utah-Colorado border. The soaring sandstone formations amid which

228   NORTH AMERICA

Thelma and Louise are pulled over for speeding (and subsequently force the state trooper into the trunk of his car) are the Courthouse Towers within Arches National Park. And the police chase scene was shot in the endless-seeming desert around the ghost town of Cisco, a railway refill station founded in the 1880s but long abandoned and since reduced to ramshackle ruins and windblown sagebrush – though, in 2015, an artist bought the place and it's now become home to an unusual and solitary artists' retreat.

The spot where Thelma and Louise – grubby, determined, clutching hands – make their final drive, off into the golden sunset, is Fossil Point, a lookout east of Canyonlands National Park, just south of Dead Horse Point State Park and looming over the Gooseneck bend of the green-blue Colorado River. It sits within a swathe of layered mesas, pinnacles, bluffs and buttes carved out of the Colorado Plateau over millions of years. A soul-stirring, scorched-earth land with no limits; a place of fenceless precipices, literally on the edge – the edge of danger and of freedom.

Reaching Fossil Point is only possible via the unpaved Shafer Trail–Potash Road, a drive requiring Thelma and Louise levels of pluck – the Shafer Trail section in particular, which switchbacks steeply down a precipitous cliff. Adapted from a Native American track, it was later used by sheep drovers, and then truckers shifting uranium; it's now a white-knuckle 4WD adventure.

You can get a sweeping view of Fossil Point from the more easily accessible Dead Horse Point State Park, a slim peninsula of land protruding off a vast plateau that lies just to the north; in the nineteenth century it was used as a corral for wild mustangs – cowboys would kettle the horses across the narrow neck leading onto the point's tip, then fence them in. The park's West Rim overlook trail gazes across to the movie's fateful outcrop, a startling vista over rugged ravines and across the twisting river.

Revving their engine, Thelma and Louise chose the deliverance of the abyss here. And the final shot – their car freeze-framed against the timeless red rock, not yet dropping but flying – feels oddly optimistic. Not death but freedom.

Coyoacán

Artistic

Where? Mexico
Which? The Two Fridas (1939) by Frida Kahlo
What? Sultry, magical neighbourhood steeped in history

In the lazy afternoon heat, the scent of orchids, dahlias and honeysuckle hangs in the air, fruit ripens on trees and cicadas chirrup. Hugged by a sapphire sky, the borough of Coyoacán – (meaning place of coyotes) – in Mexico City retains much of its original sixteenth-century layout, with narrow streets, cobblestoned plazas and vibrant markets, selling fruit, flowers and handcrafted goods. Its epicentre is a pair of plazas, the larger, cobblestoned Plaza Hidalgo and the Jardín del Centenario, with rustling trees and exotic plants, a central fountain where coyotes frolic, and the sixteenth-century Baroque parish church of San Juan Bautista – one of the oldest churches in Mexico, dating to the mid-sixteenth century, which blends the influences of indigenous Indian craftsmen with Spanish Baroque building styles. Leading on from the Plaza Hidalgo, is Coyoacán's main plaza, Plaza de la Conchita – a leafy colonial town square. All around are street vendors, bars, cafés, and people enjoying the colourful atmosphere.

It was here in Coyoacán, at La Casa Azul (The Blue House), named after its cobalt-blue walls, that Frida Kahlo (1907–54) grew up. Built in 1904, La Casa Azul is, like most of the other buildings in the area, formed around a central courtyard and garden. Over two floors, it incorporates bedrooms, studio space, a large kitchen and a dining room. Everywhere is painted with rich, vivid colours, and the entrance hall is decorated with mosaics. Now preserved as the Museo Frida Kahlo, it was made into a museum in 1958, four years after Kahlo's death. On entering, Kahlo's spirit can be felt everywhere – her paints are still in her studio by her easel, and the house is filled with paintings, period furnishings and pre-Columbian artefacts. Today, it is one of the most popular museums in Mexico City, with queues of Frida fans flocking to explore her home, work and fascinating life, immersing themselves in the creative living space she inhabited.

Kahlo spent much time in Casa Azul convalescing, first in 1918 after contracting polio, then when she suffered a terrible accident aged 18 while on her school bus that left her permanently physically damaged. She spent almost two years confined to her bed and endured 32 operations over the rest of her life. During her convalescence, she began to paint, and after she met Diego, she invited him to the Casa Azul to see her work. Rivera began visiting regularly, and soon other artists started meeting at the house. After her marriage to Rivera in 1929, Kahlo began wearing traditional Tehuana costume and drew greater artistic inspiration from Mexican folk art. Yet the marriage was not happy. Diego's infidelities took a toll on Kahlo's fragile health. She plunged into affairs with men and women, miscarried twice, had two abortions, suffered an appendectomy and had two gangrenous toes amputated.

Influenced by her health and personal problems, Kahlo produced soul-searching, introspective paintings such as the double self-portrait *The Two Fridas* (1939) that expressed her feelings of being broken by physical and psychological pain. At La Casa Azul, you can see where Kahlo lived, painted and also, sadly, where she died. An urn in the form of her face lies on her bed, holding her ashes. Beside this is the mirror in which she observed herself to paint her famous self-portraits. Her clothes, jewellery and personal objects remain where she left them. Book your tickets in advance and give yourself a few hours to explore. Then stroll into the cobbled streets or take the red tram that passes through Coyoacán. The charming Cantina La Guadalupana was a favourite local bar often frequented by Kahlo and Rivera, and while it's now closed, you can still see the original signage marking the spot. To the north is Coyoacán's colourful market, brimming with the scent of flowers, exotic fruits and delicious Mexican street food, including crispy tostadas and spicy quesadillas. Nearby is the Coyoacán Mexican Artisans Bazaar and the Museo de las Culturas Populares, where the diverse artistic heritage of Mexico can be seen. In the Frida Kahlo Park are life-sized bronze statues of Kahlo and Rivera. Wherever you go in this vibrant place, you will take in the same sights, sounds and scents that were experienced by Kahlo herself.

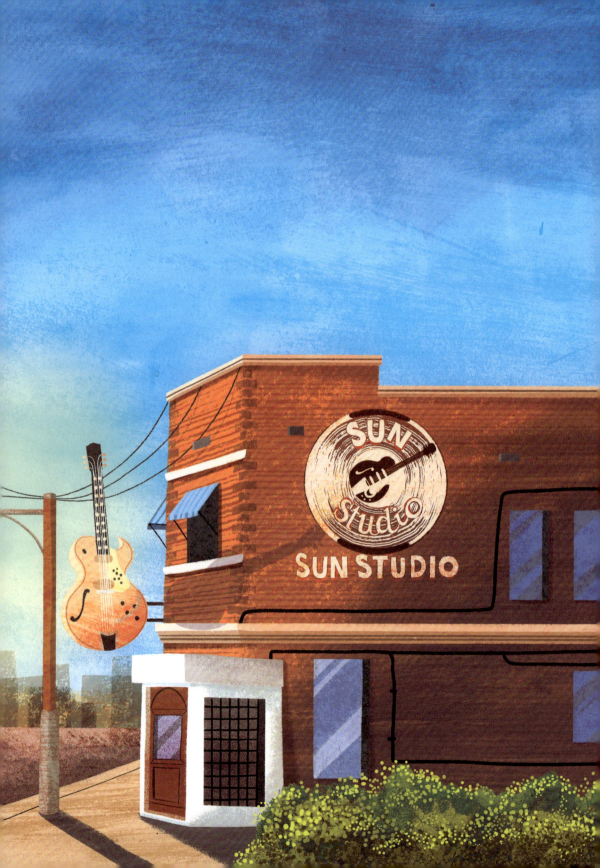

Memphis

Where? Tennessee, USA
Why? Riverside rock-and-roll

Ah, that muggy Memphis air – heavy with heat and humidity, heavier still with sound. Here, music is inescapable; melodic strains pour from the open doorways of café-clubs, juke joints, honky-tonks, piano lounges, barbecue shacks and handsome old theatres – a harmonious cacophony that seems to reverberate through every sidewalk. Yes, Memphis has a pulse, and it's a propulsive four-beats-per-bar signature, tapping out the story of this city. For Memphis is the stomping ground of legends, the very birthplace of rock and roll . . .

Memphis is a big city with a small-town feel; down-to-earth, sociable, edgy, artistic. It sits on the Chickasaw Bluffs above the mighty Mississippi River, at the point where Arkansas, Mississippi and Tennessee meet. The area was first inhabited by the Chickasaw Nation, but the city was formally founded in 1819 and named for the Ancient Egyptian city on the Nile (meaning Place of Good Abode). It boomed off the back of cotton, an industry powered by enslaved workers; however, free people of colour also came here to seek jobs. Thus, Memphis became a nexus of Black culture, especially music – it was a place where traditional spirituals, Delta blues and jazz from New Orleans started to swirl with rural country twangs. Something new began to stir.

At the centre of this was Beale Street, an iconic thoroughfare that has helped brand Memphis as one of the world's foremost music cities. Established in 1841, running from the Mississippi towards the east, it was once the southern boundary of the main Memphis business district. Black people were largely barred from shopping downtown, unless via designated 'coloured' doors, but on Beale there were many Black-owned businesses, some of the first in the South. And there was also the First Baptist Church, founded by a congregation of freed slaves, and headquarters of *Free Speech*, the first Black newspaper.

At the turn of the twentieth century, Beale Street was a refuge for African Americans moving to the city. Among them, musician W. C.

Handy – known as the 'Father of the Blues' – who came to Memphis with his band in 1909. It was in clubs on Beale that he played his sweet and soulful music, a new sound inflected with folk, Latin, ragtime and minstrel shows but ultimately its own thing. Then, in the following decades, more young Black musicians continued experimenting, developing rhythm and blues and ultimately, rock and roll.

For rock and roll ground zero, you need to walk a block north of Beale. Here, on Union Avenue, is Sun Studio, founded by pioneering promoter Sam Phillips. This is where, in 1951, Jackie Brenston and his Delta Cats recorded 'Rocket 88' – considered by many to be the first rock and roll song. And it's where many a musical legend was discovered: B. B. King, Howlin' Wolf, Jerry Lee Lewis, Elvis Presley. Phillips once said, 'If I could find a white man who had the Negro sound and the Negro feel, I could make a billion dollars'. With Elvis, he found his pay check.

Sun Studios has barely changed in the intervening decades; it remains a small block of brick and concrete, its modesty belying its immense cultural significance. You can take a tour, hum a tune in the spine-tingling studio, sit at a piano played by Johnny Cash, stand at a microphone used by Elvis. For the mother-lode of Presley memorabilia, though, you need to head a few miles south of downtown, where The King's Colonial-Revival mansion, Graceland, is also open to visitors. Elvis bought the place in 1956 and styled it to his taste – green shag carpet in the Jungle Room, stained-glass peacocks in the lounge, a kitchen stocked with Pepsi, meatloaf, peanut butter and fudge cookies. He died here in 1977 and is buried in the grounds, his grave a place of pilgrimage.

But the heart of Memphis is back on Beale. The street's fortunes have ebbed and flowed over the years, the historic façades variously ignored and crumbling, lovingly restored or turned into tourist traps. There is flashing retro neon and over-commercialisation, yet still the music endures – it remains the city's entertainment hub. B. B. King's Blues Club still packs them in every night; King's Palace is the place for jazz, Zydeco, crawfish and gumbo; the Jerry Lee Lewis Cafe and Honky Tonk is always rocking; the Rum Boogie is always a-buzz. Plus, now the story is explored further at the Rock and Soul Museum on the corner of Beale and Route 61 (the 'Blues Highway'). Here, exhibits honour those Memphis pioneers who overcame race and socio-economic barriers to make music that shook up the world.

Part Three:

South America

Cartagena

Where? Colombia

Which? *Love in the Time of Cholera* by Gabriel García Márquez (1985)

What? Colonial Caribbean-lapped city in Colombia where magic is made real

The city is steaming. The downpour has stopped and now the temperature's high as hell, the air hanging heavy with humidity, jasmine, birdsong and expectation. Yellow-red-pink walls burn in the sun. It seems barely a city at all but a lurid painting created in a fever dream; blurred brightness, hidden meanings. The shade of the square provides little escape. You're still assaulted by the Caribbean heat, by the sound of heels clattering the cobblestones, by pecking pigeons, hawkers touting Cuban cigars, the sickly smooch of lovers. A hot breeze blows through, carrying not respite but stories – stories from out at sea, from the cannon-topped battlements, from behind closed shutters, from centuries past. Cartagena: a city of stories, where magic dances down every street . . .

Gabriel García Márquez was born in the Colombian river town of Aracataca, lived peripatetically between Europe, Cuba and Mexico City but is inextricably linked with Cartagena. He arrived in the coastal city in 1948, just as La Violencia – a ten-year civil war – broke across the country. He studied at Cartagena University, and worked as a newspaper reporter, but left after only a year, never to live there full time again. And yet, this city – its palette, its pulse – infuses his writing. Márquez once confessed that 'all of my books have loose threads of Cartagena in them'.

This is never more apparent than in *El Amor en los Tiempos del Cólera – Love in the Time of Cholera*. The novel, based on the love affair of Márquez's parents, is set in the 'city of the Viceroys', a port on the Magdalena River somewhere near the Caribbean Sea – unnamed by the author but oozing with the essence of Cartagena. The streets and squares are fictitious, but wandering the real-life city it's impossible not to see the stage of Márquez's love story: that of odd young romantic

Literary

LITERARY 241

Florentino Ariza and his sweetheart Fermina Daza. After one 'casual glance' at 14-year-old Fermina, Florentino falls impossibly in love. He stalks Fermina across the city, mounting a vigil outside her half-ruined house, going places she might be, playing violin to her in church. When Fermina marries staid, respectable Dr Juvenal Urbino instead, Florentino continues to lurk around the city – on trams, down alleys, by the docks – racking up hundreds of sexual encounters while still proclaiming fidelity to Fermina. He waits 51 years, 9 months and 4 days to win her back.

Cartagena was founded by the Spanish in 1533. It was a literal treasure chest, used to store looted New World gold and silver before it was shipped back to Europe. The Spanish wrapped the city in sturdy ramparts to fend off attacks from buccaneers and Brits; these protective *murallas* (walls) were bolstered over subsequent centuries, becoming the most extensive fortifications in South America. Today, they continue to safeguard the Old Town's cluster of handsome churches, bright-hued houses, tropical courtyards and terracotta tiles. It's a confined, candy-coloured bubble, where magic might brew.

Cartagena is in better shape now than when Márquez arrived. The state of ruination, when 'weeds hung from the balconies and opened cracks in the whitewashed walls of even the best-kept mansions' has been reversed. Long known for guerrilla fighting, drugs trafficking and corruption, Colombia has cleaned up its act in the early twenty-first century. In Cartagena, houses have been restored and weeds replaced by tamed creepers and neat window boxes.

Indeed, the Old Town is as colourful, sensual and multi-sensory as Márquez's imagination. *Cumbia* music pumps from bars and spills into the streets. Food is everywhere, from rainbow-bright lollipops to fried snacks sizzling in vats of hot oil on the pavements. Dark-skinned *palenqueras*, descendants of the first free slaves, sashay in their vibrant full-skirted dresses and costume jewels, balancing bowls overflowing with tropical fruit on their heads. They'll pose for photos in exchange for money from tourists. But then, the whole city is photogenic, from the elegant wrought-iron lampposts to the balconies dripping with bougainvillea. Flowers of all kinds – roses, gardenias, camellias – symbolise love in Márquez's novel, and flourish in abundance on the real streets of Cartagena.

It's possible to seek out Florentino and Fermina. Entering the Old Town via the main gate, walking under the clock tower, you enter the Plaza de los Coches, once used as a slave market. Across the square is the Portal de los Dulces, the colonnaded and tangerine-hued passageway that became Márquez's Portal de los Escribanos, or Arcade of the Scribes. Florentino, rejected by Fermina, employed his literary powers here, writing missives for 'unlettered lovers', free of charge. You won't find poets under the shade of the arches today, but rather a line of little stalls selling a tooth-stinging array of sweet confections: sugary pastries, caramel swirls, glass jars jammed with *muñecas de leche* (milk dolls) and coconut *cocada* sweets.

A little further north is leafy Plaza Fernández de Madrid, inspiration for the Parquecito de los Evangelios – the Little Park of the Evangelists – where love-lorn Florentino spent many hours, hoping to glimpse Fermina. There are benches where you can sit, like Florentino, 'pretending to read a book of verse in the shade of the almond trees'. The Daza house was supposedly based on the white, vine-smothered mansion on the square's eastern side.

Just like Márquez's fictional city, Cartagena is a cauldron in which magic can brew. Where love can explode, colours can blind, parrots can kill. It is lyrical, vibrant, sweet and strange. It has, as Dr Urbino states, 'no equal in the world'.

Foodie

Lima

Where? Peru

Why? Go to the ground zero of super foods, where centuries of history can be read in raw fish

A feast for eyes, stomach and brain, Mercado de Surquillo is Lima – all Peru – in microcosm; both bustling local market and colourful culinary education. So much for sale here is a mystery to anyone from the outside. There's prickly *guanábana* (soursop fruit) and butterscotch-sweet *lucuma* (eggfruit), tart *camu camu* berries bursting with antioxidants and fragrant *cherimoya*, the flavour-child of a banana and a pineapple. There are chilli peppers of all fire levels and corn in every hue – zest yellow, blood red, bruise purple. There's oil pressed from *sacha inchi* (the star-shaped Inca peanut) and piles of knobbly *maca*, the virility-boosting root revered by Inca kings. And, in this ocean-facing city, there are fish stalls, salty and slippery with sea bass and giant squid, where they'll concoct a dish that provides the ultimate taste of a nation . . .

Peru isn't a country, it's a larder. Its geography, topography and multitude of microclimates means a diverse bounty thrives here. Off the lengthy Pacific coast, the cold Humboldt current meets warm tropical waters, resulting in an extraordinary array of seafood. Inland, the Andes soar, their rich, fertile soil supporting giant corn and amaranth, guinea pigs and alpaca, 300 types of *ají* (chillies) and 4,000 varieties of potato. Beyond that, the Amazon basin simmers, nurturing wild fruits and vegetables, nuts and spices, game and freshwater fish. What the rest of the world has come to call super foods – quinoa, sweet potato, avocado – Peruvians just call, well, food.

The capital Lima is the gateway to all this gastronomy. The city lies in a confluence of river valleys in the coastal desert, by the Pacific. It was founded by Spanish conquistador Francisco Pizarro in 1535 and from 1543 it became capital of the Viceroyalty of Peru. Lima is now one of the continent's most populous conurbations. A sprawl of sea smog, traffic jams, shantytowns, glitzy suburbs, a UNESCO-listed historic centre – and some of the world's best cuisine.

And Limeños love food – eating it, talking about it, talking and eating together. It's more than just sustenance. Peru's *cocina criolla* (creole food) is the result of centuries of cultural evolution. After the civil war of the late twentieth century, food was championed as a unifying force. As Peruvian chefs – notably the trailblazing Gastón Acurio – gained worldwide acclaim, the country became the foodies' 'Next Big Thing'. Here was something of which every Peruvian, regardless of class or ethnicity, could be proud, because they all had a part to play.

The country's modern menu has been shaped by its diversity of raw ingredients, its indigenous pre-Colombian traditions and its layers of immigration. For instance, the Spanish brought onions, pork, lamb and grapes, the latter giving rise to pisco, Peru's national spirit. African slaves came up with *anticuchos*, the skewered beef hearts that are now the country's favourite street food. An influx of Chinese labourers in the nineteenth century means Lima now has one of the continent's largest *Barrios Chinos* (Chinatowns). Then, in the twentieth century, Japanese immigrants arrived, birthing Nikkei, a marriage of Peruvian food and Japanese techniques, and elevating the country's national dish, *ceviche*.

Dishes similar to ceviche, in which acidic foods are used to denature and 'cook' fish proteins, can be found elsewhere in the world, but more often it's the Moche, who roamed Peru's coastal regions almost 2,000 years ago, who are credited with ceviche's creation. They cured their catch with the juice of the tumbo, seaweed and chilli. Later, the Inca did their preservation with *chicha*, a fermented Andean corn beer. When the Spanish introduced citrus fruits, these were used instead.

However, it was Japanese immigrants who perfected ceviche. With a history of preparing sushi and sashimi, they knew how to handle raw fish. They filleted it into smaller pieces to decrease the marinating time: while the fish used to bathe in acidic juices for hours, rendering it more like chicken, Japanese chefs exposed it for just a few seconds and served it right away, preserving the delicate textures and clean, light, taste.

In Lima you can find as many different versions of ceviche as there are *cevichería*. Wherever you choose to eat it, go for lunch not dinner – ceviche is best served early to display the full freshness of fish from that morning's catch. The most basic recipes consist of raw fish – often sea bass, or maybe bonito, scallops or shrimp – lime juice, salt and ají, plus red onion and coriander. The sour-spicy liquor in which the fish is marinated is called *leche de tigre*, or tiger's milk, and should be drunk alongside the ceviche. And it's good for everything: a hangover cure, a refreshing respite from the city's subtropical heat, an excuse to gather and gossip, and the most delicious mouthful of cultural history.

FOODIE   245

Salvador

Where? Bahia, Brazil
Why? Cultural diversity delivered in musical form

Welcome to Salvador, the party that never ends. There's scarcely a moment that the streets of this gritty, electrifying city aren't alive with drummers drumming, speakers blasting, bossa nova oozing, percussion crews jangling, capoeiristas flipping, booties twerking. Not to mention when Carnaval – even longer, bigger, more intense and more orgiastic than Rio's – takes over the place. As long as they're awake, *Soteropolitanos* (as locals are known) are likely playing, making, listening to or thinking about music in some way; if they're asleep, it's probably soundtracking their dreams. Music is a social glue that helps this multicultural city stick together. It's a connection to the past, a way of dealing with the present, a beat to follow into the future . . .

Magnificently sited on the wide, deep-blue sweep of Baía de Todos os Santos (All Saints Bay), Salvador – a city of 2.9 million people – is sizzling, vivacious and quick to get under the skin. Strategically sited on the northeast coast and founded by the Portuguese in 1549, it was Brazil's first capital (until 1793), and is still the capital of Bahia state. It is also the enduring capital of the Brazilian music scene.

European, African and American Indian cultures have long converged here. The city has the dubious claim to fame of hosting the New World's first slave market. The influx of African peoples profoundly influenced the cultural landscape, shaping Salvador's religion, language, music and cuisine – dishes heavy in palm oil, peanuts and coconut milk. For instance, the city has a strong connection to Candomblé, an Afro-Brazilian religion incorporating traditional Yoruba and Bantu beliefs with some aspects of Catholicism. Secretive Candomblé ceremonies see dancers whirl to syncopated claps, ritualistic call-and-response chants and the expressive taps and booms of *atabaque* drums, while respects are paid to the *orixás* (deified ancestors).

However, most of the city's music is more out in the open air. It's not unusual to happen upon a troupe practising capoeira, the most balletic martial-art, performed to the bowing of a *berimbau*, the jangle of the tambourine-like pandeiro and the reco-reco's earthy scrape. Or to hear axé tunes blasting from the sound system of a *trio elétrico* (electric float), the truck-back mobile stages that were invented in the city.

Indeed, in the 1980s, Salvador became the epicentre of *axé* – a fusion of reggae, samba, calypso and more, its name deriving from a Yoruba word meaning 'energy' or 'good vibrations'. The city has also produced some of the biggest artists of the *Música Popular Brasileira* (MPB) movement, including Gilberto Gil and Caetano Veloso. A blending of elements of bossa nova, samba, jazz, rock and regional folk, MPB is a rich and eclectic sound that reflects the cultural diversity of Brazil itself.

And that's Salvador to a tee – cultural diversity. Visitors come for the glorious beaches, of which there are many. And for the rich history, especially in the old Pelourinho district – this is where slave auctions once took place, but now the wide plazas and pastel-hued colonial-era buildings have been souped up and UNESCO-listed. But they leave most moved by the human mix; by the taste of *vatapá* shrimp porridge and *acarajé* (deep-fried bean cake); by the sounds of the drums, by the outpouring of unbridled joy.

A great way to feel the soul of the city is to catch Olodum in full flow. This legendary bloco-afro – one of the community musical groups that takes part in Carnaval festivities – was founded in 1979, during the rising Black Consciousness Movement. Their sound, comprising powerful, booming drums, rootsy African rhythms, and inflections of reggae and funk, comes with socially conscious lyrics, addressing issues of slavery and racism, getting to the heart of Salvador's cultural identity. When Paul Simon (of 'and Garfunkel' fame) heard them playing on the streets, he enlisted them to perform on his album Rhythms of the Saints. But Olodum are best heard live. Handily, they hold weekly rehearsals in an open courtyard in the historic centre. The crowds are heaving, the atmosphere is electric, the vibe 100 per cent Salvador.

La Pampa

Where? Buenos Aires Province, Argentina
Why? Eat like the original plains cowboys

Around a tabletop massacre of gnawed bones and wine stains, the cry goes up: *'¡Un aplauso para el asador!'* 'An applause for the asador!' Praise be to the cook who has provided this feast for the ages; a gargantuan grill of ribs, flanks and filets from the cattle reared on the grasslands outside. But it's been more than a meal: bellies are bulging, cheeks are glowing and spirits are high, not only on meat and Malbec but on national pride . . .

Buenos Aires, capital of Argentina, is cosmopolitan and cultured, a city of elegant boulevards, manicured parks, art galleries, opera houses and tango bars. By contrast, much of the surrounding namesake province – and vast swathes of land beyond – are open, rolling, rural countryside, an antidote to urban life. This is La Pampa, the region of highly fertile and seemingly endless plains stretching from the Atlantic coast to the Andean foothills. It is Argentina's agricultural heartland and home of its legendary *gauchos*.

Gauchos are the cowboys of South America. The origin of the word isn't certain, but may stem from the Quechua *huachu* (meaning orphan or vagabond). They appeared in the seventeenth century, poor men of mixed Spanish and indigenous blood who moved into La Pampa's lawless wilds. Cows and horses, brought by the Spanish and perfectly suited to the terrain, thrived here, and escapees from wealthy *estancias* (ranches) soon roamed wide and multiplied. The gauchos – variously considered itinerant drifters or outright bandits and crooks – were skilled riders and hunters; they tamed wild horses, caught, drove, traded and smuggled cattle, and lived by their own rules.

At first these outlaws were feared and vilified. But, following the Argentine War of Independence (1810–1818), when gauchos joined the patriotic flight against Spanish loyalists, the perception changed. They became romantic figures, free-spirited folk heroes adventuring on horseback in wide-brimmed hats and *bombachas* (baggy trousers),

FOODIE   251

sleeping on ponchos beneath the stars. Men who, when they grew hungry, would eat what was available: beef.

Gauchos had no access to complicated apparatus or ingredients. They would slaughter a cow and cook it *a la cruz*, hanging large hunks of fresh meat onto cross-shaped struts that were tilted towards a fire, ideally made from the long-burning hardwood of the quebracho tree. The meat would roast slowly, for hours, staying juicy and tender. The concept of *asado* – from the Spanish 'to grill' – was born. And it has become the defining dish of Argentina.

Today, asado is more commonly prepared on a *parrilla*, a horizontal grill mounted above hot coals – never flames: the key is low, indirect heat. The operation is ruled by an asador, the individual responsible for the perfect cooking of every cut. This is not simple barbecuing: an expert asador develops a sixth sense for working the fire and the flesh. *Vacuno* (beef), seasoned with nothing other than salt, is still the meat of choice. *Bife ancho* (ribeye), *tira de asado* (short ribs), *vacío* (flank) and *lomo* (tenderloin) are popular cuts, though the whole cow is eaten, down to the *achuras* (offal). Meat portions are cartoonishly huge. On the side, expect a simple salad, bread rolls and chimichurri; a herby sauce heavy on parsley and garlic. At the end of this gluttony, it is customary for someone to raise a toast and start a lengthy round of applause for the asador's endeavours.

You won't struggle to find authentic neighbourhood parrilla across Buenos Aires; places messy with grease and chimichurri and chatter and Malbec. But to fully embrace the life – and the gastronomy – of the gaucho, head for La Pampa. There you'll find the market town of San Antonio de Areco, which has retained its historic centre and its cowboy traditions. A gaucho festival is held here every November. Or seek out a working estancia, one of the ranches built here by colonial aristocrats that still employ modern-day gauchos to marshal the cattle, lead horseback hacks and, with luck, cook up a meat feast.

Chile

Where? South America
Which? *The House of the Spirits* by Isabel Allende (1982)
What? Mysterious Latin nation terrorised by dictators and laced with magic

The landscape seems but a dream; a hazy memory. The shrouded sky part conceals the fruitful valley, with its twisted vines, dashing stream, distant mountains; only the snow-slathered peak of a volcano stands proud and clear. A vast estancia – a huge swathe of hopeful farmland – lays vague claim to this patch of wildness, but remains at the mercy of Mother Nature in this half-forgotten country at the end of the earth . . .

Though its location is never stated, *La Casa de los Espíritus – The House of the Spirits* – breathes Chile. Author Isabel Allende declined to place her story of three generations of the Trueba family; it plays out in an unnamed country in Latin America. But despite its magic-realist flights of fancy and geographic unspecificity, there's little question of the setting. The novel is part personal saga, part document of the country's twentieth-century history.

Allende has admitted as much; she once said that in writing *The House of the Spirits*, she 'wanted to recover all that I had lost – my land, my family, my memories'. The Chilean author had spent long periods of her early life living in Santiago. But when the military coup of 1973 saw the toppling of President Salvador Allende – the world's first democratically elected Marxist president and Isabel's first cousin once removed – she fled to Venezuela. *The House of the Spirits*, which began life as a letter to her dying grandfather, was written while the author was in exile and her homeland – 'that country of catastrophes' – was in the grip of Augusto Pinochet's brutal dictatorship.

The novel begins around 1920, at a time when Chilean politics were in flux. It spans more than 50 years and two main locations: the 'big house on the corner', in the centre of the nameless capital, and Tres Marías, the Trueba's countryside estate. Real events creep into the narrative. The earthquake that tears down Tres Marías and saw 'buildings fall like

254   SOUTH AMERICA

wounded dinosaurs' echoes the 1939 earthquake that devastated Chile, killed nearly 30,000 people and yet caused limited international stir: 'the rest of the world, too busy with another war, barely noticed that nature had gone berserk in that remote corner of the globe'. Politics are ever present too – from issues of women's rights and socialism to the build-up to the coup. But there's also joy and beauty, from the conjured spirits, to the girl with the long green hair to the wild expanses of the sun-baked *campo* (countryside).

As Allende doesn't name her country, it's impossible to follow a Trueba trail with precision. But you might start in Santiago's Plaza de Armas – the name of many a Latin city's main square – where violent patriarch Esteban Trueba first sees 'Rosa the Beautiful' buying liquorice, and where you can stroll past the palm trees, chess players and towers of the Neoclassical cathedral. You could visit the museum at Las Chascona, former house of Pablo Neruda, who 'appears' in the novel simply as the Poet, or the Museum of Memory and Human Rights, which commemorates victims of the Pinochet regime. You might even explore the Brasil and Yungay *barrios* (municipalities), where the wealthy built fine mansions in the nineteenth and twentieth centuries – less eccentric versions, perhaps, of the twisted, protuberance-encrusted house where clairvoyant Clara Trueba spoke to spirits.

Then, like Esteban, you could leave the metropolis. The Chilean train network has shrunk to a handful of lines, but the southbound service from Santiago's Gustave Eiffel-designed Alameda Station still offers an escape into the *campo*. Out the train window, Esteban watches 'the passing landscape of the central valley. Vast fields stretched from the foot of the mountain range, a fertile countryside filled with vineyards, wheatfields, alfalfa and marigolds'. Similarly, the long, thin plain south of Santiago, flanked by the Andes and the coastal range, is Chile's most fertile region. This rural riot of orchards, pastures and grape-heavy vines – where horse-drawn carts still clop along the highway – is just the place to imagine Tres Marías appearing on the horizon.

Cinematic

Cusco & Machu Picchu

Where? Peru
Which? *The Motorcycle Diaries* (Walter Salles, 2004)
What? Iconic high points of the extraordinary journey that helped create a legend

All that can be seen is the dust on the road and the men on their waspish motorbike, driving through the wilderness and into history. On they press, via pampa, lakes, mountains and deserts. Even to mighty ruins – the mightiest in the land – which serve as a reminder of all that has been lost . . .

The Motorcycle Diaries is the story of Ernesto Guevara before he became Che, the revolutionary legend. Based on Che's own memoir of the epic 8,000-kilometre (5,000-mile) trip he took with Alberto Granado in 1952, it's a coming-of-age road movie about two friends venturing abroad for the first time who, alongside their buddy hijinks, become increasingly aware of social injustice; who have their eyes opened to both their continent and themselves.

Ernesto (Gael García Bernal) and Alberto (Rodrigo de la Serna) set off on a 1939 Norton 500 – christened *La Poderosa*, the Mighty One – from the refined streets of Buenos Aires. Ahead lies the whole of Latin America: oxcarts and *gauchos*, heavy snow and beating sun, colossal peaks and dusty plains, myriad *mestizo* faces; new lands, new ideas. The journey takes them through northern Patagonia's Lake District, over the Andes, across Chile's lunar-like Atacama Desert, into Peru's Inca heartlands, down the Amazon River and, finally, to Venezuela. It's a striking unfurling of the continent and, as far as possible, director Walter Salles aped the duo's actual route, shooting in the same locations. So we see – as Che did – the dazzling waters of San Martín de los Andes (where there is now a Che Museum); the picturesque Chilean port of Valparaíso, with its vintage funiculars and unexpected poverty; the

256 SOUTH AMERICA

cavernous Chuquicamata copper mine near Calama (still operating, and visitable on pre-booked tours).

We also watch the pair enter Peru, the camera panning from its jungly slopes to its dispossessed indigenous peoples and into Cusco, 'the heart of America'. Founded around 1100 CE, Cusco was the capital of the Inca, who constructed splendid palaces with perfect precision here; when the Spanish captured the city in 1533, they erected fine buildings of their own, including the elaborate churches of the Plaza de Armas. In *The Motorcycle Diaries*, the pair see both, and they find descendants of the mighty Inca now living in poverty among them, including local women in traditional dress who give them coca leaves to chew – they're said to alleviate the altitude sickness so common in a city that teeters at 3,400 metres (11,000 feet).

While some of these scenes were filmed in Cusco, others were shot in Ollantaytambo, northwest along the Sacred Valley, by the Urubamba River, where the old streets are even narrower, even more atmospheric. Ollantaytambo is also the gateway – by foot or train – to the only South American image more iconic than Che himself: Machu Picchu.

The fabled 'Lost City' was built around 1460 in the remote hinterland where sheer, lush peaks slip into the hot Amazon basin. Never found by the Spanish, Machu Picchu was 'rediscovered' by explorer Hiram Bingham in 1911. Ernesto and Alberto visited on 5 April 1952 and, in the movie, have the site's tumbling terraces, plazas, storehouses and temples to themselves – unlike today, in the 1950s tourist numbers were incredibly low. The duo wouldn't have found it quite so tidy, though – many of the now-restored outlying buildings were just piles of stones back then. But it still made quite an impression; Che called it 'the pure expression of the most powerful indigenous race in the Americas – untouched by a conquering civilisation'. It fed into his developing ideas of one united Latin America, from Mexico to the Magellan Straits.

The change in Machu Picchu's fortunes has been stark, rising from obscurity to global must-see in less than a century – in 2007, it was named one of the world's New Seven Wonders. The site has also become a powerful symbol of the Peruvian nation, greater than the sum of its parts and, much like Che himself, a legend larger than life. *The Motorcycle Diaries* shows how, through his wide-ranging, eye-opening, soul-stirring travels across a continent, the legend was born.

Part Four:
Asia

Literary

Kabul

Where? Afghanistan
Which? *The Kite Runner* by Khaled Hosseini (2003)
What? Afghan capital and Silk Road city of ancient culture cut down by modern tragedy

Life picks itself up, shakes itself off and continues at the bazaar. Despite the ever-present mess and menace, crowds still throng to the pastry shops, spice sacks and rails of knock-off T-shirts – even in times of turmoil, one needs to dress and eat. People flow around the bloody, hook-hung carcasses and the severed sheeps' heads. They step around loaded wheelbarrows and the spewed pulp of pomegranates, oozing like entrails. They crouch on their haunches, haggle for phones and sit in cafés, sipping glasses of sweet black tea. They breathe in the smells of grilling lamb, diesel, dust and destruction – the intoxicating perfume of the ancient city and its current troubles . . .

The Kite Runner is as close to Afghanistan as most of us will ever get. This nation of harsh desert, breath-stealing mountains and tribal loyalties is one of the most dangerous in the world. But no government travel advisory precludes taking a trip there via the words of Khaled Hosseini, whose debut novel speaks of both the vibrancy of late-twentieth-century Afghanistan and the horrors that have torn it apart.

Kabul has existed for around 3,500 years. Tucked between the mighty Hindu Kush mountains, it was long a strategic stop for traders toting their silks and spices between Europe and Asia. It became capital of Afghanistan in 1776.

The Kite Runner begins in 1970s Kabul, the story of young friends Amir, a wealthy Pashtun, and Hassan, a poor Hazara, whose lives are shaped by loyalty, cowardice, ethnicity and political upheaval. Their passion is kite-fighting, which sees boys – always boys – send their missives of bamboo and bright tissue paper into the skies to do battle with other fliers. The string is coated with a resin of glue and crushed glass, rendering it sharp enough to cut down an opponent; running to collect the vanquished kite from where it falls is the ultimate trophy.

LITERARY 263

This early Kabul is a revelation. Not only is the air filled with playful, colourful kites, the city seems far from the extremist war zone its name conjures today. The Kabul of the 1950s, 60s and early 70s was surprisingly cosmopolitan and liberal in outlook. There were cocktails and short skirts; the foreigners browsing the bazaars weren't soldiers but hippies, who flocked to the 'Paris of Central Asia'. Hosseini was born in 1965 into this 'golden age' of culturally rich Kabul. He left in 1976 and was later forced into permanent exile in the USA.

The events that shaped the author's life also shape The Kite Runner. In 1973, the Communist PDPA staged a coup, Afghanistan's monarchy fell, revolution flared and, in 1979, the Soviet military invaded. Thousands fled to Pakistan and beyond – just like Amir and his father, Baba. After nine blood-soaked years, the Soviets withdrew and civil war erupted. In 1996, the Taliban took control, at first a welcome relief from the infighting. But then the fundamentalist laws rolled in. Thieves were punished by amputation. The 'un-Islamic' flying of kites was banned. Adulterers were stoned to death – in *The Kite Runner*, adult Amir witnesses such an atrocity during halftime at a football match, when he returns to Kabul in 2001. After years of living in the USA, Amir says Kabul is like 'running into an old, forgotten friend and seeing that life hadn't been good to him, that he'd become homeless and destitute'. The city he remembers has become a husk roamed by beggars, strewn with rubble, ruled by fear.

The Kite Runner ends in 2002 – after September 11 and the US invasion of Afghanistan. NATO officially ended its combat mission in the country in 2014, but the country remains complicated, the Taliban resurgent. So Kabul is dangerous – but life rolls on, as it must for those who have no choice. And boys may fly their kites again, over the rooftops and bomb craters, up towards the sun-scorched mountains. Flashes of colour against the dust and the debris, continuing the fight.

Foodie

Jeonju

Where? North Jeolla Province, South Korea
Why? Feast on the most colourful dish, to feed the stomach and the spirit

Bibimbap: it's like the most perfect edible pie chart. Each segment of the sizzling bowl bright and distinct. A consumable colour wheel – rice white, sunny yolk yellow, deep spinach green, danger-red chilli, inky-black mushrooms. But it's also a national philosophy in a dish, equal parts wisdom, health, history, aesthetics and tradition. A food for muscles, mind, gut, senses and soul . . .

Sitting in the southwest of the Korean Peninsula, Jeonju is a relatively small city of big substance. It was here, in the late fourteenth century, that King Taejo founded the Joseon Dynasty, which went on to rule Korea for more than 500 years. Jeonju is considered the country's spiritual capital, inextricably entwined with its history, and the site of some of its finest achievements. Not least in relation to food.

Jeonju – the 'Taste City' – is a UNESCO City of Gastronomy, renowned for its culinary heritage and quality local ingredients. Fertile mountains rise to the east, providing a diversity of farmed vegetables, wild fungi and foraged greens. A little west is the Yellow Sea, which serves up a bounty of fresh fish, shellfish and tangy seaweed. All around are the rich Honam Plains, the historic rice-basket of Korea. Everything is on hand to create mouth-watering dishes, of which the most beloved is bibimbap.

Bibimbap is Korea's signature dish, found countrywide – but perfected in Jeonju. To make the Jeonju version, rice is cooked in beef bone broth in a hot *dolsot* (stone bowl), then topped with a rainbow of ingredients – no fewer than ten, usually more like 30. These vary with the season but might include beansprouts, gingko nuts, chestnuts, *namul* (greens), shiitake mushrooms, carrots, turnips, seaweed, sliced raw beef, mung bean jelly and vibrant *gochujang*, a red chilli paste that might be fermented for several years. A raw egg is cracked on top, before being stirred through with chopsticks, the heat of the fiery pot cooking everything through.

266   ASIA

It looks divine, with all five cardinal colours (and elements) present, conferring their alleged health-boosting properties. White (metal) ingredients such as lotus roots, beansprouts and radishes are considered good for the lungs; black (water) components like bracken, mushrooms and laver seaweed are good for the kidneys; yellow (earth) produce such as squash and soybeans are good for the stomach; red (fire) carrots, peppers, gochujang and beef help the heart; green/blue (wood) elements like spinach and parsley improve liver function.

The idea of combining multiple, mostly vegetarian, items is nothing new here. It stems from the longstanding Korean culinary concept of *banchan* (side dishes). This may have developed as Buddhism spread across the region, from around the fourth century CE; for a time, the consumption of meat was banned. Or it may have been more of an economic imperative – meat was precious and expensive.

Either way, from around the tenth century, it became increasingly common for tables to heave with a colourful spread of small plates. Common concoctions include spicy cucumber salad, steamed aubergine, seasoned soybean sprouts and sautéed fiddlehead ferns. And there will always be kimchi, the punchy fermented cabbage dish – available in an array of varieties and levels of funkiness – that's integral to Korean life.

Jeonju offers both the greatest diversity and quality of banchan and the most thoughtfully prepared bibimbap – not to mention innovative twists on the original dish. The city even hosts an annual bibimbap festival every October, which combines food demos, cultural events and the cook-up of a giant bowl of bibimbap, fit to feed 400 people.

But even outside of the festival, no one goes unsated in Jeonju. The best place to graze is along the tight-packed, gingko-tree-lined streets of the city's *hanok* village. Many of its 800-odd *hanok* (traditional slope-roofed and wood-beamed houses) are now restaurants, cafés, guesthouses or artisan workshops – as well as being a capital of gastronomy, Jeonju is a Cittaslow hub, recognised for its efforts to preserve ancient traditions.

Look out for *hanji* (paper) makers and *makgeolli* bars, which sell this milky, lightly sparkling rice spirit in bright copper bowls. Then head to Nambu Market, a maze of mind-boggling eateries and food stalls, where you'll find just about anything it's possible to eat. Tuck into street food staples like *tteokbokki* (rice cakes) and shrimp dumplings; order things on skewers, from chicken to cheese to octopus; try *bingsu* (shaved ice) and nutty *beondegi* (boiled silkworm pupae); and put your faith in *danpatjuk* (sweet red bean porridge), purported to ward off bad spirits. But don't forget the bibimbap, Jeonju's most colourful creation.

Cinematic

Tokyo

Where? Japan
Which? *Lost in Translation* (Sofia Coppola, 2003)
What? Madcap capital of blazing lights, blaring machines, bustling crowds and unexpected silence

Bright lights, bleary eyes: jet-lagged new arrivals are smacked by this big, brash, brain-messing city. The world outside the window is a flashing, bleeping, blinding otherworld. A densely packed place of skyscraping glass and neon; of car-jammed tarmac pulsing through concrete canyons; of kanji characters and LCD screens glowing, scrolling, screaming, selling. A discordant land where, surrounded by a population of millions, it's possible to have never felt more alone . . .

Lost in Translation is the sort-of love story of American actor Bob Harris (Bill Murray), who travels to Japan to make a whisky advert while in the midst of a mid-life crisis, and young graduate Charlotte (Scarlett Johansson), who has accompanied her husband to Tokyo on a business trip and feels equally adrift. Both seem lost, not only within the unfamiliar metropolis but within their own lives. As such, the capital's Shinjuku and Shibuya districts – which represent modern Japan, dialled up to 11 – provide the ideal location for capturing just how alienating a foreign city and culture can be.

Shinjuku is Tokyo's business and entertainment nexus, and home to many of its tallest buildings – this is one of the few seismically stable areas in the earthquake-prone city. It's centred on Shinjuku Station, the world's busiest rail hub, through which 3.5 million passengers pass each day; it's surrounded by malls and department stores, and encompasses Kabukicho, Japan's craziest red light district. Shibuya lies just south of Shinjuku and is Tokyo's noisiest, lairiest, busiest ward, popular with hip young things and heaving with fashion stores, sushi bars, tiny *izakaya* (old-style pubs), neon nightclubs and love hotels, where guests pay by the hour.

Bob and Charlotte are both staying at Shinjuku's luxe Park Hyatt Tokyo, a high-end hangout of the rich and famous that occupies the

268   ASIA

upper 14 floors of a 52-storey tower. The plush lobby, the minimalist-chic rooms (with their wide window ledges, ideal for wistfully gazing out like Charlotte) and even the large 47th-floor swimming pool all feature in the film. But the most iconic place is the hotel's low-lit, smokey and jazz-cool New York Bar & Grill, right at the top, where the two meet. The views from up here, through the vast floor-to-ceiling windows, stretch right across the city, taking in the NTT Docomo Yoyogi Building (Tokyo's answer to the Empire State) and – on a clear day – even Mount Fuji. This is the place (if funds allow) to nurse a Suntory whisky, just like Bob, and listen to live music as the sun sets outside.

When the two lonely leads do leave the closed-off sanctuary of the hotel, they spend most of their time in the surrounding neighbourhoods. They take taxis past Yasukuni-dori avenue's avalanche of commercial neon. They sing into the small hours at the Shibuya branch of Karaoke-Kan (filming was done in rooms 601 and 602). They eat a dismal meal at Shabu-Zen, a Shibuya basement *shabu-shabu* restaurant where kimono-wearing ladies serve thin slices of raw beef that you cook in a hot pot yourself. Charlotte also visits Jogan-ji in Shinjuku, a peaceful Buddhist temple, off the beaten track, that dates back 600 years and nods to how this dynamic city still holds on to its spiritual past.

Bob and Charlotte also both negotiate Shibuya Crossing – the Times Square of Tokyo, located outside Shibuya Station's Hachiko exit. Up to 3,000 pedestrians scramble over this heaving intersection every time the lights change, while animated billboards flash on all sides. The crew grabbed their shots, filming guerrilla-style from the second-floor windows of the junction's Starbucks. It's still the best spot to look down on what's become a symbol of this unique city's ability to somehow impose order on chaos.

Lost in Translation could only have been made in Tokyo. It's only amid the confusing, intriguing, mesmerising maelstrom of this remarkable place – which somehow succeeds in combining the thrustingly modern and enduringly traditional – that Sofia Coppola's odd couple can find each other and themselves.

Literary

Kerala

Where? India
Which? *The God of Small Things* by Arundhati Roy (1997)
What? Lush South Indian state where love and tragedy brew amid the languid backwaters

The afternoon is heavy, hazy, lazy; the viscid air, damp as an unwrung sponge, awaits the imminent squeeze of the monsoon. For now, it's curry-hot, the sun beating indiscriminately on red ants and yellow bullfrogs, whooping coucals and long-legged lily-trotters. It glitters on the corpses of silver fish. It nurtures the mango and jackfruit. Then, finally, the sky cracks. The heavens empty onto Kerala. Under this deluge, the paddies, palm trees and plantations flush even greener. And the channels swell to their limits, no longer languid but deceptively angry. The sort of spate that might make bad things – small bad things, big bad things – occur . . .

Indian author Arundhati Roy trained as an architect, which perhaps shouldn't come as a surprise. Because her debut novel, *The God of Small Things*, is like a 2D blueprint conjured into 3D reality. Kerala oozes off its pages. It's less a book than a deep pool of colour, fragrance, heat, history and politics stirred by love and loss, sentences rippling like backwaters.

The novel, which won the 1997 Booker Prize, takes place largely in the village of Ayemenem, shifting in time between 1969 and 1993 in a series of flashbacks and foreshadowing. It follows boy and girl twins, Estha and Rahel, who live with their mother Ammu and her family – grandmother Mammachi, grand-aunt Baby Kochamma – and whose lives are upturned when their half-English cousin, Sophie Mol, drowns in the nearby river. The waterways that attract so many outsiders to this dream-like patch of the subcontinent – touted by the Keralan tourist board as 'God's Own Country' – become a deadly heart of darkness.

The book is as sensorially delicious as one of Mammachi's Paradise Pickles & Preserves. It is a mouth-waterer of banana jam, fresh coconut, hot *parippu vadas* (lentil fritters), cardamom and cinnamon, red fish curry, black tamarind. There are crows feasting on fat mangoes and

LITERARY 273

fireflies flickering in the darkness. There are vibrant saris and tucked-up *mundus*. There are shanty huts leaning into the heat and colonial, teak-shuttered bungalows with deep verandas where it's always cool. There is the 'sicksweet smell of old roses on a breeze'.

But *The God of Small Things* also draws bigger issues into focus. For around 3,000 years Indian society was shaped by the caste system. Among the world's oldest forms of social stratification, this class structure divided Hindus into four main groups: at the top, Brahmins (intellectuals), Kshatriyas (warriors and rulers), Vaishyas (traders) and Shudras (labourers). Outside of this were the Dalits or 'untouchables', the lowest of the low. Members of different castes lived apart, drank from separate wells, could not marry, often would not touch.

Although the Indian Constitution of 1950 outlawed the caste system and status-based discrimination, the old ways proved hard to shake. This long-standing hierarchy, which extended beyond Hinduism into wider society, persisted; unwritten rules continued to be upheld and individuals remained limited by their rank. Certainly in *The God of Small Things*, the caste system still determines what Roy calls the Love Laws: 'the laws that lay down who should be loved and how. And how much'. For Ammu, a higher-class Syrian Christian, to be in a relationship with the handyman Velutha – a Paravan, one of the 'untouchables' – is not conscionable at all. When the 'laws' are broken, tragedy ensues.

Ayemenem is a fictionalised version of Aymanam, in Kerala's Kottayam District, where Roy spent time as a child. The village name (meaning five forests) refers to the woodland that once thrived here, alongside the Meenachil River. Now paddy fields cloak much of the area and frenetic, traffic-jammed Kottayam town has seeped towards the old village, injecting greater bustle.

There are a few old Hindu temples to visit – the Vishnu-dedicated Sree Narasimha Swamy and mural-daubed Pandavam Shasta temples. However, you won't find an exact replica of the novel's 'Ayemenem House', though the building is not entirely made up. Roy borrowed parts of two family homes to construct her fictional nexus. Puliyampallil House and Shanti House stand on adjacent plots at the end of a path of rubber trees, along from the village school. Puliyampallil is a fine early-twentieth century home 'with its steep gabled roof pulled over its ears like a low hat', while Shanti dates from the 1960s. The river flows across the fields behind, towards Lake Vembanad.

The 'History House', where the book's most tragic events occur, is not on the other side of the river in the middle of an abandoned rubber estate. The real home of 'Kari Saipu' – aka Alfred Baker, one of a family of English missionaries who'd 'gone native', spoke Malayalam (Kerala's official language) and wore *mundus* – is actually a little way away, in the Kumarakom Bird Sanctuary. The Bakers developed the sanctuary in the mid-nineteenth century, and it's now a haven for Indian darters, white Ibis, Siberian cranes and other resident and migratory birds. The 'History House' bungalow is now part of the Taj Garden Retreat.

In her novel, Roy laments how Kerala has kowtowed to tourist tastes: the heritage buildings that are now hotels, the hours-long kathakali dances that have been abridged for impatient foreigners. It's true that *kettuvallam* houseboats now tote visitors rather than rice and spice along the backwaters. But while boarding one of these restored-for-tourists vessels for a slow cruise has become a cliché, it remains the best way to see Kerala – the best way to spot its wonderful small things.

Foodie

Sichuan

Where? Southwest China
Why? For eating on the edge, a challenge to preconceptions and tastebuds

This isn't just eating. It's oral electrification. Chopstick a carefully prepared morsel into your mouth here – a cube of tender tofu, fragrant pork slivers or ribbons of ox tongue – and your lips start to vibrate, a curious pins-and-needles tingle, akin to a jolt of 50 watts. They call this eating *ma la* – a pleasure-pain combination of numbing and spiciness. The soul of Sichuan cooking . . .

Sichuan Province sprawls across southwest China, sloping from the high mountains in the west into the upper Yangtze valley. Vast, damp and fertile, it's the country's breadbasket. It's also home to *chuancai*, one of the eight recognised schools of Chinese cuisine – and the best-loved.

The roots of Sichuan cuisine date back to the Qin and Han dynasties (from around 220 BCE), when China's distinctive cuisine types started to emerge and when influences from the northern and western regions began enhancing the food of the central plains. As new ingredients and ideas were introduced – first via the many-stranded Silk Road, later through sea-trading routes – the food culture continued to evolve.

The menu here already had heft, thanks to the liberal use of Sichuan pepper, a berry harvested from the prickly ash tree containing a compound – sanshool – that delivers the distinctive ma. But the arrival of chilli peppers from the New World in the late seventeenth century injected an extra kick that the Sichuanese fully embraced. Food has always been closely connected to medicine in China, and the Sichuan combination of heat and spices is thought to have detoxifying effects, helping to balance the body in the local climate, which can be oppressively humid in summer and then chilly in winter.

Today, *chuancai* is sweet, sour, bitter, spicy, pungent, aromatic and salty. There's a local saying: 'one dish, one style, a hundred dishes, a hundred flavours'. The true strength of Sichuan cuisine is its depth and diversity. It is fiery and bold, infused with the likes of fennel, aniseed,

FOODIE   277

cinnamon, clove, garlic, ginger and fermented bean pastes. It also features a mind-broadening array of ingredients – from stir-fried rabbit-heads to goose intestines – and challenging textures: silken, slippery, sinewy, cartilaginous.

The provincial capital is Chengdu, a modern metropolis that was founded on the plains by the Jin River as far back as the fourth century BCE. Known for its aeons-old teahouse culture and giant pandas (the Giant Panda Breeding Research Base is here), it is primarily a place of food. In 2010 it became the second UNESCO City of Gastronomy, a global acknowledgement of the breadth and sophistication of the region's cuisine, which numbers more than 6,000 dishes. This includes classic sweet-sour kung pao chicken, *yu xiang rou si* (fish fragrant pork slivers) and twice-cooked pork (the meat is boiled, then fried), which is said to have been served up at meetings of Sichuan's secret societies in pre-Communist days. Hot pots – when people gather around a boiling pot of broth and take turns dipping in wafer-thin pieces of meat and vegetables – are a millennia-old social-bonding tradition.

One of the most popular Sichuan staples is *mapo doufu* – pockmarked grandmother's tofu. This unappetisingly-named but rich, intense and fragrant speciality is said to date back to the 1860s. Some say it was invented by a blemished and outcast old woman who quickly conjured it up from her modest food cupboard when she received an unexpected visitor. Others reckon it was first made by smallpox-scarred Mrs Chen, who ran a restaurant in Chengdu – which still exists today on the Qinghua Road. Either way, it's the city's signature dish, comprising cubes of soft, tender tofu and ground meat stir-fried and then simmered with Sichuan peppercorns, *doubanjiang* (a spicy paste made from fermented broad beans) and chilli oil, which adds even more heat, plus the trademark redness. In China, red is an auspicious colour, symbolising luck, happiness and prosperity. With its *ma la* hit and layers of contrasting flavours, this is the ultimate in Sichuanese comfort eating.

Mount Fuji

Where? Japan
Which? *The Great Wave off Kanagawa* (c.1829) by Katsushika Hokusai
What? Nature's power before a sacred mountain

Even on the clearest of days, Mount Fuji, Japan's highest mountain and an active volcano, is usually enshrouded in mist and clouds. With its perfect conical shape, it has long been considered the sacred symbol of Japan and an essential part of national identity. In Buddhist and Daoist tradition, it was thought to hold the secret of immortality.

From a distance, Fuji can sometimes be seen in its full splendour during the colder months and in the early mornings or late evenings, when the air is clearest. Rising between Yamanashi and Shizuoka prefectures, it can be viewed from the window of the Shinkansen bullet train that runs from Tokyo to Osaka, and particularly from the Shin-Fuji station. It is actually a composite of three successive volcanoes: at the bottom is Komitake; in the middle is Ko Fuji (Old Fuji); and at the top is Shin Fuji (New Fuji). On its northern slopes are the Fuji Goko (Five Lakes), all formed by lava flows, and to the south-east are wooded areas and hot springs. As it is such a sacred place, it is surrounded by temples and shrines, and climbing to the shrine at the peak has long been a religious practice for Buddhists, Daoists and especially those who follow the Shinto religion. Every summer, mostly during July and August, thousands flock there, often setting out at night in order to reach the summit by dawn.

Famously, Mount Fuji has been captured as a majestic, remote spectacle in a series of woodblock prints created by the Ukiyo-e (Pictures of the Floating World) painter and printmaker, Katsushika Hokusai (1760–1849). Originally published between 1830 and 1833, his *Thirty-Six Views of Mount Fuji* depict Fuji in different seasons, weather conditions, times of day and from different locations. Hokusai was 70 when he began the series, and he added 10 more after the first 36 had been printed and were being sold, making it actually Forty-Six Views, only he kept the original title. Born in Edo (now Tokyo), Hokusai started painting when he was six years old and was nationally renowned before he created this series. He produced it both as a response to a domestic travel boom at the time and because he was obsessed with the sacred powers of Mount Fuji. The mountain appears in each view in different ways. Sometimes prominently in the centre, sometimes as background detail. The first five in the series were printed entirely in shades of blue (a combination of traditional indigo and Prussian blue, which was a recently invented chemical pigment), suggesting the mountain at dawn. Then more colours were added, including delicate and rosy pinks, warm greys and gold, to show the illumination of the world as the sun rises. His process of woodblock printing was complex and precise, requiring the use of a separate block for each individual colour.

Of all the 46 images, the most famous is *The Great Wave off Kanagawa*, which made Hokusai internationally recognised. The scene depicts three boats being threatened by a large wave in front of Mount Fuji. The huge wave about to break dominates the composition and creates a sense of tension. Amid the waves are three *oshiokuri-bune* (fast boats) that carry fish from the Izu and Bōsō peninsulas to the markets in the bay of Edo. Eight rowers are in each boat, each clinging to their oars, with two passengers in the front. The boats and figures convey the enormity of the wave and so the might and power of nature. In the foreground, a small wave forms the shape of a miniature Fuji and, through perspective, is larger than the distant mountain. Storm clouds hang in the sky, while the sun rises from behind, illuminating the mountain's snowy peak. A dark outline around Mount Fuji suggests that it is early morning. Hokusai's colours are restricted: three shades of blue for the water; yellow for the boats; dark grey for the sky behind Fuji and on the boat below; pale grey for the sky above Fuji and on the foreground boat; and pink clouds in the sky, glowing over the venerated distant mountain. Climbers can take any of the four challenging trails that lead to the summit of Mount Fuji. Once reaching the peak, the magnificent landscape stretches out before you; a view that inspired so many faithful followers and such an epic series of images.

Seoul

Where? South Korea

Why? Home of polished, pulsating pop that's found fans across the world

If music be the food of love, K-pop is the sugar-rush. It's like aural jellybeans, bright and kaleidoscopic, frothily irresistible, dizzyingly upbeat. All flawless faces, finger-hearts, waving glowsticks, big smiles, great hair. Sweet as *dalgona* sponge candy. But, for all its high-energy fizz, K-pop is no junk food. Production values are first-class, performances polished, dance moves razor-sharp – this is billion-dollar business. K-pop is the vanguard of *Hallyu*, the 'Korean Wave', the term coined for the explosion in popularity of contemporary Korean culture. It encompasses everything from movies and cartoons to video games, but music – K-pop – is the biggest hit. And the gateway drug into unpicking the culture of the country as a whole . . .

Back in the annals of Korean history, music wasn't merely entertainment, it was part of the dance between heaven and earth, a profound expression of the nation's soul. The rhythmic beats of traditional instruments like the *janggu* (hourglass-shaped drum) and the melodious *gayageum* (zither) echoed from grand palace to simple hanok house, weaving themselves into the fabric of everyday life. The poetic song genre of *gagok*, with its refined melodies and advanced composition, was so significant in helping to establish the Korean identity that it's now recognised on UNESCO's Intangible Cultural Heritage of Humanity list.

But it was in the latter half of the twentieth century that something clicked. A cultural renaissance swept through South Korea, fuelled by rapid industrialisation and a newfound global outlook. Traditional sounds collided with the influences of western pop, rock and hip-hop, igniting a musical revolution that burst beyond the country's borders, in a very big way.

The birth of contemporary K-pop can be traced to a specific date: 11th April 1992, when the Seoul-based group Seo Taiji and Boys performed on

TV for the first time. The band were pioneers, incorporating rap, dance moves, distinctive outfits and subversive lyrics that questioned and criticised strict social norms. They were huge. In the decades since, this uniquely Korean brand of popular music – with its infectious melodies, genre-blending style, insanely in-sync choreography and trendsetting looks – has achieved world domination.

The centre of it all is the South Korean capital, Seoul, a live-wire metropolis of nearly ten million people bestriding the Han River. It's a city of enduring ancient traditions that lie secreted among the gleaming skyscrapers, screaming billboards, mega-malls and karaoke bars. Trendy Gangnam, on the south side of the river, is ground zero of K-pop. The rapper Psy put it on the map for foreigners in 2012 with his kitschy, catchy 'Gangnam Style', a jab at the posers in this chi-chi neighbourhood. Gangnam is full of big-brand designer stores, high-rises, multiplexes and funky coffee shops, but also the leafy temple of Bongeun-sa, founded in 794 CE. It's also home to some of the most important K-pop pilgrimage sites.

The genre's most influential record labels are based in Gangnam's Apgujeong area, including SM Entertainment, JYP and Big Hit Entertainment, label of super-watt boy band BTS, the best-selling musical act in South Korean history. Legions of K-pop devotees camp out around these buildings, hoping to spy their idols – the name for K-pop's artists and groups. Some of the labels run their own cafés, where fangirls and boys can buy everything from idol-themed cupcakes and ramen to endless piles of merch. There are also chances to join K-pop dance classes, flashmobs and make-up lessons. Or be in the studio audience of a K-pop show, if you can secure a hot ticket – entry might be via lottery, fan-club membership, a long queue, or on production of a hard copy of a group's latest album and official glowstick. However, anyone can walk the K-Star Road on Apgujeong Rodeo Street. This is the 'Hallyuwood Walk of Fame', where the biggest idols are honoured with 'GangnamDols', cartoonish bears made human-size.

Mapo-gu is another neighbourhood for music-lovers to hit, especially its hip Hongdae district. This is where many of Seoul's universities are – and therefore its students; Hongdae bubbles with youthful energy, creativity and a rebellious spirit. Indeed, there is edgier music to be found in the bars and clubs here, but still, plenty of K-pop too. For instance, the sleek headquarters of YG Entertainment sits here; fans might catch a glimpse of idols like BigBang and Blackpink popping in. Or some might head to one of Hongdae's small music joints, hear K-pop trainees honing their craft, maybe spot the idols of the future.

Cinematic

Hong Kong

Where? China
Which? Enter the Dragon (Robert Clouse, 1973)
What? Pulsatingly modern island metropolis where kick-ass traditions can still be found

It's a city of blended contradictions: concrete high-rises dwarfing sweeping tiled roofs; noisy taxis vying with hand-pulled rickshaws; billionaires' yachts moored next to old wooden junks; the air filled with jumbo jets and temple gongs – as well as the high shrieks and fluid fighting wisdom of the first Asian superhero . . .

Hong Kong is where East meets West. Long part of the Chinese empire, then ceded to the British in 1842 following the first Opium War, this Pearl River Delta fishing-village-turned-metropolis is where centuries of Chinese heritage mix with the legacy of colonialism. It's where ancient lore meets modern commerce; where 'Oriental mystique' meets a degree of western familiarity. And it's where Enter the Dragon was made, the American–Chinese co-production that brought martial arts – and its star Bruce Lee – to the world.

As the city provides a gateway to Asian culture, so too did Lee. Born in San Francisco, but raised in Kowloon, he straddled both traditions and knew how to connect to both audiences – no mean feat when the Korean and Vietnam Wars had stigmatised Asian faces. Lee had some success in the US but returned to make Enter the Dragon, his greatest film.

In it, he plays Lee, a Shaolin monk recruited by British intelligence to spy on Mr Han (Shih Kien) – a cartoonishly villainous monk-turned-crime lord – by entering a martial arts competition on Han's private island. Lee travels to the tournament with a multicultural kung fu crew and proceeds to infiltrate Han's underground lair. He unleashes lightning-quick whoop-ass on an army of henchmen (played by hundreds of extras, some members of rival Hong Kong gangs with real scores to settle) and, finally, in a secret room of mirrors, on Han himself.

The city, old and new, is revealed in the first few scenes. There's the travel-brochure pan across the busy, skyscraping business districts of

Admiralty and Central, and iconic Victoria Harbour. But there's also the sea-breeze and birdsong of hillside Tsing Shan Monastery, the city's oldest temple, founded, they say, in the fifth century by a monk who sailed from India in a wooden cup; it's here, in the leafy grounds, that Lee discusses philosophy, weaving his own interpretation of Chinese thinking into this Hollywood action flick.

Aberdeen Harbour, from where the junk leaves for Han's island, was traditionally home of the boat-living Tanka people and remains a thrilling hive of activity where life is still largely lived on the water. You'll find a whole village of houseboats strung with laundry and drying fish, hotel-size floating restaurants, a seafood market and women punting sampans with babies strapped to their backs, still keen to offer a ride.

The city of Hong Kong comprises the Kowloon Peninsula and over 260 islands. So it's fitting that Han's base should lurk out in the harbour somewhere – though in the movie it's no one place, but an amalgam of several. The aerial shot is of lush, uninhabited Kau Yi Chau isle. The fortress supposedly looming there is striking King Yin Lei, a 1930s red-brick, green-roofed mansion back on Hong Kong Island that is a rare surviving example of Chinese Renaissance style. Another East–West hybrid, King Yin Lei is now a designated official monument and is opened occasionally for guided visits.

The island's dock, where Lee lands, is really at Tai Tam Bay, on Hong Kong Island's south coast. You can still see the pebbly beach, granite overhang and little pillbox (there was heavy fighting here during the 1941 Battle of Hong Kong). New development has subsumed the land immediately behind but the wider Tai Tam Country Park is a lovely place to hike alongside streams and into densely wooded hills. This contrast sums up Hong Kong: a pulsing urban centre and a coastal wilderness; a city of two sides, bridging worlds – just as *Enter the Dragon* did, spanning America and Asia, East and West, to become the most influential kung fu movie of all time.

Foodie

Where? Karnataka, India
What? The pilgrim town that became a whole, wholesome way of eating

Food for the gods, food for the people. Udupi cuisine began as ambrosia for divine beings and is now fuel for a nation of over a billion people. Simple, seasonal, nutritious, harmonious, it's served to priests and paupers alike . . .

Located on the Arabian Sea coast, Udupi is both a small city and a big culinary movement; a temple town whose creations have spread from its holy kitchens out across Karnataka state and the country beyond. Udupi is no longer just a place, it's a brand name for well-balanced, plant-based, soul-nourishing South Indian food.

Long a place of pilgrimage, Udupi's importance grew with the founding of the Shri Krishna Temple in the thirteenth century. According to legend, it was here that the Hindu philosopher Shri Madhvacharya discovered a flawless image of Krishna – the Hindu god of food – inside a lump of yellow clay. He built a shrine to house it; 700 years later, a bustling complex of eight *mathas* (monasteries) flank the primary pyramidal temple. It is one of South India's most sacred sites, believed to hold the *sannidhya* (essence) of Krishna himself.

In the past, devotees worried that this adventurous young deity might simply up and leave. So, to convince him to stay, they began presenting the sacred idol with an elaborate array of treats. Today, this *naivedya* (food offering) is given at 14 separate *puja* (worships). These are performed by the temple's swami, starting at 5.30 a.m., finishing at 8.50 p.m., and each involving rituals such as the flapping of fly-whisks and *aarati* (the circulating of flames).

Betel nut, jaggery sugar, tender coconut and copper pots brimful with steaming rice are proffered along with dishes cooked up by Shivalli Brahmin priests. They toil away from pre-dawn in a spotlessly clean kitchen; slicing, chopping, shredding, steaming and stirring vast piles of local-grown gourds and pumpkins, jackfruit and coconut, pulses and

FOODIE 289

grains – the temple uses 5,000kg (11,000lb) of rice a day. Cauldrons of sweet-sour rasam soup simmer, steam rises from tangy lentil sambar stew, platters are piled with cooling *kosambari* salad. All staples of what has become known as Udupi cuisine.

The kitchen doesn't feed only Krishna. Every day a free meal is served to hungry visitors in the simple *bhojanshala* dining hall – a slurry of rice, sambar, veg curry, rasam and *payasam* (sweet milk pudding) dolloped onto metal plates or banana leaves. The dishes offered to the deity himself end up as lunch for the head priest and any visiting VIPs.

Respectful non-Hindus are allowed into the temple complex. They can breathe in the cumin, sandalwood and incense-scented air and wander amid the musicians, pilgrims, sacred cows and prayer bead-sellers. They can receive blessings at the Kanakana Kindi, a peephole through which Krishna is said to have revealed himself to a low-caste devotee in the sixteenth century. And they can eat with the masses – on a regular day, the dining hall might serve 6,000 people; on a festival day, perhaps 10,000 or more.

However, while the Shri Krishna temple is ground zero for Udupi cuisine, the cooking style has long since escaped its confines. In the early twentieth century, as a number of Shivalli Brahmin sought wage-paying employment elsewhere, they took their recipes to big cities and found jobs doing the only thing they knew: cooking. Setting up in burgeoning hubs like Mumbai and Bangalore, they began offering wholesome, low-cost vegetarian food that adhered to the principles of a sattvic diet – non-sattvic ingredients such as tomatoes, onions, cauliflower and carrot don't feature. Simple restaurants, called 'udupis', sprang up, making a hundred styles of sambar, *ajadinas* (dry curries), *pathrode* (hot rolled and spiced colocasia leaves), sugary *holidge* (sweet flatbreads), chutneys and pickles. Many also serve crisp and golden crêpe-like dosas – also thought to originate in Udupi – as well as pancake-thick *uttapam* and soft, puffy *idlis* (steamed rice cakes). Known for being open to diners of all castes, udupis became one of the most popular cheap-eat choices in the country – and remain so to this day.

Saigon (Ho Chi Minh City)

Literary

Where? Vietnam
Which? The Quiet American by Graham Greene (1955)
What? Historic Vietnamese avenue evoking exoticism and espionage

The heat hangs thick as a shroud. Only the beer is cool. Sipping slowly, you gaze at the road, screwing your eyes against the flat, fierce sun – and against the passage of time. Trishaw bells are now drowned by waspish motorcycles; Versace and Burger King have replaced the silk stores and milk bars. But this old thoroughfare – with its vestiges of vintage grandeur, its constant ebb and flow – still feels like the epicentre of Saigon. A street where blood and secrets were once spilt over seven o'clocktails; where privileged outsiders chewed over the fate of a nation . . .

The rue Catinat is one of the oldest streets in Saigon, and one that's had many identities. Originally Sixth Road, in 1865 the French rechristened it Catinat after the warship that helped them conquer Indochina – an unsubtle reminder of who was now in control. After Vietnamese independence from France in 1954, the name was changed to Tu Do (Freedom) Street, and soon thronged with American GIs who took the freedom at face value. After the Vietnam War, the Vietcong titled it Dong Khoi (Uprising) Street – the name it still bears today.

But it was Catinat when Graham Greene was working as a war correspondent in the city from 1951 to 1954. And it's this incarnation of the street – opium steeped, battle scarred, on the cusp of change – that forms the spine of *The Quiet American*. Greene's tale of world-weary British journo Thomas Fowler, his Vietnamese girlfriend Phuong and the titular US government worker Alden Pyle is a love triangle, murder mystery and political parable set against the backdrop of the First Indochina War. Most of the conflicts between French forces

292   ASIA

and the communist Viet Minh occurred in northern Vietnam, but the whole country was affected, including far-south Saigon; including the glamorous expat enclave of rue Catinat.

Greene's Saigon is dangerous, languorous and vividly exotic. Beautiful girls cycle in white silk trousers, locals in 'mollusc hats' shoulder pole-slung baskets and fortune-tellers squat under trees with soiled packs of cards. It's vermouth cassis, opium smoke and the constant dice clicks of games of quatre cent vingt-et-un. Today, rue Catinat/Dong Khoi isn't so evocatively other. Big brands and sleek malls have moved in. But glimmers of the past remain.

At the top end of Dong Khoi, on Paris Square, sit the red-brick Notre-Dame Cathedral – 'hideous', according to Greene – and the Central Post Office, a handsome colonial relic with its barrel-vaulted hall and historic maps of South Vietnam and Saigon.

Heading southeastwards down the street, past shiny banks and the occasional old building, you reach the Continental. Built in 1880, this classic hotel is where Fowler always has his 6 p.m. beer on the terrace, and where he first meets Pyle; the bar is indoors and air-conditioned these days, though a handful of tables line the pavement. Greene himself used to stay here, in corner room 214, believing it best placed to observe the happenings down in Lam Son square. In *The Quiet American*, Lam Son (the Place Garnier) is where a deadly car bomb explodes. It's also home of Phuong's favourite milk bar, which Greene based on the real Givral Café – lately demolished to make way for the Union Square mall.

Further down, at 8 Dong Khoi, is the dome-topped Grand Hotel. Dating from the 1930s, this colonial-style edifice had been converted into rented apartments during Greene's tenure, and served as the model for Fowler's room over the rue Catinat. After a renovation in 1998, the Grand is now one of the city's grandest; hard to imagine the opium smoke and black-trousered women chattering on the landings now.

At 7 p.m., Fowler – like so many of Saigon's burnt-out expats – would head to the Rooftop Bar of the Majestic. You can still do the same. The hotel opened in 1925 and remains the best place to be at sundown, to sip a cocktail in the cool, unchanging breeze from the Saigon River.

LITERARY 293

Foodie

Osaka

Where? Honshu, Japan
Why? Fast food done deliciously

It's not the prettiest Japanese picture but it is mouth-watering. Down neon streets, billboards flash at migraine-inducing levels, each screeching: eat here, eat here! Barbecue smoke and broth steam scent the air, sending bellies crazy. So much so that thoroughfares are clogged with snake-like queues of the insatiably hungry, chomping things on sticks, squatting with trays of sticky deliciousness. And then going back for more . . .

Sitting on the shores of the Seto Inland Sea, on Honshu's south coast, Osaka – Japan's third-largest city – throbs to its own beat. It's grittier, messier, chattier, more irreverent than the rest of this stereotypically formal, buttoned-up country. It seems to take itself less seriously. And it likes to eat.

Osaka is known as *tenka no daidokoro* – 'the country's kitchen'. The city dates back to the fifth century, but this moniker stems from the Edo Period (1603–1868), when the new Tokugawa shogunate moved its base to Edo (now Tokyo) and Osaka flourished as a trading port. Osaka was well placed: surrounded by crop-growing plains and fertile mountains; at the intersection of key sailing routes; and handily close to Kyoto, still the seat of the emperor.

Warehouses were built and goods were brought from across the country and stored here before being shipped on. The most important cargo was rice, which was used to pay taxes and measure the status of feudal lords. Also key was *kombu*, the sought-after sea kelp that gives Japanese food its deep umami punch. Later, Osaka would trade further afield; it became the main international gateway of this closed-off nation, a place of commercial and cultural exchange. And with every imaginable ingredient stacked in its store cupboards and a vast population of merchants and labourers to feed, Osaka's chefs got to work.

Tellingly, the city motto is *kuidaore*, variously translated as 'eat till you drop' or 'to spend so much on food you descend into financial ruin'.

FOODIE 295

It's true, exquisite dishes garlanded with awards are found in profusion – between them, its restaurants hold more than 90 Michelin stars. But Osaka doesn't have to be so ruinous on the wallet. The real taste of the city is its fast food.

Delicious and ubiquitous, *takoyaki* (octopus doughnuts) were invented here in the 1930s. At open-fronted stalls you can watch chefs pour fluffy wheat-flour batter into dimpled cast-iron griddles, fill them with diced octopus, crunchy tempura scraps, pickled ginger and spring onion, then artfully prod, poke and spin the mix into balls with a cocktail stick. When done, they are slathered in sweet brown sauce and Japanese mayo and sprinkled with dried bonito flakes. They're best eaten while piping hot, in one bite, the chewy exterior erupting into a scalding, gooey middle with a tender seafood chunk inside.

Follow this with *okonomiyaki* – literally 'what you like, grilled', but more specifically a frittata-thick pancake, made with flour and egg batter. It's said to have become popular during the Second World War, when rice was in short supply and alternatives were sought after. As the name suggests, any ingredient goes, but the typical Osaka version usually involves everything – shredded cabbage plus pork, cheese, shrimp or wasabi – being combined into the batter, which is fried and flipped in front of you on a teppanyaki (hot plate) and served with a dark, thick sauce.

To complete the mouth-watering 'Big Three' of Osakan fast food, finish with *kushikatsu*, bamboo skewers of breaded, deep-fried vegetables, fish and meat, served with a brown dipping sauce. A quick, easy, cheap snack for busy workers, they are found being fried on most street corners.

But while there is food everywhere in Osaka, Dotonbori is ground zero. This is the old-meets-new entertainment district, founded 400 years ago on the banks of the Doton canal and now a blaze of giant billboards and high-rises crammed cheek-by-jowl with restaurants, dumpling shops, basement *izakaya* bars, jazz clubs, *kabuki* theatres and street stalls. Come after dark to see the lights reflected in the water and to eat your way through the night.

Mumbai

Where? India
Which? The Lunchbox (Ritesh Batra, 2013)
What? Tumultuous megapolis where, somehow, there is a system of order in the chaos

The sweaty, smutty morning rumbles to life: a cock crows, bicycle bells jangle, rickshaw horns shriek, car exhausts splutter, a train, another train, then another train wheezes by, disgorging hordes onto packed platforms – commute o'clock, people legion as pigeons. And amid it all, another flock: an army of men – white-capped, pure-purposed – working their delicious, precious loads expertly around the crowds to ensure no one misses their lunch . . .

Mumbai is mayhem. A megacity of over 20 million, with India's richest and poorest all squashed in. It's a city of commotion and contradictions, of monsoonal downpours and beating heat, of oppressive crowds and aching loneliness. It's also the frenzied backdrop to writer-director Ritesh Batra's old-fashioned, modern-set romance, in which neglected young housewife Ila (Nimrat Kaur) and taciturn widower Saajan (Irrfan Khan) strike up a chaste, epistolary relationship via a rare mishap in Mumbai's mind-boggling *dabbawala* lunch-delivery system.

It began in 1890, when a Mumbai banker employed a Wakari village boy to bring a homecooked lunch to his office each day. The concept caught on: such an ethnically diverse city – crammed with Hindus, Muslims, Buddhists, Parsis and Jains – meant many workers preferred homecooking to restaurants due to their varied dietary needs. Soon that entrepreneurial boy had enlisted others from his village. Today, there are around 5,000 *dabbawalas* (literally 'one who carries a box'), delivering 200,000 lunches every day.

The Lunchbox thrusts us into the melee. We follow a tiffin tin on its improbable, multi-stage journey from doorstep to final destination – real-life *dabbawalas* were filmed performing this feat of logistics. Watching them, you're right there, in Mumbai's bewildering din; in its curry-sweat-dirt-diesel fug. The *dabbawalas* operate across the city,

298   ASIA

from Virar to Churchgate, Ambernath to Dadar. Head to any one of these stations and you might catch the moving miracle of these men in their Gandhi caps and white *kurtas* (smocks) sorting wooden trays of tiffin tins by their colour coding and alpha-numeric symbols, carrying them on their heads, loading them into jute bags and onto the handlebars of pushbikes before weaving away down traffic-clogged streets. Or contact the official Mumbai Dabbawala association, which offers a 'Day with Dabbawala' experience so that you can follow the whole operation at close quarters.

The movie works on the basis that one of these tins goes awry. In an attempt to rekindle her ailing marriage, Ila makes her husband ever-better dishes – paneer kofta, bitter gourd curry, her grandmother's spring apple sabzi – but rather than being delivered to him, these loving lunches mistakenly end up on Saajan's desk. In truth this is unlikely: a 2010 Harvard University study analysed the *dabbawala* system and concluded, incredibly, that just one in four million lunchboxes is ever sent to the wrong address.

As well as the mouthwatering immersion of tracking food around the city, *The Lunchbox* puts one of Mumbai's oldest neighbourhoods on the screen. Saajan lives in the West Mumbai suburb of Bandra, close to the Arabian Sea, in a place called Ranwar Village. Founded in the seventeenth century and now heritage-listed, Ranwar is an old, low-rise hamlet holding out against the encroaching skyscrapers. It remains Catholic dominated, and is full of churches (including Mount Carmel, where Saajan visits his wife's grave), narrow lanes and Indo-Portuguese cottages draped in bougainvillea. It has also become a canvas for street art, especially the work of the Bollywood Art Project, who have been daubing Ranwar's flaking walls with Indian movie legends; this includes a mural of Irrfan Khan, who died in 2020, painted close to where his character lived.

The Lunchbox details the quiet, special bond formed by two lonely souls, who – despite Mumbai's crowds, clamour and chaos – find each other and become exactly what the other needs. Who become proof that, even here, 'the wrong train can get you to the right station'.

Part Five:

Australasia

Melbourne

Where? Victoria, Australia
What? A metropolis of migrants, each adding their own spice to the mix

The caramel aroma of fresh-ground coffee dances with warm pizza dough, griddled roti and buttery croissants, with steaming fish dumplings, berebere spice and hot meat pies oozing beef gravy. The flavours of the globe infuse the streets of Australia's second-biggest city; here, a modern food culture thickens in a crucible of colonialism, conflict, exile, escape, fortune-seeking and entrepreneurial spirit . . .

Melbourne is a city of around five million people, over a third of whom were born overseas. The Victorian capital has the tenth-largest immigrant population of any city in the world, with residents hailing from more than 200 different countries. They speak over 230 languages, practise more than 110 religions – and all have different tastes in food. It is this staggering diversity that has made Melbourne one of the most tantalising smorgasbords on the planet.

The traditional owners of the region are the Kulin people, who've lived on the shores of Port Phillip Bay and around the Yarra River for over 40,000 years. Their diet was dictated by the environment and seasons. They gathered edible plants and flowers, hunted kangaroo, possum and birds, fished for eels, yabbies and crustaceans. The land was their larder.

Then, in 1788, Europeans arrived in Australia. They began exploring the Port Phillip Bay area from the early nineteenth century. In 1837, Melbourne was named; the first immigrants to sail directly from Britain arrived there in 1839. The first wave of incomers were largely Anglo-Celtic and brought with them their traditional tastes for the likes of beef, lamb, sugar and bread. When gold was discovered in Victoria in the 1850s, Melbourne became a boomtown. A torrent of prospectors flowed in from all over – and needed to be fed.

A notable number of these hopeful new arrivals were Chinese, largely from the country's southern Kwangtung Province. Many decided it was more lucrative to set up restaurants serving Cantonese-style dishes

302   AUSTRALASIA

– to remind their compatriots of home – rather than actually panning for gold. Gradually, Little Bourke Street filled with Chinese herbalists, grocers and cookshops. Now Melbourne's Chinatown is the longest continuous Chinese settlement in the western world. Crimson lanterns dangle above a line-up of dim sum canteens, yum cha brunch spots and white-clothed Cantonese restaurants as well as a cosmopolitan array of Thai, Malaysian, Japanese and even German additions. There's no one dish to try, though alongside classics expect invention: wontons stuffed with pork and peanut butter, *xiao long bao* dumplings with a hint of truffle, barramundi topped with *lap cheong* (Chinese sausage).

The next significant wave of immigrants (and flavours) came after the Second World War, as displaced people from across Europe were encouraged to boost the Australian population. This included Italians and Greeks who brought gyros, souvlaki and spanakopita, pasta, gelato and pizza, all made in authentic ways but, over time, tweaked for local tastes. They also brought good coffee and, with it, a new kind of café culture. Now, Melbourne is considered the coffee capital of the world, and brewing here is akin to a religious ritual, requiring the finest beans, the proper equipment and the expert skills of trained baristas. The drink is ideally served in a space that's shabby-chic or minimalist, although customers still flock to the red-vinyl bar stools of Pellegrini's, established on Bourke Street in 1954 and still serving espresso today.

The end of the Vietnam War in 1975 resulted in millions of South-East Asians fleeing the communist takeover of South Vietnam. Many sought asylum in Melbourne. That means it's easy to pick up seriously good Vietnamese food here, such as crisp *banh khot* pancakes, unctuous pork bun cha or bulging *banh mi* baguettes. From the 1980s, they were joined here by the first major influx of African refugees, largely Ethiopians escaping the Derg military junta. Little Africa is the place to scoop up fiery, peppery curries with injera flatbreads, chow down on *tibs* (cubed meat) and drink coffee the Ethiopian way: poured from a *jebena* clay pot into small cups, in three servings.

Many more cultures have added their spice to the Melbourne mix. So perhaps the best place to taste it all is Queen Victoria Market. Built on the site of the Old Melbourne Cemetery, the market officially opened in 1878 and has been feeding the city ever since. It sprawls over two blocks and has 600-plus stalls, from Greek, Polish, French and African delis to counters cooking up Turkish borek, American doughnuts, German bratwurst and Japanese sando sandwiches. All the flavours rubbing along together, innovating for an open-minded and adventurous clientele eager to savour the world, with a Melbournian twist.

FOODIE   303

Cinematic

Karekare Beach

Where? New Zealand
Which? The Piano (Jane Campion, 1993)
What? Wild sweep of sand, where noisy nature meets pioneer spirit

White rollers crash in, frothing and furious, pounding the dark crags and black sands into submission. It's a crescendo of nature – violent, deafening. The angry voice of a sea that is carrying an unspeaking woman to a harsh, far-distant world . . .

If *The Lord of the Rings* movie trilogy portrayed New Zealand at its most magical, *The Piano* shows it at its most real. This haunting period romance winds back to colonial times when Aotearoa was no enviable holiday spot but rather a place of hardship: isolated, untamed, fierce.

The film is set in the mid-nineteenth century – the exact date is unspecified. We don't know, for instance, if it is before or after the 1840 Treaty of Waitangi, New Zealand's founding document, which promised to protect Maori culture and give the right of governance to the British Crown. The location is unspecified too. It is simply somewhere in the bush, by the coast, a slurry of mud and rain, wild and slightly sinister, also a little enchanted, verging on primeval. Unfamiliar birds sing through the tangled supplejack vines, the mosses and ferns and the thick forests of tawa, rimu and kauri trees. And there are Maori, wearing *moko* (tattoos), speaking their own tongue and paddling their *waka* (canoes) – though, reduced to secondary characters, their function seems mainly to help signify the otherness of this land.

Into this land arrive Ada McGrath (Holly Hunter), her young daughter Flora (Anna Paquin) and her beloved piano. Ada, who hasn't spoken since she was six, has been sold off by her father, forced to leave Scotland to marry emotionally cold frontiersman Alisdair Stewart (Sam Neill). Still confined inside her civilised bonnet and crinoline, Ada is rowed ashore with Flora and left on a black cliff-backed beach that might as well be the edge of the earth, their tiny, fragile forms dwarfed by the elemental enormity of nature.

CINEMATIC   305

When Stewart appears, he decides the piano is too cumbersome to bother carrying to his house inland, so leaves it there, at the mercy of the wind and waves. It's a haunting image: the instrument inside the wooden crate, abandoned on the desolate sands. It seems emblematic of Ada's loneliness and vulnerability. It's also a symbol of the European expansionist quest.

In the end, Stewart trades the piano to George Baines (Harvey Keitel) – a rougher-around-the-edges type who's gone slightly 'native'. Ada is livid but strikes a strange, unsettling bargain with Baines in order to get it back. There follows a story of love, repression, sexual obsession, expression beyond words.

A few different farm estates on New Zealand's North Island were used to create the miry woodlands where Stewart and Baines live. But the most memorable location is the dramatic beach on which Ada first washes up. This is Karekare, an isolated strand and rural settlement (population circa 270 people) fringing the Waitakere Ranges. Despite its in-the-booay feel, Karekare is only a short drive west of Auckland, New Zealand's biggest city. Surfers come to ride the swells, others to visit the waterfall just inland or simply to stride along the shore.

The rugged landscapes here were formed millions of years ago by the ructions of a huge undersea volcano. The Waitakere Ranges are what remains of the volcano's upthrusted and eroded eastern flank; Karekare's great Watchman rock and pyramidal Paratahi Island, which sits offshore, also remain, in defiance of the indefatigable Tasman Sea.

The Karekare area was occupied from the thirteenth century. In the seventeenth century the Te Kawerau ā Maki settled here, building a *pa* (hillfort) on the Watchman, planting kumara and fishing from the rocks. But in 1825 they were attacked by the Ngapuhi, a Northland tribe armed with muskets who slaughtered almost the entire community. After this, Karekare earned a second name: Mauaharanui, the Place of the Great Wrongdoing. A dark history that seems an apt match for this melancholy yet mesmerising film.

Tahiti

Where? French Polynesia
Which? *Where Do We Come From? What Are We? Where Are We Going?* (1897) by Paul Gauguin
What? Exotic, allegorical meanings in dense, tropical surroundings

Trees top-heavy with bananas and giant flowers greet you. Glorious colours and perfumes pervade; a blend of coconut, hibiscus, jasmine, ginger, frangipani, vanilla and the lemony scent of the national tiare flower. Even in the early morning, the warmth is palpable. A gentle breeze hovers expectantly, sometimes warm and humid, sometimes mild and light, and always heavy with fragrant floral notes.

With high mountains, coral reefs, turquoise lagoons, palm-fringed beaches, tropical vegetation and sparkling waterfalls, the islands of Tahiti in the South Pacific Ocean, epitomise the luxuriance of the tropics. Papeete, the capital, is a lively, bustling port with markets selling local produce and a mix of languages. Leaving his wife and children, this is where Paul Gauguin (1848–1903) arrived in June 1891 from Paris, in search of artistic regeneration. An inherent traveller, Gauguin lived in Peru, Martinique, Paris, Arles and Copenhagen. After joining the merchant navy, he sailed the seas from Le Havre to Rio de Janeiro, and on returning to Paris, worked as a stockbroker for 11 years. But his early travels left him with a loathing of modern cities, and he yearned for mystical, distant lands where he could immerse himself in ancient cultures, abundant nature and simple living. However, his romantic image of Tahiti as an untouched paradise was dashed when he saw the extent of French colonisation there. He had moved to Tahiti in search of new, exciting motifs and to escape European civilisation, and was disappointed that it was not what he had dreamed of.

Gauguin spent the first few months in Papeete, then moved approximately 45 kilometres (28 miles) down the coast to the remote village of Mataiea. There, he lived in a native-style bamboo hut with no windows and a roof made of pandanus leaves, close to the beach,

308 AUSTRALASIA

surrounded by tropical vegetation, shaded from the sultry heat. From the door of his hut, Gauguin could see the distant mountains at the centre of the island, and from the beach, he could see the peninsula of Taiarapu. Mataiea was quiet, inhabited only by natives to the island, and so was closer to the island life he had hoped for. Almost as soon as he arrived, using a palette of tropical colours, he began painting images of Tahitian life.

Although Tahiti became Gauguin's home for most of the last 12 years of his life, he stayed there for just two years on his first visit, producing paintings that broke with traditionally accepted art. They included richly coloured, flat-looking idyllic landscapes and evocative figures, suggesting mystical notions through his own personal symbolism. Due to increasing poverty, he used coarse canvases and thinly applied paint, and his imagery emulated local Oceanic styles, with a deliberately crude, naïve appearance. With darkly outlined, sinuous contours, his palette of jewel-bright colours convey joy, serenity, mystery and hope. In order to communicate an extra sense of exoticism to European viewers, he gave his works Tahitian titles, such as Fatata te Miti (By the Sea) and Manao Tupapau (The Spirit of the Dead Watching), both of 1892.

In 1897, Gauguin painted his largest work. With *Where Do We Come From? What Are We? Where Are We Going?* he aspired to compare with great fresco painters of the past, including Giotto. Calling the vast painting his 'testament', he explored the human condition and his personal struggle with the meaning of existence. In three main sections, the painting presents Tahiti as an earthly Garden of Eden. The first part represents Eve as an old woman holding her head, conveying the guilt of humanity. Towards the centre, a figure picks fruit, referencing the Tree of Knowledge and the forbidden fruit of the Old Testament. On the right, a baby suggests new beginnings. In the background is the vibrant vegetation of Tahiti, including flowers, plants and banana trees.

In 1901, Gauguin moved to Atuona on the island of Hiva Oa, in the Marquesas Islands, where today you can visit a reconstruction of his two-storey thatched home in the Paul Gauguin Cultural Centre. He died there in 1903 and was buried in the local Calvary Cemetery, situated at the top of a steep hill, but the climb is worth it as once there, you can enjoy spectacular views of the bay below.

Literary

Hanging Rock

Where? Victoria, Australia
Which? *Picnic at Hanging Rock* by Joan Lindsay (1967)
What? Sinister Australian formation where literature has created a new legend

There is the Rock – shrouded in mist, shrouded in mystery. It's an anachronism in the bush, spewed from the earth's belly but now rising from the plains like a man-made Gothic castle of towers and crenellations. At first the Rock seems empty, but really it scuffles and creeps: snakes coiled, wallabies hunched, grubs rifling the rotten bark, koalas and kookaburras in the eucalyptus trees. And something else. Something that haunts the inky hollows, something that seems able to stop clocks, chill bones and call young girls to their doom . . .

Hanging Rock looms large in both the landscape and psyche of Australia. Rare and formidable, it is a mamelon, a mound of stiff magma that erupted, congealed and contracted around six million years ago, and has subsequently weathered to become 'pinnacled like a fortress'. But Hanging Rock is more than a geological quirk. It's become a national symbol of the strange, a place where anything might happen – thanks to Joan Lindsay's classic novel.

According to Lindsay, *Picnic at Hanging Rock* came to her in a series of dreams, so vivid that when she woke she could still sense the breeze blowing through the gum trees and the laughter resounding through the hot air. It tells the story of a fateful boarding-school outing to Hanging Rock on Valentine's Day 1900. Four girls and one of the mistresses disappear without a trace, up-turning life at Appleyard College and sending ripples through the wider community. As the book continues, and the mystery remains unsolved, so the 'shadow of the Rock [grows] darker and longer . . . a brooding blackness solid as a wall'.

The Rock was a place of loss long before Lindsay's novel. From the 1830s its traditional owners – the Dja Dja Wurrung, Woi Wurrung and Taungurung tribes – were eradicated from the area, either murdered, killed by disease or forced into Aboriginal reserves. Their ancestors

LITERARY 311

had lived on this land for more than 25,000 years and felt deep connections with what they called Ngannelong; initiation ceremonies and corroborees were held here, important rituals that connected indigenous people to their creator-spirits. Yet in an instant those ancient bonds were severed by European colonisers who'd been here no more than 50 years. Hanging Rock had always been viewed as special, even supernatural; now it was laced with tragedy. The perfect setting, then, for Lindsay's puzzling, terrible tale.

Some readers have become so obsessed with the myth of the missing girls that, for many, it's become reality. Lindsay herself was ambiguous. In a brief prologue she states: 'Whether *Picnic at Hanging Rock* is fact or fiction my readers must decide for themselves'. Either way, the monstrous Rock is just as described. Located northwest of Melbourne, a little north of Mount Macedon, it rises 105 metres (345 feet) from the Hesket Plains, as extraordinary now as when Miranda, Irma and the rest of the Appleyard girls laid eyes on it over a century ago.

The schoolgirls, surely sweltering in their prim lace collars, corsets and petticoats, travel to Hanging Rock in a covered drag. You'll no longer kick up fine red dust as you drive the Melbourne–Bendigo road but you could pause, as they did, for refreshment in the village of Woodend – the 1896-built hotel is still a serving brewhouse. And, as you drive, you'll still look out at the lines of stringy bark trees, cloud-tufted Mount Macedon and, eventually, the terrible bulk of Hanging Rock itself, which sits within Hanging Rock Recreation Reserve.

Like drag-driver Mr Hussey, you could go to the horse races here – the first official meeting was held at the Hanging Rock track in 1886, and continues twice a year, on New Year's Day and Australia Day. The Reserve also encompasses a visitor centre and, of course, picnic grounds where, like the girls, you can spend an afternoon in exquisite languor, dozing and dreaming, breathing in the wattle and eucalypt, basking with the lizards. There are hiking trails too, leading under the boulders, along precipices and up and around the Rock's summit, which you can follow. If you dare.

Cinematic

Outback

Where? Australia

Which? The Adventures of Priscilla, Queen of the Desert (Stephan Elliott, 1994)

What? Bold, boundless bush at its most striking and outrageous

A desert holiday! Hip, hip, hip hooray! All aboard the big silver bus taking three bling drag queens into the Outback. Along the way ABBA songs, Spandex, glitter and platform heels clash with kangaroos, red rocks and rednecks. A classic journey of transformation played out in a landscape that thinks it's seen it all – but hasn't seen anything quite like this . . .

The Adventures of Priscilla, Queen of the Desert hit cinemas with a brash, trailblazing bang in 1994 – the same year the Australian government passed the Human Rights (Sexual Conduct) Act, which finally legalised sexual activity between consenting adults throughout the country. This is the sociopolitical backdrop to Stephan Elliott's cult road movie, which follows two drag queens and a transgender woman – Mitzi Del Bra (Hugo Weaving), Felicia Jollygoodfellow (Guy Pearce) and Bernadette Bassenger (Terence Stamp) – as they drive from Sydney to middle-of-nowhere Alice Springs in a knackered Hino RC320 that they crown Priscilla. Ahead of its time, this low-budget flick became a worldwide hit, a landmark for the LGBTQ+ movement, an exploration of Australian male identity and a dazzling delve into the country's Outback.

The action kicks off at the Imperial Hotel Erskineville, with the be-sequinned Mitzi and Felicia lip-syncing on the bar. An Art Deco classic, the Imperial has been a stalwart of Sydney's LGBTQ+ scene since the 1980s, providing a safe, sometimes scandalous, space for the community when homosexuality was still illegal. The Imperial now hosts a Priscilla-themed bar and regular drag events.

But the movie quickly leaves Sydney. There are brief glimpses of the Opera House and the Harbour Bridge before it's bye-bye cosmopolitanism, hello bush. The trio bump and bitch along empty roads, surrounded by an eternity of scrub and sky, and eventually

314   AUSTRALASIA

trundle into Broken Hill, Australia's oldest mining town in deepest New South Wales. Desert-edge and isolated, Broken Hill proves largely accepting of these outlandish outsiders once the pub crowd has been won over by Bernadette's killer put-downs – though homophobic graffiti is sprayed onto Priscilla's side. In reality, Broken Hill, the country's first heritage-listed town, has a thriving creative scene and a welcoming reputation. The main drag, Argent Street – where the queens go shopping – is lined with cafés, galleries and boutiques as well as the Palace Hotel, where they spend the night. The kitsch murals seen in the film still festoon the foyer and the hotel's owner launched Broken Heel, a three-day drag festival of cabaret, comedy and cross-dressing fun.

Just beyond Broken Hill is the ghost town of Silverton (where many an Aussie movie has been made, now home to a Mad Max Museum) and, further still, the Mundi Mundi Plains, where a ribbon of tarmac trails off into the flat horizon. It's a nothingness of terrifying proportions, and not a place where you'd want to break down – as Priscilla does.

If Broken Hill turns out to be relatively open-minded, the same is not true of Coober Pedy (white man's burrow), where the trio receive a reception as hostile as the terrain. The land around this South Australian town, home to the largest opal mines in the world, looks like the moon, or the aftermath of the apocalypse. Toothpaste-white mounds pepper the yellow-red earth, baking under temperatures that can top 50°C (122°F). To escape the heat, the hard-bitten residents live in subterranean dwellings; even the church and hotels – such as the White Cliffs Motel, where the queens stay – are dug into the earth.

Alice Springs, Priscilla's ultimate destination, is the gateway to some of the most quintessentially Australian landscapes: Uluru-Kata Tjuta National Park and Kings Canyon. In the original script, Felicia's dream was to stand triumphantly atop Uluru in a full-length Gaultier dress and heels – 'a cock in a frock on a rock' – but with the site so sacred to indigenous Australians, the notion of filming men in drag there was out of the question; in 2017, all tourists were banned from climbing Uluru. Instead, the trio hike to the top of Kings Canyon, a ravine some 400 million years old and home to the Luritja Aboriginal people for more than 20,000 years. In full, flashy regalia, the queens make the Rim Walk, up 500-odd steps, through a narrow gap – now known as Priscilla's Crack – and to the canyon lookout, with views across the eternity of Australia: 'It never ends, does it?' says Bernadette. 'All that space.'

The image – three sparkled, feathered figures conquering this raw, primeval land – couldn't be more Australian: unashamedly irreverent, bluntly funny, progressive, rough-edged, uplifting and spectacular. An Australia with space for everyone.

Part Six:
Africa

Tangier

Where? Morocco
Which? Paysage Vu d'une Fenêtre (*Landscape Viewed from a Window*) (1913) by Henri Matisse
What? City filled with evocative North African light

The light is distinctive in Tangier. At dawn, it pierces through the early morning mist; at midday, it splinters into shafts of light; the golden sunset transforms everything into glowing embers; and at night, silver studs punctuate the deep velvet sky. Just before sunrise, the call to morning prayer echoes from numerous towers across the city, rising in volume before darkness melts into day.

Tangier sits on the northernmost tip of Africa, overlooking both the inky Mediterranean Sea and the azure Atlantic Ocean. Not far away is the Strait of Gibraltar, and these geographical cross-currents result in a synergy of nationalities and languages, mainly French, Arabic and English. Blending these influences and its unique location, Tangier is Europe's gateway to Africa. For a time, it was semi-independent from Africa as an international zone, which attracted diplomats, artists, writers and holiday-makers. After the 1950s, its popularity dipped, but its charm is once again rising. Now you can appreciate anew the same sights that attracted French artists Eugène Delacroix in 1832 and Henri Matisse in 1912 and 1913.

Many different civilisations have occupied Tangier, starting from before the tenth century BCE when it was a Phoenician trading post and later became a Carthaginian settlement. It has been a Berber town and was occupied by the Romans, captured by the Byzantine Empire, and it has also been under Spanish and British rule. This eclectic mix of cultures has resulted in a rich diversity of inhabitants and influences. Tangier combines old and new, with its *kasbah* (citadel), *medina* (old walled city), colonial-era neighbourhoods, high-speed train line and regal, elaborate palaces. The medina is a network of alleyways, brimming with lively shops filled with trinkets, artisanal goods, carpets and local food, as well as teahouses serving tea from delicate filigree glasses.

In the early twentieth century, Tangier attracted the avant-garde Fauve painter Henri Matisse (1869–1954), seeking a new direction for his art. He was charmed by the cosmopolitan city, its bright and luminous light, vivid colours, variegated sunshine and striking, exotic architecture. With his ardent appreciation of Persian art, and his admiration of Delacroix's North African paintings, as well as advice on colour that he was given by Paul Gauguin, Matisse was delighted with his visits to the city and they had a profound effect on his work and career. He described the light of Tangier as 'mellow' and the city as 'a painter's paradise', and he interpreted it all with rich pigments, animated brushwork and contrasting patterns. The landscapes of Tangier were far more luxuriant than any he had seen before. On his arrival, he went almost immediately into the gardens of the Villa Brooks, a private estate not far from his hotel, and spent weeks painting the acanthuses, palms and periwinkles that grew there.

While in Tangier, Matisse produced approximately 20 oil paintings and even more sketches, using bold shapes and vibrant, expressive colours. On his arrival in the city, it was raining, and he painted a vase of irises in his hotel room, emphasising the pattern created by the flowers against the dressing table and mirror, but among his most evocative paintings of Tangier are his 1912 landscapes *Vue sur la Baie de Tangier (View of the Bay of Tangier)* and *La Porte de la Casbah (Entrance to the Kasbah)*, and *Paysage Vu d'une Fenêtre (Landscape Viewed from a Window)* of 1913. Mainly captured in brilliant blue, evoking the reflection of the sky on the stark white buildings, this last image was painted directly from his window in Room 35 of the Grand Hôtel Villa de France, looking out over St Andrew's Church to the kasbah beyond. Most of Matisse's Tangier paintings feature vivid pinks, yellows, blues and greens, circles, stripes and other shapes, all created with thin washes of pigment. Although he spent only a few months there, the experiences and inspiration remained with Matisse for the rest of his life and completely shaped his subsequent art. Later in the 1920s, his paintings of odalisques that he produced in Nice, of reclining females set against patterned cushions, wallpaper and carpets, are clearly the direct result of the way in which the magical light of Tangier affected him.

Soweto

Where? South Africa
Which? *Burger's Daughter* by Nadine Gordimer (1979)
What? Turbulent township at the centre of South Africa's apartheid-era struggles

Sprawling across the veld, this confusing, suppurating place sits apart from the bright, big city, separated not just by geography, but by dilapidation and the sharp end of history. Here in the township, rotten roads crawl through ordered ugliness, row upon row of unlovely houses. Tin shacks lean on each other like drunks; drunks sway between old cars and half-crazed chickens; junk piles up down dirty alleys where tramps forage and stray dogs cock a leg. The air smells of urine, offal, liquor, despair. This is the land across the divide; the Black backyard. A dumping ground. A crucible for social change . . .

In the second half of the twentieth century, South Africa was a deplorably fractured nation. The Afrikaner National Party adopted the policy of apartheid (separateness) in 1948, institutionalising existing racial discrimination. People were required to live in areas according to ethnicity; Black-only townships were created and millions were forcibly moved. Mixed marriages were prohibited, and schools, buses, even park benches were segregated. Nadine Gordimer's *Burger's Daughter* was published in 1979, when apartheid – 'the dirtiest social swindle the world has ever known' – still wracked the country. Initially banned for being dangerous and indecent, it's a striking work of historical fiction in which the suffering is all too real.

The novel centres on Rosa Burger, daughter of prominent white Afrikaner anti-apartheid protesters – both of whom are imprisoned for their beliefs, both of whom die in prison cells. Rosa has been raised in a highly politicised household in Johannesburg, where races splashed together in the pool and shared *boerewors* (sausages) and ideologies around the *braai* (barbecue). With her parents gone, Rosa is forced to find her own identity – but, whatever her personal struggles, she can't escape the political realties of her homeland. Racism is an intrinsic part

322   AFRICA

of daily life at this time. And nowhere is this more evident than in the township of Soweto.

The South West Townships, southwest of Johannesburg, were first created to move Black people away from the city and its white suburbs to areas separated by *cordons sanitaires* (sanitary corridors), such as rivers or railways. Soweto quickly became the largest Black city in South Africa, deprived and angry. Rosa speaks of its 'restless broken streets' filled with the 'litter of twice-discarded possessions first thrown out by the white man and then picked over by the Black'. In Soweto, families try to get by in small, overcrowded homes surrounded by ordure, urchins and *tsotsi* (thugs), while enraged youths denounce the regime. In both real life and Gordimer's novel, the situation erupted in 1976, when a ruling that the Afrikaans language be used in schools triggered the Soweto Uprising. The riots were violently quashed – 176 students were killed – but trouble continued on and off until South Africa's first multiracial elections in 1994.

Soweto, like South Africa, has moved on since. The huge township has areas of desperate poverty but also middle-class suburbs and millionaires. And where once only the bravest traveller ventured here, now it's a Johannesburg must-see. Joining a tour is safest, and will take in key sites: the Hector Pieterson Memorial and Museum, named for the first child killed during the 1976 Uprising; Vilakazi Street, where two Nobel Peace Prize winners – Nelson Mandela and Desmond Tutu – once lived; the graffitied cooling towers of the Orlando power station, now used for bungee jumping. There's also a chance to see ordinary Soweto – to drink a mug of *umqombothi* (maize beer) at a shebeen, to join a hallelujah-ing congregation in a tin-roofed church, to browse stalls selling sweets and intestines and ingenious items crafted from trash.

In 1991, the year after Mandela was released from prison and the year apartheid was officially repealed, Nadine Gordimer won the Nobel Prize in Literature for 'epic writing . . . of very great benefit to humanity'. *Burger's Daughter* merges fiction and fact, using stories to help heal the real world.

LITERARY   323

Matmata & Tozeur

Where? Tunisia
Which? Star Wars: A New Hope (George Lucas, 1977)
What? Stark Sahara-edge lands that look out of this world

It feels like a galaxy far, far away, no doubt. Most colours have been erased, leaving only apricot sands stretching to a distant horizon and a piercing-blue sky. The harsh wind has sketched ripples in the grains and sculpted mighty *yardangs* (desert ridges); elsewhere, salt flats dazzle, ravines gouge and those who live here are forced underground in an attempt to escape the heat. The overall sense is hostility. Not somewhere you'd want to end up or linger long. To quote the first impressions of an anxious droid, 'What a desolate place this is' . . .

Orbiting somewhere in the Outer Rim Territories of the complicated *Star Wars* cosmos, Tatooine is a hardscrabble world. The planet of Luke Skywalker in George Lucas' low-budget good-versus-evil space opera, it is desiccated, bleached-out and savage, peopled by smugglers, scavengers and outcasts. 'If there's a bright centre to the universe,' says Skywalker to C-3PO, 'you're on the planet that it's farthest from.'

When Lucas was location scouting for his hero's home, the real-world location chosen for filming was Tunisia, the smallest country in North Africa and, when the crew arrived in 1976, only independent for 20 years. Ironically, given its otherworldly feel, it was Tunisia's proximity to civilisation that appealed: here were epic desert landscapes that looked alien but were conveniently close to Europe.

Tatooine sets the tone for the entire *Star Wars* series. It's the first planet to appear on screen, aiming to convince viewers – in a time when computer-generated imagery was in its infancy – that this sci-fi universe could be believed. In southern Tunisia Lucas found just the thing: a hot, barren Sahara-edge emptiness of remote Berber villages, traditional *ksour* (fortified granaries), lunar-looking rock formations and troglodyte houses dug out of the earth. A realm where reality and fantasy could, with pioneering visual effects, easily merge. He also found his name, which was adapted from the actual Tunisian desert city of Tataouine.

However, filming didn't take place there. Instead, a cave house in the town of Matmata stood in for the interior of the Lars Homestead, where Luke Skywalker (Mark Hamill) begins *Star Wars: A New Hope* living a quiet life with his aunt and uncle. Matmata is pocked with these underground dwellings: man-made craters burrowed into the ground, with windowless rooms and tunnels leading off central courtyards. Most residents have lived in them for generations, scraping a living from olive farming, rug weaving or, more latterly, tourism. The Sidi Driss Hotel – which stood in for the movie's homestead – now caters to *Star Wars* fans, who come to stay in its simple, Jedi-austere rooms and admire the original set props and paraphernalia.

The Lars Homestead's exterior was actually shot just outside Naftah, near the city of Tozeur, on the striking salt pan of Chott el Djerid (the Lagoon of the Land of Palms); it's the largest salt pan in the Sahara and largely dry, though speckled in parts by vivid, multi-coloured saltwater pools and the odd flamingo. Harsh in the extreme, yet ethereally beautiful. You can still see the simple domed structure that was supposedly the homestead's entrance, and where Luke stared longingly into a spectacular purple-hued double sunset. The set wasn't built to last, especially not within this merciless environment, but having been remade for later movies in the *Star Wars* series, it endures. For now.

Complete your galactic wanderings at nearby Sidi Bouhlel – aka Star Wars Canyon – a dramatic ravine in Dghoumès National Park (also featured in *Raiders of the Lost Ark*). Known in the movie as the Jundland Wastes, this is where R2-D2 is captured by the cowled, junk-collecting Jawas and Luke is attacked by the Tusken Raiders. In reality you're more likely to find a small, white *marabout* (shrine), ancient crocodile fossils and a swirl and crumple of stark, strange, sun-baked sandstone crags that, for a moment, make you feel you are indeed on another planet.

Dakar

Where? Senegal
What? Rhythms brought back to their roots

The city's air is full to bursting – car horns honk, motorbikes cough and splutter, sheep bleat and traders hawk their wares in a dozen languages. There's the tang of *yassa* chicken and the smoky char of grilling fish; a haze of sand swept in from the Sahara, salt from the sea and, of course, music. Plenty of music, from crackly radios to smooth jazz, *kora* twangs to *sabar* drumbeats. Some say everyone in Senegal is a musician, that Dakar is Africa's most vibrant music hub, and that understanding the country's rhythms is the best way to understand its culture as a whole . . .

Dakar sprawls over the Cap Vert peninsula, West Africa's western-most tip, an arrowhead of land aimed across the Atlantic. And for a long time, that's what it was: focused westward, cruelly pointing the way of travel to the enslaved people who were traded to the New World. From the fifteenth to the nineteenth century, the notorious Île de Gorée, a small speck off the peninsula, was the largest slave-trading centre on the African coast; millions of enslaved people passed through. Now, by the Maison des Esclaves (House of Slaves) museum, there is a monument there to honour them: a woman embraces a man with arms raised in defiant joy as he breaks the shackles that bound him. Notably, the couple stand atop a huge *djembe*, a traditional goblet-shaped wooden drum. The *djembe* has been at the heart of West African spiritual life, community and storytelling for centuries; it's a symbol of harmony and heritage. It's no coincidence that it features in the statue here.

Ethnic groups, including the Wolof, Serer and Fulani, have occupied the land around the Senegal River for as long as anyone knows. Europeans arrived in the fifteenth century, setting up trading posts along the coast, with France eventually becoming the ruling colonial power. Senegal finally gained independence in 1960. Throughout that time music was always present, and West African rhythms travelled overseas with the slaves, influencing cultures in faraway lands – genres

MUSICAL 329

like blues, soul and reggae all trace their roots back here. But it was in the decades after gaining autonomy that the country began to make its mark. Music was even written into the first line of the fledgling nation's new national anthem, 'Le Lion Rouge': *'Pincez tous vos koras, frappez les balafons'* – 'Everyone strum thy koras, strike thy balafons'.

A cultural revival swept through, sparking a musical renaissance; local musicians – like iconic Afro-Cuban dance band Orchestra Baobab – started to add traditional instruments to popular Latin rhythms, producing something more distinctly Senegalese. Then came mbalax, the dynamic and electrifying genre, rooted in the sabar drum rhythms of the Wolof people, that blends traditional sounds with contemporary jazz, funk and rock. Youssou N'Dour, the 'King of Mbalax', seduced audiences with his lustrous tenor voice and innovative sound – not to mention his political activism. Similarly, soulful singer-musician Baaba Maal – born into a poor Fulani fishing family – studied music in Dakar and has travelled with his music ever since, using it to give a voice to his community and his country. In Senegal, musicians have long been oral historians, and more and more they are protestors and campaigners, leading the way on issues such as the environment and human rights.

For all this depth of musical talent, finding live music in Dakar can be tricky. The nightclub scene isn't as buzzy as it was; now it is bars and restaurants that host impromptu events. The best gigs are often staged at a moment's notice – knowing people and people-who-know-people is key to finding out who is playing where and when. It's worth swinging by spots like the Institut Français and the Djoloff hotel to see if anything's going on.

But music-seekers could do worse than just keeping an ear to the ground while wandering the wave-lapped Corniche Ouest or the bougainvillea-rambled lanes of the Plateau district. Or while exploring the Île de Gorée, where the darkness of the past has been swapped for peace – the island is now a hub for artists of all stripes, who gather amid the narrow, car-free streets and peeling buildings to paint, create and, of course, make music of their own.

Foodie

Marrakesh

Where? Morocco

Why? Mouth-watering memories of the Maghreb, served up at the greatest nightly show

As sunset slides into a deepening twilight, the square starts to fizz. Bare bulbs flicker, swaying in a desert-sent breeze; awnings splay, parasols unfurl, cartwheels clatter on the slabs, jostling into position for the night. Meat is skewered, snails boiled, peanuts roasted, oranges squeezed; kettles whistle, pots bubble, frying pans spit and sizzle. The fuzzy warmth of fresh-baked bread, onions reduced to caramel sweetness, lamb hunks charred, a spritz of fresh mint, a hundred spices in a thousand combinations. Steam rises above it all, as if the whole place is simmering, a huge stew in the heart of the old city . . .

The merest thought of Marrakesh can make your mouth water. Historically a key North African trading post, food cultures have mixed here for centuries. The ancient culinary traditions of the Berber (Amazigh), Arab flavours from the east, ingredients brought up through the Saharan trade routes by camel caravans, influences brought down from Moorish Andalucía, a soupçon of French colonial seasoning – all have been stirred together over the years in Morocco's 'red city'.

The nomadic Berber have long lived in the surrounding mountains and desert, but the city itself was first founded in around 1070, when Youssef Ibn Tachfine, leader of the Berber Muslim Almoravid dynasty, created a basecamp. This camp grew to become the capital of the Almoravid Empire. Defensive walls, mosques and the fortified Ksar al-Hajjar palace were eventually built. And while virtually nothing of these original structures remains today, they continue to shape the layout of modern Marrakesh. The city's souks still occupy the area northwest of the principal mosque, and the market square that once spread before the ancient ksar is still the site of the main square, the Djemaa El Fna.

The Djemaa El Fna is Marrakesh's preeminent entertainment hub since the eleventh century. A carnivalesque menagerie of backflipping acrobats, Gnaoua musicians, fortune-tellers, henna tattooists and

332   AFRICA

snake charmers pack out this vast plaza. But it's also where you can taste the soul of the city. Come dusk, the food stalls are brought in by mule carts; communal tables are set out; coal braziers are fired up; a smorgasbord appears. There are tourist trap stalls touting grilled chicken and so-so tagines, but most of the diners here are local and should be followed to more interesting eating – everything from spicy merguez sausages to chunky *harira* (chickpea soup), from spicy snail broth to boiled offal, sheep brain and whole goats' heads.

One ubiquitous dish is couscous. One of the earliest written references to it is in an anonymous thirteenth-century tome, *The Book of Cooking in Maghreb and Andalus in the Era of the Almohads.* It contains a recipe from Marrakesh for *Kuskusû Fityâni* (Soldiers' Couscous), in which meat and vegetables are cooked, before the couscous is simmered in the broth and served with a sprinkle of cinnamon. While this dish is named for military men, couscous was foremost the food of nomads. The task of preparing it – always a woman's job – involves hand-rolling the hard grains with a little water to create the granules, over and over until every grain is done. Once it's made, it's easy to transport, quick to cook, cheap and filling.

To sample the very best couscous, you'll need an invitation to a party or wedding. It's an essential part of Moroccan and wider North African culture. In 2020, UNESCO placed the 'knowledge, know-how and practices related to the production and consumption of couscous' in Morocco, Algeria, Mauritania and Tunisia on its list of Intangible Cultural Heritage. In Marrakesh you can learn to make it with a *dada*, a local woman who holds all the secrets of Moroccan food, learned not by formal training but by a lifetime's experience.

That said, Marrakesh's signature dish is very much male. Tangia – not to be confused with tagine – is a tender meat stew specific to the city, and named for the tall, urn-like clay pot in which it's cooked. Tangia is considered the 'bachelor's meal', traditionally eaten by souk traders, who would eat together on their day off. The night before, they would load their tangia pots with meat, including bones, tendons, oxtails and trotters (the fat and gelatin are essential to create the confit-like texture); saffron and cumin, preserved lemons, garlic, a splash of oil, a little *smen* (clarified butter). Then they would take it to the ovens that heat the public *hammams* (bathhouses). There, the stoker would leave the tangia to cook slowly overnight, so the succulent dish would be ready for the next day's lunch. Follow your nose (and the long line of Marrakeshi men) to Mechoui Alley, just off the Djemaa El Fna, to give it a try for yourself.

FOODIE   333

Part Seven:

Middle East

Literary

Cairo

Where? Egypt
Which? *Palace Walk* by Naguib Mahfouz (1956)
What? Medieval Egyptian labyrinth of mosques, souks and secrets

Peek through the *mashrabiya* window: what lies beyond? This boxed-in balcony, concealed by a carapace of woodwork and lattice, allows glimpses to the bustle below. Down there is another world – of barbers and bean-sellers, street hawkers, brass workers, human traffic; of lamb kofta on hot coals, bitter-black coffee and sacks of spice; of the sweet smoke of *sheesha* pipes, wafting like restless *jinns* (genies). Out there, life ebbs and flows, roars, revolts, moves on. A world whizzing by, oblivious to the eyes peering down from behind the screen . . .

Naguib Mahfouz's *Palace Walk* is a literary look through the *mashrabiya* – gazing out and gazing in. Part one of Mahfouz's Cairo Trilogy, it demystifies the rituals, rhythms and ructions present in the Arabic world at the beginning of the twentieth century. Indeed, it's less a novel than a rich carpet, woven with both the story of Egypt at a time of upheaval and the intricacies of urban Muslim family life, with its faith, fears, love and oppression.

This was a tumultuous period in Egyptian history. Britain had grasped control of the country in the 1880s and, in 1914, it became an official British protectorate. However, when the First World War came to a close, but hoped-for Egyptian independence did not come with it, nationalist fervour began to bubble. All strands of society – educated elite and working-class masses, Cairenes and country dwellers, Muslims and Christians, men and women – were united in a bid to be rid of their colonisers. It was the original Arab Spring.

Mahfouz witnessed the chaos first-hand. As a child he lived in the al-Gamaliyya area of Islamic Cairo, the city's oldest neighbourhood, and saw protests outside his window. Later, having learned his literary skills from the storytellers of the *ashwa* (coffee houses) – then great hubs of cultural debate and exchange – he wove these early experiences into his epic trilogy: *Palace Walk, Palace of Desire and Sugar Street*. Palace Walk, which runs from 1917 to the 1919 nationalist revolution, is a story of the sights, sounds and souls of Islamic Cairo at a defining moment.

The novel was published in 1956 under the Arabic title *Bayn al-Qasrayn (Between the Two Palaces)*, the name of the old city's chief thoroughfare but also a nod to Egypt's cultural and political transition. The wider public turmoil is channelled through the personal saga of the al-Jawad family: despotic, philandering patriarch Abd al-Jawad, his subjugated wife Amina and their five children. Since marrying 25 years previously, Amina has been a virtual prisoner in her own home, viewing the world beyond only through the latticework windows. But one day, when her husband is away, she ventures out . . .

Amina, face veiled, draped in black cloth and escorted by her younger son, leaves the house on Bayn al-Qasrayn to walk along the backstreets of Islamic Cairo and visit the Al-Hussein Mosque, supposed burial spot of the head of Hussein, Mohammed's grandson. Here, Amina, so long locked up, proceeds to 'devour the place with greedy, curious eyes: the walls, ceiling, pillars, carpets, chandeliers, pulpit, and the *mihrab* niches . . . How often she had longed to visit this site.' The mosque is off limits to non-Muslims. But a stroll amid the same timeless alleys is not.

While the Egyptian capital is now a mega-sprawl – the biggest in the Arabic world – in Islamic Cairo, the streets narrow and modernity melts away; in parts it feels little different from when the Fatimid Caliphate first founded their new city here in 969 CE. From the tenth to the twelfth centuries the Fatimids constructed a great walled citadel, sliced by the main thoroughfare of Bayn al-Qasrayn. This 'Palace Walk' runs north–south linking Bab al-Futah and Bab Zuweila; between these turreted medieval gates lies an open-air museum of dishevelled palaces, dusty caravanserais, *adhan*-calling minarets, forgotten tombs, underground cisterns and fit-to-burst bazaars. From it, alleyways run off into quiet squares and Aladdin's caves of tat and treasures.

Working northwards from Bab Zuweila, you first pass the Al Ghouri *wikala*, a beautifully restored sixteenth-century hostel for African merchants where Sufis still gather to do their whirling dance and where artisans sell local crafts. Comprehensive shopping possibilities lie a little further to the east, where, adjacent to the Al-Hussein Mosque is the crazy maze of Khan el-Khalili. Turn two corners in this labyrinthine souk and you're lost amid an avalanche of bric-a-brac, stuffed into an impossible tangle of alleys. Mahfouz used to write and people-watch in the El-Fishawy Café, Khan el-Khalili's oldest coffee house, though these days its scuffed wooden chairs and cracked marble-topped tables are more frequented by tourists than Nobel laureates.

338   MIDDLE EAST

Beyond this is the gold-sellers' souk, the awesome mausoleum and *madrassa* (Islamic school) of Qalawun, the twelfth-century Al-Aqmar Mosque and the tenth-century Al-Hakim Mosque, the street's oldest building. And somewhere in the middle is Beshtak Palace. This fourteenth-century home of a rich *amir* occupies the site of Mahfouz's fictional al-Jawad family home. The interior is exquisite, with its marble floors and coloured glass. You won't, of course, find Amina trapped inside, but you can imagine it: at first-floor level, dark-wood *mashrabiya* windows project over the street, exactly the sort of secretive boxes from which she might have viewed the comings and goings of a world both unchanged for centuries and in dangerous flux. A world she wasn't permitted to enter.

LITERARY 339

Foodie

Tel Aviv

Where? Israel
Why? Dip into the great hummus dispute

Cicer arietinum. The humble chickpea. Cheap pulse, health food, alleged aphrodisiac. They are one of the earliest cultivated legumes, consumed by humans for at least 10,000 years. And, at some point, they were blitzed into their earthy, zesty, unctuous apotheosis: hummus. No one knows when or where this delectable dip originated. But, in a region that scarce needs more to argue about, the debate rages on . . .

Cosmopolitan Tel Aviv is a serious contender for culinary capital of the Middle East. Infused with Mediterranean breezes and a hedonistic vibe, the coastal city offers world-class fine dining, lip-smacking street food and a vibrant vegan scene – including a love for all things chickpea.

Hummus does not hail from Tel Aviv. Some reckon the dip is referenced in the Bible; recipe books suggest something similar might have been eaten across Egypt and the Levant in medieval times. It certainly predates 1948, when the State of Israel was created. But while hummus may not be an Israeli invention, the nation has adopted it with unrivalled gusto. Considered a side dish across much of the Middle East, in Israel it's often the main event. The country now has the highest hummus consumption per capita in the world, with the average resident devouring 10kg (22lb) a year. It's become the unofficial national dish.

The word 'hummus' is Arabic for 'chickpea'. The dip is more accurately called *hummus bi'tahina*, chickpeas with tahini (sesame paste). The basic recipe is very simple: chickpeas, tahini, lemon juice, garlic. The diversity – of which there is infinite – stems from the way these elements are mixed and served. Are the chickpeas hand-mashed or machine blended? Is the garlic roasted or raw? Is the consistency runny, creamy or paté-thick? Is it drizzled with olive oil, sprinkled with onion, speckled with cumin, sumac or paprika? Is it served with *ful* (broad beans), *beitza* (egg), dried sausage, pita or pickles? No matter the details, it's inexpensive, kosher, nutritious, delicious. Packed with minerals like potassium and zinc, it's said to boost energy and sexual function, too.

340   MIDDLE EAST

Tel Aviv's hummus heartland is Jaffa, the ancient port – one of the oldest in the world – from which Israel's capital has emerged. Now designated a neighbourhood of the Israeli capital, Jaffa's maze of narrow, crumbling streets meanders in the shadow of the modern city's tower blocks, feeling a world apart. The population here is around a third Arab; and this is where you'll find the finest *hummusia*, the no-frills canteens that specialise in hummus. They open from early morning until the last dregs of that day's batch have been scooped from the pot. The best hummusia run out before lunch.

And the very best of all, so they say, is Abu Hassan, on Ha'Dolphin street. You'll recognise it by the unruly queue snaking away from the door and by the people scoffing from take-out tubs on the pavement outside, too impatient to walk far before digging in. Palestinian entrepreneur Ali Karawan (aka Abu Hassan) started hawking his wife's homemade hummus from a handcart in the 1950s; now his son runs this cramped, noisy, shoulder-bargy joint, serving the salivating masses of every race, class and creed. It's a place where, for a moment at least, issues of nationality and politics might be forgotten; hostilities swapped for the harmony of flavours in each bowl. Where maybe every diner could agree that, while hummus is claimed by many a country, it's owned by none at all.

Note, it's not all about hummus. The chickpea is central to another of Israel's most popular foods: falafel. These deep-fried balls of ground chickpeas, garlic, coriander and spice are also of heavily contested origins. Their meatless simplicity works for Lent-observing Christians, kosher Jews and fast-breaking Muslims. It's a food for all religions and none; a snack for breakfast, lunch, mezze platter or midnight feast. And the best way to eat them? Crisp and moist, in fresh pita, with a good dollop of hummus on top.

Cinematic

Wadi Rum

Where? Jordan
Which? Lawrence of Arabia (David Lean, 1962)
What? Dramatic desert of otherworldly landscapes and controversial legends

The desert is a fiery furnace. On the horizon, magicked from the trembling heat and swirling dust, a dark speck appears. It floats in the mirage. Tiny, but growing. Near-silently approaching, the only sound is soft, steady hoofs hitting pale-yellow sand. It is a figure on camel-back, drawing slowly – unbearably slowly – closer to the screen. In movie terms it takes eons for the stranger to arrive. The audience is forced to wait, to adjust to this alien world, where time, temperature, scale and even the nature of life itself play to a different beat . . .

David Lean's *Lawrence of Arabia* is epic in every sense: the tale of a larger-than-life man, told in ambitious fashion, over a prodigious 210 minutes, filmed in fathomless deserts under enormous skies. It is the dark-edged adventure biopic of British army officer Thomas Edward Lawrence (Peter O'Toole) who, as a well-educated young lieutenant with expertise in Arabic culture, is posted to the Levant during the First World War to serve as a liaison between the British and the Arabs in their fight for freedom against the Ottoman Turks – the aftermath of which has shaped western relations with the region ever since. The film contains a swashbuckle of military strategy and dramatic battles but is centred on the main man: an unlikely hero, variously judged brilliant, mendacious, enigmatic, self-aggrandising, courageous and controversial.

The movie takes some liberties with history. For instance, the timeline of the Arab Revolt is sometimes dubious, and the unfolding of the attack on Aqaba is fictionalised for dramatic effect. And, despite appearances, large parts were filmed in Morocco and Spain – indeed, the Red Sea port of Aqaba was recreated on a beach near Almería. However, the most visually striking segments are right where they ought to be: shot on the same Jordanian soil where Lawrence did indeed wage guerrilla-style war against the Turks from 1916 to 1918.

CINEMATIC 343

Then, what is now Jordan was part of the Hejaz Kingdom, and Britain had promised King Ali of Hejaz that if the Ottomans were defeated, a single independent Arab state would be created, that would include modern-day Syria, Iraq, Palestine and Jordan. Instead, thanks to the hush-hush Sykes–Picot Agreement, the region was actually divided between the British and the French. The British-supervised state of Transjordan was created in 1922; Jordan became an independent country in 1946.

While aspects of Jordan have changed immeasurably in the century since Lawrence's feats of derring-do, some have changed barely at all, including the desert landscapes of Wadi Rum. They remain as cinematic now as when Lean shot them and when Lawrence was charging through. Indeed, in *Seven Pillars of Wisdom*, Lawrence's autobiographical account of his exploits in Arabia, he calls this great, dry valley 'vast, echoing and God-like'; he talks of its 'stupendous hills', its landscapes 'greater than imagination', of the 'innumerable silence of stars'.

Cutting through the deserts of southern Jordan, Wadi Rum has been formed and shaped over around 30 million years. It is an otherworldly land of granite, basalt and sandstone mountains weathered into monstrous bulging mounds, strange ridges, sheer cliffs, slender gorges and precarious arches, all lapped by blood-orange sand. The area has been inhabited since prehistoric times – petroglyphs dating back 12,000 years can be found on the rocks – and is laced with ancient trade routes, long used by travelling caravans. Bedouin nomads continue to roam with their goats and camels, though far fewer live traditionally now: since Hollywood has shown Jordan's good looks to the world, many local Zalabia and Zuwaydeh Bedouin – sub-clans of the eminent Howeitat tribe – have turned to tourism to make a living. What Lean started in 1962 has only been reinforced by a long list of other movies made here, from *Star Wars* instalments to *The Martian* – Wadi Rum is especially good at looking like outer space. Indeed, it is sometimes called the Valley of the Moon.

In *Lawrence of Arabia*, though, Wadi Rum and the wider desert regions of southern Jordan play themselves. It is here that Lawrence jolts across wind-raked dunes on his camel; where he witnesses the unforgettable entrance of Sherif Ali (Omar Sharif) appearing slowly out of a shimmering mirage; where he first meets Prince Faisal (Alec Guinness); where he flounces vainly in freshly acquired Arab robes; where he successfully leads an army across miles of merciless sand. The camera sucks up and spits out the country's punishing heat, desiccating aridity, terrifying scale and scenic punch. The colours pop: bright orange,

344   MIDDLE EAST

coral pink, deep red, golden yellow. And the details are rich: a boy sinking into quicksand, elongated shadows cast onto flawless dunes, a struck match merging into a burning desert sunrise.

It is not so hard to survive in Wadi Rum these days. At least, it's not hard to experience a tiny taste of its old ways for a day or two. Now a UNESCO World Heritage site and travel hotspot, Wadi Rum caters ably for Lawrence pilgrims – to the extent that, in the 1980s, Jabal al-Mazmar (the Mountain of Plague) was renamed Seven Pillars of Wisdom, after Lawrence's book (though there is no connection). It's possible to stay at a Bedouin camp, sleep in a wool tent, break bread with families whose ancestors have lived here for generations, ride a camel into unearthly canyons, gather round a campfire and gaze up into the timeless starry skies – just as Lean's crew, and Lawrence himself, once did.

Index

A

Acurio, Gastón 245
Adventures of Priscilla, Queen of the Desert 314–315
af Klint, Hilma *Paintings for the Temple* 143–144
Aiello, Danny 194
Alberta, Canada 223–225
Allende, Isabel *The House of the Spirits* 254–255
Allende, Salvador 254
Amélie 158–159
Andalucía, Spain 149–150
Anderson, Wes 45–47
Andersson, Bibi 104
Andress, Ursula 191
Andrews, Julie 121
Arles, France 155–157
Arnalds, Ólafur 56
art 6–9
    Arles, France 155–157
    Bern, Switzerland 118–119
    Brussels, Belgium 98–99
    Cascais and Estoril, Portugal 28–29
    Catalonia, Spain 42–43
    Coyoacán, Mexico 232–233
    Delft, Netherlands 58–59
    East Bergholt, Suffolk, England, UK 184–185
    Elbe Sandstone Mountains, Germany 35–36
    Giverny, France 173–174
    Guernica, Spain 69–71
    Lake Attersee, Austria 82–83
    Lake Mälaren, Sweden 143–144
    London, England, UK 161–163
    Mount Fuji, Japan 280–281
    New Mexico, USA 197–198
    New York, USA 206–207
    Oslo, Norway 137–138
    St Ives, Cornwall, England, UK 12–13
    Tahiti, French Polynesia 308–309
    Tangier, Morocco 319–320
    Venice, Italy 107–109
Art Nouveau 83, 98–99
Artusi, Pellegrino 62
Arzak, Elena 183
Arzak, Juan Mari 183
asado 252

B

Baker, Alfred 274–275
Baquero, Ivana 85
Basquiat, Jean-Michel *Per Capita* 206–207
Bath, England, UK 64–67
Batra, Ritesh 298
Beatles, The 8, 25–26
Beethoven, Ludwig van 8, 131–132
Belchite, Spain 86
Bellini, Giovanni 107, 108
Berger, Georgette 99
Bergman, Ingmar 104–105
Bergman, Ingrid 43
Berlin, Germany 124–125
Bern, Switzerland 118–119
Bernal, Gael Garcia 256
bibimbap 266–277
BigBang 284
Bingham, Hiram 256
bistros and *bouchons* 48–49
Björk 56
Blackpink 284
blues 235–236
Bologna, Italy 61–63
Bonaparte, Napoleon 215
Bond, Michael *Paddington* 95
Bosch, Hieronymus *The Last Judgement triptych* 177
Botticelli, Sandro 179
bouillabaisse 19–20
Brahms, Johannes 132
Brando, Marlon 17
Breughel, Jan, the Elder 98
Brontë, Anne 111
Brontë, Charlotte 111, 112
Brontë, Emily *Wuthering Heights* 7, 111–112
Brooklyn, New York, USA 194–195
Brosnan, Pierce 191
Bruges, Belgium 176–177
Brunel, Isambard Kingdom 95

Atomic Kitten 26
Augustus 156
Austen, Jane 66
    Northanger Abbey 64, 66, 67
    Persuasion 66, 67
Avildsen, John G. 212

Brunelleschi, Filippo 179
Brussels, Belgium 98–99
BTS 284
Buena Vista Social Club 210
Buñuel, Luís 42
Burton, Richard 191

C

Cairo, Egypt 337–339
Campion, Jane 305
Canaletto, Giovanni Antonio Canal 107–109
    The Entrance to the Grand Canal, Venice 107
Capote, Truman 191, 227
Cartagena, Colombia 241–243
Cascais and Estoril, Portugal 28–29
Cash, Johnny 236
Castro, Fidel 210
Catalonia, Spain 42–43
Catherine the Great of Russia 141
Cervantes, Miguel de *Don Quixote* 50–51
ceviche 245
Chanel, Coco 43
Chile 254–255
Christian IV of Denmark–Norway 137
cicchetti 30–31
Cipriani, Giyseppe 108
Clark, William 223–224
Clouse, Robert 286
Columbus, Christopher 50
Connery, Sean 190
Constable, John *Flatford Mill (Scene on a Navigable River)* 184–185
Constantine 155, 156
Copenhagen, Denmark 75–77
Coppola, Sofia 268, 269
Coyoacán, Mexico 232–233
Cuba, Caribbean 209–210
Cusco and Machu Picchu, Peru 256–257

D

da Gama, Vasco 116
Dakar, Senegal 329–330
Dali, Salvador *The Persistence of Memory* 42–43
Dalton, Timothy 129

Davis, Geena 228
Davis, Ossie 194
Davos, Switzerland 78–79
De Danann 102
Dead Horse Point State Park, Utah, USA 228–230
Deitch, Jeffrey 206
del Toro, Guillermo 85–86
Delacroix, Eugène 319, 320
Delft, Netherlands 58–59
Destino 43
Diakonova, Elena Ivanovna 43
Diaz, Al 206–207
DiCaprio, Leonard 7, 224
Dickens, Charles 140, 162
  Oliver Twist 152–153
Disney, Walt 43
Do the Right Thing 194–195
Döblin, Alfred *Berlin Alexanderplatz* 124–125
Dolce Vita, La 16–17
Dostoevsky, Fyodor *Crime and Punishment* 140–141
Dr. No 190–191
Dublin, Ireland 22–23
Duchamp, Marcel 42, 98
Dumas, Alexandre 91
Dumfries & Galloway, Scotland, UK 170–171

E

East Bergholt, Suffolk, England, UK 184–185
Echo and the Bunnymen 26
Eiffel, Gustave 182–183, 255
Ekberg, Anita 17
El Greco 50
Elbe Sandstone Mountains, Germany 35–36
Elliott, Stephan 314
Ensor, James 98
Enter the Dragon 286–287
Expressionists 36

F

Fabritius, Carel 58
Farm, The 26
Fårö, Sweden 104–105
Farrell, Colin 176

Fellini, Federico 16
Ferrante, Elena *My Brilliant Friend* 164–165
Fiennes, Ralph 45, 46, 176
films 6–9
  Alberta, Canada 223–225
  Belchite and the Sierra de Guadarrama, Spain 85–86
  Brooklyn, New York, USA 194–195
  Bruges, Belgium 176–177
  Cusco and Machu Picchu, Peru 256–257
  Dead Horse Point State Park, Utah, USA 228–230
  Dumfries & Galloway, Scotland, UK 170–171
  Fårö, Sweden 104–105
  Görlitz, Germany 45–47
  Hong Kong, China 286–287
  Karekare Beach, New Zealand 305–306
  London, England, UK 95–97
  Matmata and Tozeur, Tunisia 325–326
  Montmartre, Paris, France 158–159
  Mumbai, India 298–299
  Outback, Australia 314–315
  Philadelphia, USA 212–213
  Rome, Italy 16–17
  Salzburg, Austria 121–123
  Tokyo, Japan 268–269
  Wadi Rum, Jordan 343–345
  Wells, England, UK 128–129
flamenco 149–150
Fleming, Ian *Dr. No* 190–191
Flöge, Emilie 82–83
Florence, Italy 179–181
Flynn, Errol 191
food 6–9
  Bologna, Italy 61–63
  Copenhagen, Denmark 75–77
  Jeonju, South Korea 266–267
  Kraków, Poland 146–147
  La Pampa, Buenos Aires, Argentina 251–252
  Lima, Peru 244–245
  Lisbon, Portugal 115–116
  Lyon, France 48–49
  Marrakesh, Morocco 332–333

Marseille, France 19–20
Melbourne, Victoria, Australia 302–303
Montréal, Québec, Canada 200–201
New Orleans, Loisiana, USA 215–217
Nuremberg, Germany 92–93
Oostduinkerke, Belgium 38–39
Osaka, Japan 295–296
San Sebastian, Spain 182–183
Sichuan, China 277–278
Tel Aviv, Israel 340–341
Tusheti, Georgia 134–135
Udupi, India 289–290
Valencia, Spain 167–168
Venice, Italy 30–31
Franco, Francisco 69, 85, 86
Frankie Goes to Hollywood 26
Freud, Sigmund 43
Friedrich, Caspar David *Wanderer Above the Sea of Fog* 35–36
Frost, Nick 129

G

Gainsborough, Sir Thomas 184
Gainsbourg, Serge 6
Galway, Ireland 101–102
Gaudí, Antonio 42
Gauguin, Paul 156, 308–309, 320
  Where Do We Come From? What Are We? Where Are We Going? 309
Gehry, Frank 213
Genghis Khan 134
Gerry and the Pacemakers 26
Ghiberti, Lorenzo 179
Gil, Gilberto 248
Giotto de Bondone 179, 309
Giverny, France 173–174
Glass, Hugh 223
Gleeson, Brendan 176
Goebbels, Joseph 73
Goldin, Nan 207
Gordimer, Nadine *Burger's Daughter* 322–323
Görlitz, Germany 45–47
Grand Budapest Hotel, The 45–47
Greene, Graham *The Quiet American* 292–293
Guernica, Spain 69–71
Guevara, Ernesto 356
gumbo 216

INDEX   347

H

Hamada, Shōji 13
Hamill, Mark 326
Hamsun, Knut *Growth of the Soil* 72–73
Handy, W. C. 235–236
Hanging Rock, Victoria, Australia 311–312
Harald Hardrada 137
Haring, Keith 207
Haussmann, Georges 90, 182
Haydn, Joseph 131
Hayworth, Rita 183
Hemingway, Ernest 157
Hepburn, Audrey 17
Hepworth, Barbara 13
Hitler, Adolf 73, 121, 122, 124, 125
Hokusai, Katsushika 280–281
    The Great Wave off Kanagawa 281
Holzer, Jenny 207
Homer *Odyssey* 22
Hong Kong, China 286–287
Hooch, Pieter de 58
Horta, Victor 99
Hosseini, Khaled *The Kite Runner* 263–264
Hot Fuzz 128–129
Howlin' Wolf 236
Hugo, Victor *Les Misérables* 6, 89–91
hummus 340–341
Hunter, Holly 305

I

Icelandic music 55–56
In Bruges 176–177
Inglourious Basterds 46
Isabel II of Spain 182

J

Jackie Brenston and his Delta Cats 236
Jadwiga of Poland 147
Jamaica, Caribbean 190–191
James, Henry 157
Japanese fast food 295–296
jazz 209–210
Jeonju, South Korea 266–267
Jeunet, Jean-Pierre 158
Jewish cuisine 200–201
Johansson, Scarlett 268

Joyce, James *Ulysses* 22–23
Julius Caesar 155, 156–157

K

K-pop 283–284
Kabul, Afghanistan 263–264
Kahlo, Frida *The Two Fridas* 232–233
Kaleo 56
Karekare Beach, New Zealand 305–306
Kassovitz, Mathieu 158
Kaur, Nimrat 298
Keitel, Harvey 306
Kerala, India 273–275
Khan, Irrfan 298
khinkali 134–135
Kidman, Nicole 97
King, B. B. 236
King, Paul 95
Kitzmiller, John 191
Klee, Paul 118–119
    Mount Niesen, Egyptian Night 119
Klimt, Gustav 82–83, 132
    Lake Attersee 83
Kokoschka, Oscar 163
Kraków, Poland 146–147
Kutschera, Maria Augusta 122

L

La Mancha, Spain 50–51
La Pampa, Buenos Aires, Argentina 251–252
La's, The 26
Lacroix, Christian 157
Lake Attersee, Austria 82–83
Lake Mälaren, Sweden 143–144
Lawrence of Arabia 7, 343–345
Lawrence, T. E. *Seven Pillars of Wisdom* 344, 345
Leach, Bernard 13
Lean, David 343, 345
lebkuchen 92–93
Lee, Bruce 286–287
Lee, Christopher 170
Lee, Harper *To Kill a Mockingbird* 226–227
Lee, Ruby 194
Lee, Spike 194–195
Leeuwenhoek, Antonie van 59

LeWars, Marguerite 191
Lewis, Meriwether 223–224
Lima, Peru 244–245
Lindsay, Joan *Picnic at Hanging Rock* 311–312
Lippi, Filippino 179
Lisbon, Portugal 115–116
literature 6–9
    Bath, England, UK 64–67
    Berlin, Germany 124–125
    Cairo, Egypt 337–339
    Cartagena, Colombia 241–243
    Chile 254–255
    Davos, Switzerland 78–79
    Dublin, Ireland 22–23
    Hanging Rock, Victoria, Australia 311–312
    Kabul, Afghanistan 263–264
    Kerala, India 273–275
    La Mancha, Spain 50–51
    London, England, UK 152–153
    Mississippi River, Missouri, USA 203–204
    Monroeville, Alabama, USA 226–227
    Monterey, California, USA 188–189
    Naples, Italy 164–165
    New York, USA 218–219
    Nordland, Norway 72–73
    Paris, France 89–91
    Saigon (Ho Chi Minh City), Vietnam 292–293
    Soweto, South Africa 322–323
    St Petersburg, Russia 140–141
    Yorkshire Moors, England, UK 111–112
Liverpool, England, UK 25–26
London, England, UK 95–97, 152–153, 161–163
Longhena, Baldassare 109
López, Sergi 85
Lord of the Rings, The 305
Lost in Translation 7, 268–269
Lott, Willy 185
Lubezki, Emmanuel 223
Lucas, George 325
Lucy, Autherine 226
Lunchbox, The 298–299
Lyon, France 48–49

348   INDEX

M

Maal, Baaba 330
Machu Picchu, Peru 256–257
Madhvacharya, Shri 289
Magritte, René 42, 98
  The Empire of Light 99
Mahfouz, Naguib *Palace Walk* 337–339
Mahler, Gustav 132
Mandela, Nelson 323
Mann, Katia 79
Mann, Thomas *The Magic Mountain* 78–79
Mantegna, Andrea 107
Márquez, Gabriel Garcia *Love in the Time of Cholera* 241–243
Marrakesh, Morocco 332–333
Marseille, France 19–20
Martian, The 344
Mastroianni, Marcello 16
Matisse, Henri 42, 159, 319–20
  Paysage Vu d'une Fenêtre 320
Matmata and Tozeur, Tunisia 325–326
mbalax 330
McDonagh, Martin 176, 177
Medici, Lorenzo de' 180
Melbourne, Victoria, Australia 302–303
Memphis, Tennessee, USA 235–236
Merseybeat 26
Meyer, Claus 76
Michelangelo *David* 179–181
Miró, Joan 42
Mississippi River, Missouri, USA 203–204
Mondrian, Piet 58
Monet, Claude 8, 107, 159, 163, 173–174
  The Water Lily Pond: Green Harmony 174
Monroeville, Alabama, USA 226–227
Monterey, California, USA 188–189
Montmartre, Paris, France 158–159
Montréal, Québec, Canada 200–201
Motorcycle Diaries, The 256–257
Mount Fuji, Japan 280–281
Mozart, Wolfgang Amadeus 8, 121, 131–132
Mumbai, India 298–299
Munch, Edvard *The Scream* 137–138
Munnings, Sir Alfred James 184

Murray, Bill 268
music 6–9
  Andalucía, Spain 149–150
  Cuba, Caribbean 209–210
  Dakar, Senegal 329–330
  Galway, Ireland 101–102
  Liverpool, England, UK 25–26
  Memphis, Tennessee, USA 235–236
  Reykjavik, Iceland 55–56
  Salvador, Bahia, Brazil 247–248
  Seoul, South Korea 283–284
  Vienna, Austria 131–132
Myers, Polly 226

N

N'Dour, Youssou 330
Naples, Italy 164–165
Neill, Sam 305
New Mexico, USA 197–198
New Nordic Cuisine 75–77
New Orleans, Louisiana, USA 215–217
New York, USA 206–207, 218–219
Nicholas I of Russia
Nicholson, Ben 13
Nordland, Norway 72–73
Nunn, Bill 194
Nuremberg, Germany 92–93

O

O'Keefe, Georgia 197–198
  My Front Yard, Summer 198
O'Toole, Peter 343
obwarzanki 146–147
Of Monsters and Men 56
Olbracht of Poland 147
Olodum 248
OMD 26
Oostduinkerke, Belgium 38–39
Osaka, Japan 295–296
Oslo, Norway 137–138
Outback, Australia 314–315

P

Paddington 95–97
paella 167–168
Pan's Labyrinth 85–86
Paquin, Anna 305
Paris, France 89–91
Parks, Rosa 226

pastéis de nata 115–116
Pearce, Guy 314
Pegg, Simon 128
Penn, William 129
Persona 104–105
Peter the Great of Russia 140
Philadelphia, USA 212–213
Phillips, Sam 236
Piano, The 7, 305–306
Picasso, Pablo 42, 157, 163
  Guernica 7–8, 69, 70–71
Pieterson, Hector 323
Pinochet, Augusto 254, 255
Pizarro, Francisco 244
plant-based food 289–290
Presley, Elvis 236
Psy 284
Pushkin, Alexander 134

Q

Quisling, Vidkun 73

R

Raiders of the Lost Ark 326
Reader, The 46
Redzepi, René 76
Rego, Paula *The Dance* 28–29
Renoir, Auguste *Luncheon of the Boating Party* 159
Revenant, The 7, 223–225
Revolori, Tony 45
Rey, Félix 156
Reykjavík, Iceland 55–56
Ricketts, Ed 189
Rivera, Diego 233
Roberts, Aldwyn 96
Rocky 212–213
Rome, Italy 16–17
Ronan, Saoirse 46
Rossetti, Dante Gabriel 111
Roy, Arundhati *The God of Small Things* 7, 273–275
Ruskin, John 162

S

Saigon (Ho Chi Minh City), Vietnam 292–293
Salinger, J.D. *The Catcher in the Rye* 218–219

INDEX   349

Salles, Walter 256
salsa 209–210
Salvador, Bahia, Brazil 247–248
Salzburg, Austria 121–123
San Sebastian, Spain 182–183
Santesso, Walter 17
Sarandon, Susan 228
Sargent, John Singer 107
Schjerfbeck, Helene 12
Schubert, Franz 132
Scott, Ridley 228
Seo Taiji and Boys 283–284
Seoul, South Korea 283–284
Serna, Rodrigo de la 256
Sharif, Omar 344
Shire, Talia 212
shrimp 38–39
Sichuan, China 277–278
Sickert, Walter 12
Sierra de Guadarrama, Spain 85–86
Sigur Rós 56
Simon, Paul 248
Sinatra, Frank 17
Sound of Music, The 121–123
Soweto, South Africa 322–323
spaghetti bolognese 61–62
St Ives, Cornwall, England, UK 12–13
St Ninian 171
St Petersburg, Russia 140–141
Stallone, Sylvester 212
Stamp, Terence 314
Star Wars 7, 325–326, 344
Steen, Jan 58–59
Steinbeck, John Cannery Row 188–189
Strauss, Johann 132
Strauss, Richard 132
Sugarcubes, The 56
Surrealists 36, 43, 99
Swinging Blue Jeans, The 26

T
tagliatelle al ragú Bolognese 62–62
Tahiti, French Polynesia 308–309
Tangier, Morocco 319–320
Tarantino, Quentin 46
Tautou, Audrey 158
Taylor, Elizabeth 191
Tel Aviv, Israel 340–341
Thelma & Louise 228–230

Three Coins in the Fountain 17
Through a Glass Darkly 105
Tiepolo, Gianbattista 107
Titian 107
Tokyo, Japan 268–269
Toulouse-Lautrec, Henri 159
Tozeur and Matmata, Tunisia 325–326
Tusheti, Georgia 134–135
Tutu, Desmond 323
Twain, Mark Adventures of Huckleberry
    Finn 203–204

U
Udupi, India 289–290
Ullman, Liv 104

V
Valencia, Spain 167–168
Van Eyck, Jan 177
Van Gogh, Vincent 155–157
    Café Terrace at Night 156
Vasari, Giorgio 180
Velázquez, Diego 50
Veloso, Caetano 248
Venice, Italy 30–31, 107–109
Vermeer, Johannes 58–59
    View of Delft 59
Veronese, Paolo 107
Vienna Secession 83, 132
Vienna, Austria 131–132
Vliet, Hendrick Corneliz van 59
Von Trapp, Georg 122

W
Wadi Rum, Jordan 343–345
Warhol, Andy 163, 207
Waterhouse, Alfred 97
Weathers, Carl 212
Weaving, Hugo 314
Wells, England, UK 128–129
Weyden, Rogier van der 98
Whistler, Beatrice 163
Whistler, James Abbott McNeill 12,
    161–163
    Nocturne: Blue and Gold – Old
    Battersea Bridge 162
Wicker Man, The 170–171
Wilhem I of Germany
Wise, Robert 121

Wiseman, Joseph 190
Wood, John, the Elder and Younger
    64–66
Woods, Flora 189
Woodward, Edward 170
Wright, Edgar 128

Y
Yorkshire Moors, England, UK 111–112
Young, Terence 190

Z
Zola, Émile 91
Zorn, Anders 12

SARAH BAXTER is an author and journalist. She was Associate Editor of *Wanderlust* magazine, the bible for independent-minded travellers, for more than ten years and has written extensively on walking and travel for a diverse range of other publications, including the *Guardian*, the *Telegraph*, and the *Independent*. Sarah has also contributed to more than a dozen *Lonely Planet* guidebooks.

SUSIE HODGE is a UK author who has written widely on art, art history and art techniques. She has published over 100 books, including *The Short Story of Art, Why Your Five Year Old Could Not Have Done That: Modern Art Explained* and *Modern Art in Detail*.

AMY GRIMES is an illustrator based in London. Particularly inspired by nature and the natural patterns found there, Amy's work often features bright and bold illustrated motifs, floral icons and leafy landscapes. As well as working on design and publishing commissions, Amy has an illustrated brand selling prints, textiles and stationery under the name of Hello Grimes.

Quarto

First published in 2025 by White Lion Publishing,
an imprint of The Quarto Group.
1 Triptych Place,
London, SE1 9SH,
United Kingdom
T (0)20 7700 9000
www.Quarto.com

© 2025 Quarto Publishing plc.
Illustration copyright © 2025 Amy Grimes
Text of Artistic entries written by Susie Hodge, all other text written by Sarah Baxter

Material previously published in:
Literary Places, 2019
Artistic Places, 2021
Cinematic Places, 2023
Foodie Places, 2024

All rights reserved. No part of this book may be reproduced or utilised in any form or by any means, electronic or mechanical, including photocopying, recording or by any information storage and retrieval system, without permission in writing from White Lion Publishing.

Every effort has been made to trace the copyright holders of material quoted in this book. If application is made in writing to the publisher, any omissions will be included in future editions.

A catalogue record for this book is available from the British Library.

ISBN 978 1 8360 0276 5
Ebook ISBN 978 1 8360 0278 9

10 9 8 7 6 5 4 3 2 1

Design by Mylène Mozas

Publisher Jessica Axe
Senior Commissioning Editor Andrew Roff
Editor Róisín Duffy
Art Director Paileen Currie
Senior Designer Renata Latipova
Production Controller Rohana Yusof

Printed in China